Chekisty

———

Chekisty

A History of the KGB

John J. Dziak

Foreword by
Robert Conquest

Lexington Books

D.C. Heath and Company/Lexington, Massachusetts/Toronto

The views expressed in this study are those of the author and should not be construed as representing positions of the Department of Defense or the U.S. government.

Library of Congress Cataloging-in-Publication Data

Dziak, John J.
Chekisty : a history of the KGB.

Bibliography: p.
Includes index.
1. Soviet Union. Komitet gosudarstvennoĭ bezopasnosti
—History. I. Title.
HV8224.D95   1988   363.2'83'0947   84-43178
ISBN 0-669-10258-X (alk. paper)

Published simultaneously in Canada
Printed in the United States of America
Casebound International Standard Book Number: 0-669-10258-X
Library of Congress Catalog Card Number: 84-43178

The paper used in this publication meets the minimum requirements of American National Standard for Information Sciences—Permanence of Paper for Printed Library Materials, ANSI Z39.48-1984.

ISBN 0-669-10258-X

88 89 90 91 92 8 7 6 5 4 3 2 1

For

CAROLE

Contents

Foreword

J OHN DZIAK has given us one of the few valuable books ever published on the Soviet secret police over its seven decades of existence and in its various avatars.

The secret police has always played an important role, sometimes an overwhelming role, in the Soviet Union. It has been, and is today, a vast organization penetrating all aspects of Soviet life. Whoever seeks to understand the Soviet Union without considering its secret police will lack knowledge that is essential for avoiding completely misleading ideas of the regime as it is at present, and as it has been through its seventy-year history. This applies to both the internal and the international activities of the police.

Dr. Dziak traces the Soviet security organs from their rough and ready beginnings. He details the power they developed in the early Red Terror of 1918. He leads us through and clarifies the tangle of organizational change from then to this day. He describes many of the police's most remarkable and typical activities, right from the early days with such cases as those of Lockhart and Reilly, some of whose details only became known quite recently, and through the internal and external terror and deception operations of the decades that have followed.

Reading of even those early operations of the secret police, the first impression one forms is of the large resources at its disposal. Operations like the "Trust" in the 1920s could scarcely have been performed by the intelligence services of other countries, simply for want of personnel and resources.

Later on, the disproportion became far greater. The size of the "organs," starting with 20–30 men in December 1917, increased enormously over the next two decades; and it remains vast.

The present size of the KGB is not exactly known, but all estimates agree that it has several hundred thousand employees. When
we compare this with the mere thousands employed by all the Western internal security services put together, we are clearly in a totally
different world, with a different perspective. (And though the point
is different, the same, of course, would apply to a comparison of the
Soviet foreign intelligence effort's size with those of Western
nations).

Even the overt power and prestige of the KGB remain exceptionally high. Of its previous chiefs only Beria and Andropov were at
the same time full members of the Politburo. The fact that Chebrikov, the present head of the KGB, with a very low-level and limited
political background, is in a more powerful position than such comparative giants as Dzerzhinskiy and Yagoda and Yezhov and Serov
and Shelepin is a very strong indication that the secret police is now
in a condition of great strength.

In recent years oppression has, by Soviet standards, shrunk to a
comparatively low level. But, as Nadezhda Mandelstam says in the
second volume of her memoirs, *Hope Abandoned*, the police machine
remains in being, and "even when it is only idling, as today, it continues to function in essentially the same manner as before. At any
moment, after lying dormant for some time, it could start up again
at full speed."

There is much speculation on how far the present regime may
"liberalize" the Soviet Union. One very sound criterion would be
how much the size and power of the secret police will be reduced.
If and when its scope becomes no more, or not much more, than
what is regarded as sufficient by such states as our own—or even by
the tsarist regime—we would have reason to think that real and substantial progress has been made.

Until then John Dziak's account is not merely historical research,
but the presentation of the background of a real and immense phenomenon in the world today, with great power for harm not only in
its own country, but internationally as well. Dr. Dziak has thus performed a public service in forwarding an understanding of this crucial element in the affairs of the present-day world.

Robert Conquest
Hoover Institution

Acknowledgments

A SPECIAL and warm note of thanks is due to Raymond G. Rocca, who inspired this study and then freely gave help and encouragement along the way. The author expresses his deep appreciation to Dorothy Nicolosi and Frank Barnett of the National Strategy Information Center, and to Devon Gaffney, Owen A. Lock, Hayden B. Peake, Walter Pforzheimer, Herbert Romerstein, Richard H. Shultz, Robert Suggs, David L. Thomas, General James A. Williams, and Natalie Grant Wraga, all of whom helped in ways too varied to enumerate. To Jaime Welch-Donahue of Lexington Books for her great reserves of patience—thank you. Finally, to my wife, Carole, and son, Jack, for all you did to make this happen and all you gave up in the process, my loving thanks.

Introduction

THE LIQUIDATION of a people and its culture cannot be accomplished without the eradication of its memory. Similarly, the engineering of a "new" man and his enveloping culture also requires the invention of a new past following the destruction or falsification of the old. The story of the Soviet state is replete with ceaseless attempts by the Communist Party to revoke and reorder not only its prerevolutionary past but the events, personalities, and even epochs of its own seventy-year history. This endless manipulation of the past dramatically affects the "new Soviet man" the party has sought to mold. He has no reliable compass to help him fix his position relative to the massive party–state apparatus that defines his world.

This would be tragedy enough if it were confined only to the Soviet Union and its coterie of satellites and allied clone-states. Unfortunately, the effect of such efforts for nearly three-quarters of a century has also been felt in the noncommunist world. Here historians and analysts of the Soviet phenomenon face the dilemma of attempting to work against a backdrop of both denied and manipulated data. Compounding this problem is the steady percolation of Soviet interpretations into Western consciousness. For instance, few Westerners, other than specialists whose job it is to know, realize that Leon Trotsky was the founder and first commander of the Red Army and had encouraged the extralegal expansion of the powers of the Cheka, the first Soviet secret police. Fewer still remember that the Molotov–Ribbentrop Pact of 1939 helped launch World War II, with Germany invading Poland from the West joined by the USSR thrusting in from the East.[1] Or take the figure of twenty million Soviet casualties in World War II, first offered up by Moscow and then assimilated in the West as a given with little or no thought or statistical evaluation ever applied. Why were the German casualties so much lower? Was Moscow engaging in a bit of historical *maskirovka* (deception) to cover the millions of casualties *it* inflicted on its own people at the hands of state security both before and during the war? Even more disturbing is a tendency among some Western academics to rely on official Soviet accounts and documents and to dismiss accounts of participants who were anticommunist and thus "unreliable"—a type of victor's, or mugger's, justice so to speak.

The problem of historical memory is especially acute when it comes to the Soviet secret police or, more correctly, state security. For the first several decades of the Soviet state, few officially sanctioned writings emerged from state presses, with some important exceptions during the early 1920s. Though it did not deny the existence of the internal security dimension of state security, Moscow claimed that only bourgeois or fascist states engaged in espionage and covert action. Only with the need to refurbish the thuggish image of the KGB in the wake of de-Stalinization did the Soviet Union admit to foreign intelligence operations, and this in heroic superlatives. Now the KGB is officially hyped as the political action arm of the party and the watchdog of the norms of socialist legality. Its depredations against the Soviet population are attributed to a few unreconstructed agents of foreign intelligence services, that is, Beria and his lieutenants. But the man whose orders Beria was following himself has been gradually rehabilitated. We hear precious little any more about the abuses of the "cult of personality," the polite codewords for the name of Stalin.

Instead, we have been treated to the cult of F. E. Dzerzhinskiy, the near-sanctified founder of the Cheka. Because the leadership of both the party and the secret police has been so subject to the vagaries of historical rewrite, the party had to provide a symbolic anchor to fix the KGB's image and legitimacy. Dzerzhinskiy was an ideal symbol. Dying within two years of Lenin and not having been tainted by Trotskyite opposition links, he was safe, clean. But in jumping back to Dzerzhinskiy as their patron saint, the Soviets fail to explain the continuity through those years when Dzerzhinskiy's creation slaughtered millions in the name of a party-sanctioned vision of social progress. And, lest we forget the response of important, influential segments of Western opinion during that period of

great "social experimentation," recall the frequent rationale that om-
elets cannot be made without breaking a few eggs.

In the West we tend to view the KGB and its antecedents either
as a standard internal police force (albeit rather authoritarian), or we
fix on its foreign operations, its espionage and subversive dimensions. In the case of the former we mirror police functions, attrib-
uting a generic quality to all nation-states. This is especially evident
by the paucity of scholarly work on Soviet state security. And in
most history and government texts on the USSR, a chapter devoted
to the police constitutes the most one can expect to find. Fortunately,
the few exceptions tend to be outstanding examples of what can be
accomplished in keeping an honest memory alive. I have in mind
here the seminal works of Robert Conquest on the purges, the terror-
famine, and the NKVD of the late 1930s; George Leggett's classic
history, *The Cheka*; the rich deposit of defector testimony and memoir
literature; and Ronald Hingley's *The Russian Secret Police*, a solid general history, however, long out of print.

In the KGB's foreign role, we find a different reality with its own
set of problems. The publicity attendant upon disclosures of KGB
operations in the West has generated a surfeit of published materials.
But quantity does not always foster insight or good analysis. Here,
too, the scholarly community seems to have abdicated the field in
favor of a generic foreign policy analysis frequently posited on
Western-derived behavioral models. Again, defector and émigré
memoirs, coupled in this instance with respectable journalistic efforts, carry the field. John Barron's two KGB studies demonstrate a
grasp of the foreign dimension of KGB operations that few others
have yet to match.

Still, we must remember that the KGB's foreign operations are
essentially the external manifestations of its party-sanctioned role of
watchdog and guarantor of the party's power monopoly. This role
has an overwhelming counterintelligence flavor to it. Penetration,
provocation, elaborate deceptions to manipulate and disarm "enemies of the state"—these are some of the operational givens of an
organ that the party considers its political action arm. These two,
the party and the KGB, are fused in an organic union transcending
the rest of the bureaucracy of the Soviet state and even Soviet law,
such as it is. It is no accident that very shortly after the Bolshevik
Party illegally seized power in a coup (*not* a revolution), it created an

extralegal secret police to secure, expand, and perpetuate that power. The two were illicitly joined in what could properly be called a counterintelligence state, an enterprise perpetually in search of enemies, foreign and domestic. It must remain forever mobilized in this search if the union is to endure. It has no other claims to legitimacy other than the ideology that ordained and sanctioned the seizure of power in the first place. Essentially, then, the Bolshevik Party was a conspiracy that came to power and *remained* a conspiracy afterwards with the active collaboration of its secret police.

The intent of this book is to probe the history of the Soviet Union as a counterintelligence state. As such, the book focuses largely on the internal dynamics of the party–state security condominium. It makes no effort to probe foreign subversive and espionage operations in any comprehensive detail. Where it does, it is in the context of their internal interaction.

The inspiration for this book originated with a course on the history of Soviet intelligence and security I developed and have taught since 1977 at The George Washington University. I was repeatedly both elated and distressed by the continued popular response from students to the subject. At one point seventy students had registered for the course. That provided the elation. The distress came with the realization that they had heretofore been taught about the Soviet system with no, or very little, reference to the guarantor of that system. Physics minus mathematics, if you will.

As I see it, then, this book is a modest effort to preserve some bit of memory from eradication. I offer no exotic, novel sources of information. However, a lot of forgotten materials are brought to light again. This is not an exhaustive history but rather a selective and concise inquiry into the roots, creation, and maturation of the counterintelligence state. The book does not eschew a viewpoint. I see no point in pretending that I am unaffected by the several tens of millions of people killed by this party–state security amalgam. Conversely, not being of a utopian, social engineering bent, I am not impressed with omelet analogies for the creation of the perfect society.

Chekisty is the Russian for *Chekists*, that is, members of the Cheka. Today's KGB, in its claim to the Dzerzhinskiy patrimony, has revived and retained the old nomenclature for its officers. I thought this a fitting title for the book.

Abbreviations

AOD	Administrative Organs Department
Cheka, VChKa, VCheKa, VeCheKa	Vserossiyskaya Chrezvychaynaya Komissiya po Bor'be s Kontrrevolyutsiyey i Sabotazhem (All-Russian Extraordinary Commission to Combat Counterrevolution and Sabotage)
CPUSA	Communist Party of the United States
DOSAAF	Dobrovol'noye Obshchestvo Sodeystviya Armii, Aviatsii, Flotu (Volunteer Society for Cooperation with the Army, Aviation, and the Fleet)
DTU	Dorozhno-Transportnyy Upravleniye (Road and Transportation Directorate)
GAU	Glavnoye Arkhivnoye Upravleniye (Main Archive Administration)
GKES	Gosudarstvenny Komitet po Vneshnim Ekonomicheskim Svyazyam (State Committee for Foreign Economic Relations)
GKNT	Gosudarstvennyy Komitet po Nauki i Tekhnologii (State Committee for Science and Technology)
GKO	Gosudarstvennyy Komitet Oborony (State Committee of Defense)
GPU	Gosudarstvennoye Politicheskoye Upravleniye (State Political Directorate)
GRU	Glavnoye Razvedyvatel'noye Upravleniye (Main

Intelligence Directorate of the General Staff)

GUGB   Glavnoye Upravleniye Gosudarstvennoy
              Bezopaznosti (Chief Directorate, or Main
              Administration, of State Security of the
              NKVD)

GUKR   Glavnoye Upravleniye Kontrrazvedki (Main
              Administration for Counterintelligence)

Gulag   Glavnoye Upravleniye Lagerey (Main
              Administration of Corrective Labor Camps)

GUM   Glavnoye Upravleniye Militsii (Main
              Administration of Militia)

GUMZ   Glavnoye Upravleniye Mestami Zaklyucheniya
              (Main Administration of Places of Detention)

GUPO   Glavnoye Upravleniye Pozharnoi Okhrany (Main
              Administration of Fire Protection)

INO/INU   Inostrannyy Otdel/Inostrannoye Upravleniye
              (Foreign Department/Foreign Directorate of the
              Cheka, GPU, OGPU, and NKVD)

KGB   Komitet Gosudarstvennoy Bezopasnosti
              (Committee for State Security)

KI   Komitet Informatsii (Committee of Information)

KRU   Kontrrazvedyvatel'noye Upravleniye
              (Counterintelligence Directorate)

MGB   Ministerstvo Gosudarstvennoy Bezopasnosti
              (Ministry of State Security)

MI-5   British Security Service

MI-6   British Secret Intelligence Service

MOOP   Ministerstvo Okhrany Obshchestvennogo
              Poryadka (Ministry for Maintenance of Public
              Order)

MRC   Military Revolutionary Committee

MVD   Ministerstvo Vnutrennikh Del (Ministry of
              Internal Affairs)

NEP   New Economic Policy

NKGB   Narodnyy Komissariat Gosudarstvennoy

	Bezopasnosti (People's Commissariat of State Security)
NKID	Narodnyy Komissariat Inostrannykh Del (People's Commissariat of Foreign Affairs)
NKO	Narodnyy Komissariat Oborony (People's Commissariat of Defense)
NKYu	Narodnyy Komissariat Yustitsii (People's Commissariat of Justice)
NKVD	Narodnyy Komissariat Vnutrennikh Del (People's Commissariat of Internal Affairs)
NKVMF	Narodnyy Komissariat Voyenno-Morskogo Flota (People's Commissariat of the Navy)
NTS	Narodno-Trudovoy Soyuz Rossiyskikh Solidaristov (Popular Labor Alliance of Russian Solidarists)
OGPU	Obyedinennoye Gosudarstvennoye Politicheskoye Upravleniye (United State Political Directorate)
OKH	Oberkommando des Heeres (German Army High Command)
OKW	Oberkommando der Wehrmacht (German Armed Forces High Command)
OO	Osobye Otdely (Special Departments of the KGB—Military Counterintelligence); Okhrannoye Otdeleniye (tsarist Security Divisions)
POUM	Partido Obrero de Unificación Marxista (Workers' Party of Marxist Unification)
ROVS	Russkiy Obshche-Voyenskiy Soyuz; also Rossiyskiy Obshchevoinskiy Soyuz (Russian Armed Forces Union; Russian General Military Union)
RSDLP	Russian Social Democratic Labor Party
RU	Razvedyvatel'noye Upravleniye (Intelligence Directorate)

SA	Sturmabteilung (Nazi storm troopers or Brownshirts)
SD	Sicherheitsdienst (Nazi security service)
SMERSH	"Smert' Shpionam"—"Death to Spies"—popular title of Armed Forces Counterintelligence Directorate, 1943–46
Sovnarkom, SNK	Sovet Narodnykh Komissarov (Council of People's Commissars)
SPU	Sekretno-politicheskoye Upravleniye (Secret Political Directorate)
SR	Socialist Revolutionary Party
SS	Schutzstaffel (Elite Guard of the Nazi Party)
UB	Urzad Bezpieczenstwa (Office of Security [of Polish Security Service])
UOO	Upravleniye Osobykh Otdelov (Armed Forces Counterintelligence–Directorate of Special Departments)
VPK	Voyenno-promyshlennaya Komissiya (Military Industrial Commission)
VSNKh	Vysshego Soveta Narodnogo Khozyaystva (Supreme Council of National Economy)
VTsIK	Vserossiyskiy Tsentral'nyy Ispolnitel'nyy Komitet (All-Russian Central Executive Committee of the Congress of Soviets)
WiN	Wolnosc i Niepodleglosc (Freedom and Independence; remnant of Polish Home Army)

1

The Formation of the State Security Tradition

T HE SERIOUS STUDY of foreign and, specifically, Soviet intelligence and security systems is a recent development in nongovernment circles in the West and as such still has a limited literature, whether theoretical or operational. Much research and writing to date has tended to fix upon Western systems, if for no other reason (and a good one at that) than accessibility of data due to the publicity generated by investigations, oversight, leaks, and assorted controversies. Also, autocratic, dictatorial, and despotic systems are difficult to access on this subject, to say the least. The down side to this is twofold: There is an excessive amount of generalization and mirroring based on Western intelligence and security systems, with the result that the unique historical, ideological, and political ethos of a non-Western system becomes force-fit to the Western paradigm.

I propose that the twentieth century offers some unique examples of intelligence and security systems that themselves seem to be the impelling drive of the political system they appear to serve. Put another way, certain political systems display an overarching concern with "enemies," both internal and external. Security and the extirpation of real or presumed threats become the premier enterprises of such systems—and are among the few state enterprises that work with a modicum of efficiency and success. The fixation with enemies and threats to the security of the state involves a very heavy internal commitment of state resources. Further, this fixation demands the creation of a state security service that penetrates and permeates all societal institutions (including the military), but not necessarily the claimant to monopoly power, usually a self-proclaimed "revolution-ary" party. This security service is the principal guardian of the party; the two together constitute a permanent counterintelligence enterprise to which all other major political, social, and economic questions are subordinated. Indeed, the commonweal is not the prin-cipal objective of such an amalgam of ensconced power and security screen; self-perpetuation is. I would label such a system the coun-terintelligence state. In such a system foreign activities are an exter-nal variant of this security imperative. Hence, foreign intelligence in some respects takes on the dimensions of external counterintelli-gence. The security service and foreign intelligence tend to be the same organ of the state.

Clearly, the Soviet Union throughout its history, and various of the surrogates and satellites it has spawned, fit this label. Western security and foreign intelligence services are poor models for analyz-ing these counterintelligence states. The latter must be probed on their own terms and in the context of their political traditions. This chapter further explores the concept of the Soviet Union as the pre-mier counterintelligence state in a century characterized by despotic revolutionary systems, and then examines more deeply the conspir-atorial and provocational roots of both the Bolshevik Party and the state security structure that it generated.

The conspiracy-preoccupied character of the Soviet system lends a flavor to its intelligence and security structure that is unique and not easy to compare with Western services except in the most super-ficial externals. Soviet state security began as an integral feature of the party–state virtually from the inception of the Bolshevik regime. The very structure of this party–state, as well as its statecraft and harsh internal regimen, bear all the hallmarks of a dominating secu-rity service, that is, the counterintelligence state. No matter how one defines a totalitarian or totalist system one comes to police state, and the USSR is the longest-lived pervasive police state of the twentieth century—one may even argue the greatest in history.[1] But unlike the police states of authoritarian dictatorships, or even that of Nazi Ger-many—which lasted only twelve years and where security and in-telligence powers were surprisingly diffuse for most of that period—Soviet state security was and is almost coterminous with the party. There is more than mere sloganeering involved when the KGB is touted as the "shield and sword" of the party. Party and state security are intermeshed in an operational union that is too frequently misperceived by observers from a pluralist political tradition. Such observers are used to institutional boundaries that define power relationships and to security and intelligence services that are subject to rigid constitutional or traditional restraints. The counterintelligence state requires assessment on its own terms, drawing on its own conspiracy-fixed tradition.

I should explain why I see the USSR as a counterintelligence state. Prior to the appearance of the Soviet party–state, history offered few, if any, precedents of a millenarian, security-focused system. One might argue that the generic "Oriental" or "Asiatic" despotisms studied by such disparate students of social history as Karl Marx, Max Weber, or Karl Wittfogel presented compelling analogies for such a system.[2] However, certain key ingredients (such as an all-embracing, ubiquitous ideology or a continuously institutionalized secret police) were lacking in those despotisms both in scope and intensity. Certainly, intrusive claims on the totality of human existence, common to the Soviet state, were not characteristic of those despotisms.

The Bolshevik victory created a party–state structure that equated domestic opposition (and later, even apathy) with treason; declared whole classes of people as foreordained by history to destruction; and arrogated to itself a mandate to execute history's will on an international scale. Such sweeping claims were seriously held and meant to be acted upon. In a sense, a secular theocracy was born in which a priesthood (the party), served by a combined holy office and temple guard (the Cheka), sought to exercise its will: the imposition of its ideas and the elimination of those actually or potentially opposed. Such a system is pathological about enemies and makes the search for them, their discovery, and elimination an overriding state objective. Police and counterintelligence operations (such as arrest, investigation, penetration, provocation, deception, entrapment, denunciation, informants, spy mania, censorship, dossiers, and so on) soon characterize the behavior of the whole state structure, not just of the security organs. Domestic society is the first object of these operations; the millenarian imperative then carries them into the international system.

The military, above all, is subject to special scrutiny in this security system. From the creation of the Red Army in 1918 to the Soviet armed forces of the late twentieth century, state security has had the exclusive mandate for military counterintelligence (another argument against applying a Western paradigm). The Special Departments (Osobye Otdely—OOs) were formed by F. E. Dzerzhinskiy's Cheka—with the strong support and concurrence of Red Army chief, Leon Trotsky—to facilitate a special, punitive means of penetration to ensure party control of the military gun. No "Bonapartism" here! These means included a covert network of informants and hostage taking of families to guarantee the loyalty of the so-called "military specialists," former tsarist officers recruited to captain the new Red Army. Though hostage taking is no longer needed, the KGB's OOs still suffuse the Soviet armed forces under the overall direction of the KGB's Third Chief Directorate. The savaging of the Soviet officer corps by state security in the late 1930s, with little or no evidence of either guilt or attempts at self-defense by the victims, is a tribute to the mind-set, yet workability, of the counterintelligence state.

Thus, the discovery and elimination of perceived conspiracies and enemies characterized the motives and behavior of the counterintelligence state. It is my belief that the USSR is the foremost example of a counterintelligence state.

Historically, conspiracy was central to the formation of the Soviet system and the party's monopoly position in it. The long years spent underground prior to the Bolshevik coup in October 1917 (OS)[3] involved not only covert provocational and counterprovocation duels with the tsar's security service, the Okhrana, but intense struggle with the Mensheviks and even elements within the Bolshevik faction of the Russian Social Democratic Labor Party (RSDLP). The tradition of Okhrana penetration and provocation within the revolutionary parties had gone to bizarre lengths. Witness the case of Yevno Azef, a police spy who took part in the establishment of a single Socialist Revolutionary Party (SR) for the Russian Empire and who also was a founding member of the Fighting Organization, the SR's terrorist section; or that of the tsarist Okhrana police agent Roman Malinovsky, colleague of Lenin, member of the Bolshevik Central Committee and chairman of the Bolshevik faction of the Fourth Imperial Duma (or legislative assembly) of which he was a deputy.

Grigoriy Zinoviev's lament was not without foundation: "At that time . . . there was not a single organization in the areas into which a provocateur had not wormed himself, and everyone trailed each other around, one member fearing and not trusting the next."[4]

When Vladimir Burtsev, an SR writer who as a self-styled one-man security service against the Okhrana (and later the Cheka), warned Lenin that his confidant Jacob Zhitomirsky was an agent provocateur, Lenin sent Malinovsky to investigate the matter with Burtsev. Lenin protected Malinovsky almost to the end, hurling venomous charges of "malicious slanderers" at the Mensheviks Julius Martov and Theodore Dan who in 1914 demanded a nonfactional Social Democratic Party investigation of Malinovsky. Even when Nikolay Bukharin had earlier voiced his suspicions of Malinovsky to Lenin, Lenin and Zinoviev offered a spirited defense of the man. Malinovsky, it is said, told Lenin before World War I of his earlier criminal past (which led him to his police connections) to which Lenin allegedly replied, "for Bolsheviks such things are of no importance."[5] In 1917 Lenin was called to testify on Malinovsky before the Extraordinary Commission of the Provisional Government, which was probing Okhrana operations and provocations. He emphatically exonerated Malinovsky on the grounds that everything he did benefited the Bolshevik faction, which gained far more than did the Okhrana.[6] This was an interesting claim insofar as the Okhrana all along had intended to help the Bolsheviks through their use of Malinovsky so as to ensure continuation of the split between Bolsheviks and Mensheviks, thereby preventing unification of the revolutionary movement. And this was precisely the complaint of the Mensheviks—and some Bolsheviks—when as early as 1913–14 they raised the charges against Malinovsky in the first place.

When Malinovsky returned to Russia in November 1918 he noisily demanded his own arrest and that he be brought to see Lenin. He was granted his first wish but Lenin remained strangely silent, refusing to see him. Had Lenin finally grasped the truth and was he too embarrassed to persist in Malinovsky's defense in the face of the evidence? Or had Lenin known all along, in effect making common cause with the police in the interests of a "higher" objective that required a furtherance of the split with the Mensheviks and ultimately, as events turned out, an exclusive Bolshevik victory? And if he knew, did Lenin cynically drop Malinovsky at the end or was he prevented from protecting him by Bolsheviks who had been the "victims" of Malinovsky's denunciations, for example, Stalin, Yakov Sverdlov, Nikolay Krylenko?

Krylenko, the prosecutor at Malinovsky's trial, himself was suspected of both Okhrana and German intelligence connections during World War I.[7] The man who had acceded to Malinovsky's request for arrest was Zinoviev, who with Lenin had defended him against Bukharin's charges years before.

Why was Malinovsky executed so quickly, within hours of the trial, after even the prosecution sought to prove that his activities redounded more to the party than to the Okhrana? And why indeed, after all and sundry knew of his highly acclaimed bolshevizing work among Russian prisoners-of-war in German prison camps during the war? Why was Stepan Beletsky, the director of the Department of Police to whom Malinovsky reported, also shot so quickly after Malinovsky's execution?

Malinovsky's behavior in returning to Russia in 1918, fully aware of his notoriety, itself raises questions. Most police agents whose covers were blown or threatened fled to other countries, frequently with a respectable bonus from the Okhrana. Was Malinovsky's bravado driven by a stricken conscience or did he expect a deserved exoneration and welcome from a Bolshevik leadership whose double agent he really was? Did a thoroughly cynical triumvirate of Lenin, Zinoviev, and Krylenko sacrifice him in the interests of hiding a very criminal episode in Bolshevik history that could threaten the legitimacy of their revolution? And what was the role of Stalin in Malinovsky's trial and execution? Little seems to have surfaced on this point, yet, as we shall see, it would likely have been in Stalin's direct interest to have Malinovsky silenced forever. The trial itself was the last bizarre episode of the Malinovsky affair and bore an eerie similarity to those notorious theatrical productions of the 1930s, Stalin's purge trials. The more one probes the Malinovsky business, the more fragile Bolshevik historiography actually appears and becomes.

An intriguing characteristic of Malinovsky and other police-provocateurs, somewhat unique to the Russian milieu, is that such men tended to confuse their double roles. They obscured their true loyalties, thus staining the reputations both of their police sponsors and the revolutionary groups they penetrated and served. They contributed in a major way to furthering the split in the Social Democratic Party, whose Menshevik faction already feared the joint threat of Okhrana provocations and the despotic predilections inherent in Lenin's unitary organizational schemes.

It should be remembered that well before the Malinovsky controversies the non-Bolshevik left had voiced strong fears over future revolutionary developments should the Social Democrats succumb to Lenin's insistence on his recipe for the future. At the 1906 Stockholm congress of the Social Democrats, Georgiy Plekhanov's and others' fears of a despotic restoration forced a grudging Lenin to offer up "protective" guarantees calculated to inhibit the degeneration of their revolution. These were socialist revolutions in the West, which even Lenin admitted they could not call forth of their own volition; and the absence of a standing army and a bureaucracy through the "complete democratization . . . of the whole system of the state."[8] As late as 8 March 1918, at the Seventh Party Congress, Lenin broadened the institutional prohibition to include the police: "Soviet power is a new type of state in which there is no bureaucracy, no standing army, no police."[9] Already within a few short months of the Bolshevik coup of October 1917, Plekhanov's fears were realized, guarantees notwithstanding. On 20 December 1917 (NS) a far more pervasive and virulent form of the Okhrana was reinstituted as the Cheka. A massive and arbitrary party–state bureaucracy quickly emerged, evoking bitter disillusionment manifested by the Kronstadt uprising and Workers' Opposition; "democratization of the state" was terminated with the forced dissolution of the democratically elected Constituent Assembly in January 1918; and a standing Red Army based on conscription followed in April. In short order then, not only did a despotic restoration occur but it bore repressive similarities more akin to the older pre-Petrine tradition of Muscovy, Ivan the Terrible and his Oprichnina, than it did to the relatively ineffectual Okhrana and the weakened autocracy it inadequately served. Russia of 1917 simply was not the autocratic system of ages past. The tsar's powers had weakened significantly throughout the last part of the nineteenth century and the years prior to World War I. Hence, Bolshevik despotism resembles not the fragile edifice under Nicholas II, but the arbitrary powers of Ivan the Terrible.

Before leaving the business of police agents and provocateurs and their formative influence on the character of the new Soviet counterintelligence state, it is worth a brief revisit to an enduring contro-

versy that has its roots in this period. Both before and after 1917
there were persistent suspicions and rumors that Stalin also had been
an Okhrana police agent. A trail of compromises and arrests of Stalin's associates—not dissimilar to events in the Malinovsky case—
seemed to follow Stalin's activities until he supposedly was fingered
by Malinovsky in February 1913 and exiled by the police to Siberia.
Indeed, the arrest of the latter could have been the unanticipated
result of a failed attempt by Stalin initially to compromise Malinovsky.[10] The reminiscences of a former Okhrana officer, one Nikolay
Vladimirovich Veselago, have both Malinovsky and Stalin reporting
on Lenin as well as on each other. Stalin, according to this account,
was not aware that Malinovsky was also a penetration agent.[11] However, the compromising of Malinovsky may have been a provocation
by Stalin to supplant Malinovsky in his premier double role as police
agent and Bolshevik luminary in the Duma. Later, there were also
claims in Bolshevik circles of Lavrentiy Beria's dubious activities in
the Caucasus prior to Bolshevik consolidation of control there. These
ranged from criminal involvements to serving the secret police forces
of various political regimes.[12]

To be sure, the proposition of Stalin as Okhrana police agent is
controversial and the evidence incomplete, yet insistent and persistent. The implications, though, for the nature of the Soviet system
and the development of state security would be profound and highly
unsettling to several generations of Soviet leaders. Clearly it was in
the interests of Stalin and his successors that a scandal far greater
than Malinovsky's never surface. Therefore, any careful study of Soviet state security should at the very least take note of this controversy, its implications, and the sources involved.

What are some of the more notable of these sources? In addition
to the recollection of the former tsarist police officer Veselago, there
were many hints and charges from within the Soviet Union, some
of which are aired, but not accepted, by Roy Medvedev in his 1971
work *Let History Judge.*[13] Medvedev's arguments against the evidence
are themselves ambivalent and contradictory. As an example, he argues that Stalin would have or should have eliminated such people
as Lavrentiy Beria and his henchman, General Bogdan Z. Kobulov,
who were aware of Stalin's alleged Okhrana links, as Stalin had done
with others who knew the secret. Yet, earlier, Medvedev had answered his own objection by acknowledging that Stalin relied on the

likes of N. I. Yezhov, Beria, and even A. Ya. Vyshinskiy because he knew they were compromised by their own questionable political past.[14] Medvedev seems unwittingly to make a case for a criminal conspiracy as the pedigree of the Soviet system. But his methodology is somewhat inconsistent. He readily accepts as valid those sources that condemn Vyshinskiy's and Beria's pre-Bolshevik past. Yet similar evidence against Stalin is treated as hyperbole or hearsay and cavalierly dismissed. Something is wrong here.

Finally, going back full circle to the very beginnings of the Soviet regime, a study was begun under the Provisional Government but published in 1918, under the Bolsheviks, that continues to intrigue researchers. It identified twelve secret agents of the Okhrana who had penetrated the Social Democrats. The first eleven names including Malinovsky's were spelled out, but the last one was identified only by his party *klichka* or nickname of "Vasiliy."[15] Vasiliy indeed had been one of Stalin's party pseudonyms used in numerous party communications. Medvedev cites the same source, listing the twelve agents, but gives no indication that he was privy to the Vasiliy connection.[16] His historiography, in its efforts to keep the Bolshevik coup cleanly Leninist, does not come to grips with its shabby past.

Another important source in the charges against Stalin, and one difficult to write off, is General Alexander Orlov, former NKVD *rezident* (station chief) in Spain during the Spanish Civil War. Orlov claimed that the accidental discovery of Stalin's Okhrana file by the NKVD was a key factor in the purges and even precipitated a stillborn coup in 1937 by military and NKVD elements.[17] Orlov's charge appeared in the same year (1956) as Isaac Don Levine's *Stalin's Great Secret*, which claimed that a 1913 internal Okhrana classified document identified Stalin as an agent of the St. Petersburg Okhrana office.[18] Both book and document provoked a storm of controversy; many claimed that Levine relied on a forgery.

This document or Okhrana memorandum (called the "Eremin letter" [also found spelled as "Yeryomin"] after its alleged author), though most certainly a forgery, does bear a compelling air of authenticity. Despite its obvious errors, it was a far cry from such decipherable fabrications as, for instance, the Litvinov diaries (*Notes for a Journal*) attributed to Grigoriy Bessedovskiy.[19] Edward Ellis Smith, who carefully probed Stalin's pre-1917 years, concludes "that the letter was produced by someone (not a novice at operational intelligence matters) who had knowledge of Stalin's Okhrana dossier and who comprehended the interactions of the Okhrana and revolutionary movements. Most important, he was convinced that Stalin had been an agent of the Okhrana."[20] Smith also developed a persuasive argument that Stalin's Okhrana past actually dated to the early 1900s in the Caucasus. He demonstrated that there was a surprising congruence between official Soviet, Stalin-inspired accounts of Stalin's alleged 1903–4 exile and a belated (1911) Okhrana report signed by— Colonel Eremin and his Okhrana superior! The latter were building Stalin's "legend" to protect his credibility among the people he was betraying; the Stalinist hagiographers (Beria for one) necessarily had to keep the legend up.

It might be significant that Colonel A. M. Eremin had been chief of the Tbilisi Gendarme Administration, chief of the Special Section (Osobyy Otdel) at Department of Police headquarters in St. Petersburg, and, finally, chief of the Gendarme Administration in Finland when he disappeared following the February 1917 Revolution. He had long been associated with running double agents in the revolutionary movement. If Eremin was not the author of the 1913 Okhrana document, then it must have been someone with a similar quality of access and an intimate knowledge of Stalin's early life and police and Bolshevik affairs during that period. The question remains then, whose forgery and to what purpose?

Still another element of conspiracy involved the German efforts to knock Imperial Russia out of the war. These ranged from penetration of the tsarist government to support for national separatist and revolutionary elements. A complex skein of German espionage and political action, obscured by intelligence legends and missing or destroyed records, may have become intermeshed with revolutionary intrigues of the Bolsheviks and provocational manipulations of the Okhrana. One such confluence might well have included the tsarist General Mikhail D. Bonch-Bruyevich, brother of the Bolshevik revolutionary and associate of Lenin, Vladimir D. Bonch-Bruyevich. In 1916 General Bonch-Bruyevich had duties comprising both intelligence and counterintelligence, first at General Headquarters and then at the Northern Front. He had developed a reputation as a spy-hunter and figured prominently in the arrest, trial, and execution in 1915 of an alleged German spy, one Colonel S. N. Myasoedov. The case was a shocking miscarriage of justice. As one respected historian notes, Myasoedov became a scapegoat for military failures and the victim of intrigues by Generals Bonch-Bruyevich and Nikolay Batyushin, both of whom exercised major military counterintelligence and intelligence responsibilities.[21] Both generals were strongly suspected of having been agents of the Central Powers,[22] although Batyushin is believed to have been responsible for the blackmail and recruitment of the homosexual Colonel Alfred Redl of the Austro-Hungarian General Staff—an unlikely accomplishment for a German or Austrian agent.

General Bonch-Bruyevich's rendering of the Myasoedov affair is notoriously specious and self-serving, not surprising given the man's record both during World War I and after.[23] Bonch-Bruyevich maintained the reputation of a liberal yet remained in close contact with his Bolshevik brother. Historian George Katkov suggests a German–Bolshevik collusive link whereby

> secret information from the armies of the northern front reached Lenin in Switzerland at the time when M. Bonch-Bruevich was Chief of Staff to the commander of this front, General Ruzsky. Some secret documents signed "Bonch-Bruevich" and "Ruzsky" were published in Switzerland by Lenin and Zinovyev in the Bolshevik magazine *Sbornik Sotsial-Demokrata*. This material was probably sent to Lenin via the German controlled intelligence agency run by Alexander Keskula.[24]

Such linkage no doubt extended beyond espionage and into the realm of political action cum political sabotage. Bonch-Bruyevich is alleged to have been one of those responsible for the poor conduct of military planning and operations.[25] He was also connected to those tsarist generals who helped engineer the abdication of Nicholas II.

Several months after the October 1917 Bolshevik coup, General Bonch-Bruyevich became director of the Supreme Military Soviet, "entrusted with the direction of all military operations with the unconditional subordination of all military institutions and personnel. . . ."[26] His brother, M. D. Bonch-Bruyevich, headed the Soviet regime's first security organ known originally as the Committee for Combatting Pogroms, then becoming the Investigation Commission, which actually preceded the Cheka and for a while operated in parallel with it. He also organized and implemented the government's

move from Petrograd to Moscow under extreme conditions of secrecy buttressed by a superb deception plan.

Thus, the two brothers moved with great dispatch to the highest
positions of military–security affairs in the early weeks and months
following the Bolshevik putsch. Few tsarist officers of such seniority
were accorded such high Soviet rank so speedily and readily. General
Bonch-Bruyevich's wartime activities, the amazing speed of his
Bolshevization, his attainment of high Soviet rank (he is listed as a
lieutenant general as of 1944) and his phenomenal longevity despite
his tsarist service (neither he nor his brother were touched by the
blood purges of the 1930s and both died of natural causes in the mid-
to late 1950s) suggest much more than just a long streak of good
fortune. Was General Bonch-Bruyevich serving the German General
Staff on behalf of the Bolsheviks while a tsarist officer? One of Lenin's biographers, Stefan Possony, strongly suspects just such a cross
connection.[27] This would have been in keeping with the convoluted,
conspiratorial traditions of the Bolshevik Party and the determined
German political action program aimed at bringing down the Russian Empire.

For students of Soviet state security, then, there is still a pressing
question on the roots of both the service and the system itself. However historians settle that issue, it must be stressed that the formative, underground period of the Bolshevik faction was suffused by
conspiracy, counterconspiracy, and factional hostility pursued by
Lenin with a vengeance. It should not be surprising that the new
regime ushered in by the October 1917 coup bore a sharp resem-
blance to a criminal conspiracy in contrast to the benign and timorous Provisional Government it smashed.

A long-term conspiracy suddenly and unexpectedly come to
power certainly will not be inclined to assume the attributes of the
protodemocratic government it just drove out. Though superficially
it may have had more in common with the Okhrana and an older
tsarist tradition, the new Bolshevik regime certainly had no repressive models to copy from the Provisional Government. Indeed, it
may be argued that had the Provisional Government employed a
modest but true security service in democracy's defense the "inevi-
table" Bolshevik victory might well have gone the way of failed
coups or putschs by other self-appointed agents of history.

The new system tipped its hand early as to its intent and direction. Within weeks of its seizure of power it created a secret police that has since become an export commodity for repressive revolutionary regimes and movements throughout the world. On 20 December 1917 (NS), the Council of People's Commissars (Sovnarkom) issued the protocol creating the Cheka or All-Russian Extraordinary Commission to Combat Counterrevolution and Sabotage.[28] Shortly thereafter the People's Commissar of Justice, I. Z. Steinberg, issued his instruction on the Revolutionary Tribunals, which virtually became one with the Cheka and were later granted further powers, with the authority to pass death sentences in June 1918.

In short order, a fused police-security-judicial network enjoying extraordinary (read extralegal) powers reminiscent of the sixteenth-century Oprichnina, operated virtually at will on the body politic of the new party–state. It must be stressed that this was all the creation of Lenin and Dzerzhinskiy; it cannot be ascribed to the "cult of personality" or other fictive constructs for Stalin and Stalinism. Stalin may have epitomized the underclass thug-cum-provocateur, but it took the superior strategic vision of Lenin and the ascetic determination of the once-seminarian Dzerzhinskiy to create and hone a bureaucratic terror machine constrained only by a party vested with deity-like omniscience. The bloody-mindedness of both men set an operational style for the Cheka requiring little adjustment to fit Stalin's brutal temperament. Missive upon missive issued from Lenin's pen urging the Cheka to beat and shoot remorselessly. Dzerzhinskiy got down to basic principles in a candid interview with a Russian correspondent in 1918:

> [The society and the press] think of the struggle with counter-revolution and speculation on the level of normal state existence and for that reason they scream of courts, of guarantees, of inquiry, of investigation, etc. . . . We represent in ourselves organized terror—this must be said very clearly. . . .
>
> Of course, we may make mistakes, but up till now there have been no mistakes. This is proved by the minutes of our meetings. In almost all cases the criminals, when pressed against the wall by evidence, admit their crimes. And what argument would have more weight than the confession of the accused himself.[29]

New relationships of state to society with no restraints on the former; state-directed terror; the infallibility not merely of the party but of state security as well; and the fixation with forced confession as the determinant of guilt—these were the legacies that made the later phenomenon of Stalinism possible.

The priorities are instructive here. Tremendous energies were poured into the internal repressive organs even though the new regime was also beset from all sides by hostile armies. For several months the Bolsheviks equivocated in the face of these external threats until a no-nonsense approach finally cast Trotsky in the role of revolutionary drillmaster of a new conscript army. But there was no dawdling in the creation of the Cheka and the Revolutionary Tribunals, or in defining their purposes as seen by Dzerzhinskiy's interview. From the very beginning the party was single-minded and decisive when it came to protecting its monopoly of power and vesting that protection in the so-called "organs." Lenin's dictum that "a good Communist is at the same time a good Chekist" or the Chekist V. Moroz's observation that "there is no sphere of our life where the Cheka does not have its eagle eye," captured the spirit of the party–police amalgam and the fixation with state security.

Have almost seventy years of the Soviet state altered that fixation? One way of answering would be to examine the first mechanisms that Moscow exports to a new socialist client state, revolutionary movement, or satellite. Almost simultaneous with or even before the arrival of military advisors and hardware, come the state security cadres whose job it is to replicate local versions of the KGB. Of course (with the socialist division of labor) East Germans, Bulgarians, and Cubans often may stand in for their Soviet counterparts, but the purpose is the same.

The counterintelligence and security focus of early Soviet state security is underscored by the plethora of information on internal organization and operations, but much less on early Cheka foreign operations. This counterintelligence tendency is best illustrated by Lenin's lament that "our intelligence service in the Cheka, although splendidly organized, unfortunately does not yet extend to America."[30] Two weeks later, in fact on 20 December 1920, the anniversary of the Cheka, Dzerzhinskiy ordered the creation of the Inostrannyy Otdel (INO), or Foreign Department, for conducting foreign intelligence and counterintelligence operations.[31] This does not mean that Moscow ran no foreign operations before December 1920. A good deal of the mission that now belongs to the KGB's First Chief

Directorate was conducted by the Comintern with which the Cheka was intimately associated. Dzerzhinskiy himself represented both the Russian and Polish Communist Parties at different Comintern congresses. High-ranking Chekists were frequently dispatched on Comintern missions before and after the formation of the INO.

In addition, the Red Army, as early as 1918, had an intelligence service known variously as the Third Section and Registration Directorate until 1921, when it became known as the Intelligence Directorate (RU) or Second Directorate of the Red Army General Staff. It too worked with and through the Comintern, especially after the Civil War when battlefield priorities dropped off. Like all other institutions in the Soviet system, military intelligence was the subject of probing Cheka interest both in its tactical and strategic missions. Then and now it was monitored by a special state security counterintelligence network. Unlike Western systems, Soviet military intelligence never exercised its own counterintelligence responsibilities. Even during World War II, when the Armed Forces Counterintelligence Directorate (GUKR–NKO–SMERSH) was titularly removed from state security, its head, Viktor Abakumov, and personnel came from the NKVD. The organizational move most likely was made to place SMERSH directly under the State Committee of Defense (GKO), of which Stalin was chief as well as commissar of defense. After the war SMERSH was reabsorbed into the Ministry of State Security (MGB), of which Abakumov became chief. Today, military intelligence (GRU) is subject to counterintelligence scrutiny by the Third Chief Directorate of the KGB.

Another arguable indicator of state security preeminence over military intelligence is that at critical junctures of GRU history its chiefs were drawn from state security: General Yan Berzin came to military intelligence in December 1920 direct from his post as commander of the Cheka Special Department (OO) of the Fifteenth Red Army; he served as chief of military intelligence from 1924 to 1935 and again in 1937; Nikolay Yezhov, NKVD chief from 1936 to 1938 was de facto chief of military intelligence from 1937 to 1938 at the height of the military purges; from 1958 to 1963 the former KGB chief, Ivan Serov, ran the GRU; and from 1963 to the present, General Pëtr Ivashutin, a former chief of the KGB's Third Chief Directorate (Armed Forces Counterintelligence) has been GRU head.

In a very profound sense, then, foreign intelligence, from the earliest years, was more of an external projection of state security—external counterintelligence—than a "mere" foreign intelligence service in the mold of Western nation-states. To be sure, the emergence of the USSR as a world power after World War II altered that somewhat; and post-Stalin developments further modified that orientation. But even today the operational character of Soviet state security is so qualitatively different from its Western counterparts that approaching it analytically as just another intelligence or even security service will not do. "State security" connotes such an interlayering of party–KGB concerns and missions that they tend to be unintelligible when approached on the basis of Western bureaucratic or interest group models.

Swimming against fashionable academic currents, Leszek Kolakowski unabashedly—and correctly in my view—insists on still identifying this system as totalitarian.[32] The upshot of the process of Stalinist totalitarianism "was a fully state-owned society which came very close to the ideal of perfect unity, *cemented by party and police.*"[33] Two critical features of this perfect unity, the system of universal spying as the principle of government and the apparent omnipotence of ideology (conceived by Lenin and honed by Stalin) are enduring pillars of the system as it approaches the twenty-first century.[34]

Both Lenin and Dzerzhinskiy adamantly and successfully fought attempts to subordinate the Cheka to any governmental body, keeping it directly answerable to the party, because to them it was truly the party's "sword and shield." Even later name changes, which seemed to connote subordination to government commissariats or ministries, were more the result of arcane maneuverings on Stalin's part or the attempt to manipulate domestic and foreign perceptions, than they were substantive developments. Indeed, the most recent titular change in 1978 formally dispensed with the fiction of the "KGB *under* the Council of Ministers" and simply labeled it "KGB of the USSR."

Stalin's legacy, then, must be grouped with that of Lenin and Dzerzhinskiy because these two men presented him with an extralegal action arm unconstrained by any checks outside the highest echelons of the party. That he used it the way he did was in keeping with his and the party's conspiratorial roots and with the possibilities that such an unfettered instrument presented. State security was a bloody tool of repression under Lenin and Dzerzhinskiy; Stalin took it to new heights. George Leggett, in his excellent chronicle of the Cheka, observed that "the precarious and illegitimate Bolshevik regime, battling for survival in circumstances of perpetual crisis, required massive political police support."[35] That judgment seems applicable to the Soviet system throughout its history. It gets at the essence of state security.

2

The Classical Period of Lenin and Dzerzhinskiy: Defense of the Revolution through Extraordinary Measures

T HE FORMATIVE PERIOD of the Soviet state following the Bolshevik coup of October 1917 has become a touchstone of legitimacy for defenders of the Soviet system and for those Soviet officials searching for precedents for the extralegal power of today's state security. For example, in 1959 in an attempt to refurbish the image of the KGB, Khrushchev's new KGB chief, Aleksandr Shelepin, intensified a glorification of the days of Lenin and Dzerzhinskiy and claims of noble exploits of the Cheka. This was a necessary public relations element of a broader move to return state security to its originally intended role of sword and shield of the party. It was part of Khrushchev's attempt to reconstitute the symbiosis of party and police that, in his view, had been prostituted by Stalin's personal dictatorship.

It is a telling tribute to the persistence of political legends that despite a noticeable re-Stalinization since Khrushchev's fall in 1964, the myth of revolutionary purity, selflessness, and honesty associated with the halcyon days of the Cheka survives into the last quarter of the twentieth century. Yet the powers of today's KGB were honed under Stalin, who in turn took advantage of the extraordinary authority given to state security by Dzerzhinskiy and Lenin. Today's Soviet leaders, despite their gradual yet persistent rehabilitation of Stalin, still cannot bring themselves to trace the pedigree of state security back through Stalin, the purges, and collectivization. Hence their retrospective leapfrog to Dzerzhinskiy, Lenin, and the Cheka in their efforts to claim some sort of legitimacy and heroic tradition for the "organs" of repression. A benchmark in this contrived historiography came in 1975 with the publication of a collection of documents titled Lenin i VChK (*Lenin and the Cheka*) under the editorial chairmanship of the late General Semyon K. Tsvigun, then first deputy chairman of the KGB.[1] In his adulatory comments, Tsvigun declared that state security blossomed forth "under the direct influence of V. I. Lenin" and that its "basic principles . . . as well as . . . traditions, having passed the test of over a half century, have not lost their application even at the present time."[2] But by claiming this patrimony the leadership inadvertently admits the very historical truth that it has attempted to mask: the Stalinist years are integral to the state security tradition, and Lenin was the architect of it all. Hence, the "abuses" by the organs could not be pinned blithely on Stalin because the founding spirit was Lenin, who forged the traditions that "passed the test of over a half century"!

If the Soviet leaders find it awkward squaring such circles, it is even more uncomfortable for those apologists on the fringes of the system who profess a certain neo-Leninist creed. Roy Medvedev seems to offer himself as the agonized believer desperately attempting to retrieve a pure and noble faith sullied by the usurper Stalin. Yet even with Stalin, as noted in chapter 1, Medvedev will not allow himself to pursue certain avenues of inquiry. This refusal accompanies a cavalier and dismissive manner in handling evidence and sources—especially defectors and old Bolsheviks[3]—that threatens further to taint the wellsprings of Medvedev's faith. More recently, he has used a device common to Soviet historiography: relegating inconvenient events and persons to nonexistence. His *The October Revolution* ignores some of 1917's most prominent figures and events—Parvus (Dr. Alexander L. Helphand); Karl B. Radek; the Bonch-Bruyevich brothers; Karl Moor; Keskula; Fürstenberg–Hanecki; German–Bolshevik collusion; and the Malinovsky scandal, to name a few.[4] What he offers up instead more closely resembles Bolshevik boilerplate: the inevitability of the Bolshevik revolution;

the nobility and purity of Lenin's intentions; the selflessness of the Bolshevik revolutionaries. Nowhere does Medvedev address the precursor justifications for his hero's use of terror: Lenin, and even Plekhanov, "made no secret of the fact that they thought it proper to kill their ideological opponents."[5] Nor does he really address the creation of the instrument designed to act on such precepts, the Cheka. This is not to single out Medvedev. All too often Western scholarship also has tempered the central role of terror in the formation of the Soviet system.

Why, then, did terror become the logic of the new system, a system that exercised so captivating a hold on its intellectual defenders that they still ignore, or find ways to explain away, the flow of blood? Leonard Schapiro offers one answer, elegant in its simplicity: the secret police, the Cheka, "came into existence in response to the conditions that arise when a minority is determined to rule alone."[6] But there was another dimension, that of belief. The will to power was accompanied by an ideological certitude that labeled whole categories of humanity as enemies—the ones Lenin and Plekhanov thought it proper to kill. Paul Johnson observes that "once verbal hatred was screwed up to this pitch, blood was bound to flow eventually."[7]

Because this Leninist thinking was predicated on alleged scientific principles, such large-scale killing required specialized instruments, operated in a programmatic fashion. The party, the self-appointed vanguard for interpreting these scientific laws of history, was already in place. An instrument in party hands for effectively organizing violence was now an institutional requirement.

Shortly after Lenin slipped back into the country with German assistance on 16 April 1917, a Political Bureau (or Politburo) was formed to oversee the Bolshevik putsch. The putsch itself was directed by Trotsky and a "Military Revolutionary Committee" (MRC) formed out of the Petrograd Soviet. Security at Bolshevik headquarters at the Smolny Institute in Petrograd was entrusted to Dzerzhinskiy by the MRC, which detailed to his command a detachment of Red Guards and Baltic sailors. Also concerned with the maintenance of internal order were the People's Commissariat of Internal Affairs on whose collegium Dzerzhinskiy sat; a Commission for Combating Counterrevolution and Sabotage attached to the All-Russian Central Executive Committee of the Congress of Soviets (VTsIK); and a Committee for Combating Pogroms headed by M. D. Bonch-Bruyevich. Thus, a plethora of organs sprang into being, all having internal security and internal counterintelligence missions. The apparent confusion and overlap reflected both the uncertainty of the Bolsheviks in the tenuousness of their hold on power and their relationship to the VTsIK. Because the latter included non-Bolshevik leftist parties such as the Socialist Revolutionaries (SRs) and Mensheviks, Lenin did operate under a certain modicum of constraints.

The hostility and anarchy generated by the Bolshevik coup forced a hurried streamlining of this security network. As the commissariats came into being as official government bodies under the Council of People's Commissars (Sovnarkom), the MRC ordered itself dissolved on 18 December 1917 (NS), its dissolution presided over by a special liquidation commission of which Dzerzhinskiy was a member. Responding to an imminent general strike of state employees, Lenin and the Sovnarkom on 19 December ordered Dzerzhinskiy's commission to prepare recommendations for handling the crisis and to present these at the 20 December meeting.

Dzerzhinskiy's report and recommendations were approved by the Sovnarkom at the 20 December meeting. The approval was issued as a "resolution," not as a "decree," although it also has been classified as a "protocol" of the Sovnarkom by some sources.[8] Hence its nonlegal and tenuous pedigree. Regardless, the All-Russian Extraordinary Commission to Combat Counterrevolution and Sabotage, attached to the Council of People's Commissars, was created. It quickly became known by its acronym, VChKa or Cheka. Actually, the "resolution" really comprised the minutes of Dzerzhinskiy's report and a short statement giving the commission a name, establishing it, and ordering the minutes to be published. It was never published as a decree, and it had no legal basis by the Soviets' own admission. In fact, the resolution was not published at all until 1922, so that the Cheka indeed was a secret police in the most literal sense.[9] In summary, Dzerzhinskiy's minutes included:

An incomplete composition of the commission (I. Ksenofontov, N. Zhedilev, V. Averin, K. Peterson, Ya. Peters, D. Evseyev, V. Trifonov, F. Dzerzhinskiy, Sergo [Ordzhonikidze], and Vasilevskiy).

Tasks: suppress and liquidate all counterrevolution and sabotage throughout Russia; hand over for trial by revolutionary tribunal all saboteurs and counterrevolutionaries, and develop means to combat them; and conduct only preliminary investigation, as needed to suppress such acts.

Organization to comprise an information department; an organizational department to organize the struggle with counterrevolution throughout Russia; and a fighting department to conduct operational action.

Attention to be primarily focused on the press, sabotage, Kadets (members of the Constitutional Democratic Party), Right SRs, saboteurs, and strikers.

Actions to be taken: confiscation; eviction from residence; deprivation of ration cards; publication of lists of enemies of the people, etc.[10]

This was not an unrestricted mandate, but the suddenness and volatility of Lenin's October victory may account for the limitations. Likewise, there were still multitudes on the non-Bolshevik left which, at that point, probably inhibited an immediate push for broader powers. Still, Lenin proved to be the adroit political strategist. By subordinating the Cheka to the Sovnarkom rather than to the All-Russian Central Executive Committee (VTsIK), he kept it under a body that his party controlled. In the VTsIK he would have to contend with strong representations from Left and Right SRs, the Mensheviks, and other leftist groups. As with so many events in the formation of the Soviet state, fortune dovetailed with Lenin's design. The immediate pressure of a general strike impelled the Cheka's creation while Lenin ensured that he determined its subordination, extralegality, and secrecy.

It has been argued over the years that the limited mandate of the Sovnarkom's resolution was proof that premeditated terror was not part of Lenin's plan for the Cheka. Yet long before the coalescence of organized and meaningful military opposition to Bolshevik rule, his exhortations to visit violence on those who opposed his party's plans were voiced in incessant, shrill cries marked by battlefield verbiage. Well before the launching of SR violence against party and Cheka officials in 1918, the Cheka began shooting so-called speculators, counterrevolutionaries, and other social undesirables.

The precursors to Stalin's massive Gulag empire were first aired by Lenin shortly before his October 1917 coup when he declared that he would co-opt an alleged capitalist weapon, compulsory labor. Compulsory labor in the hands of the "proletarian state" would be more potent than the guillotine, for the guillotine merely terrorized and broke active resistance.[11] Passive resistance was, for Lenin, far more dangerous. Compulsory labor would break such resistance and demonstrate the omnipotence of the "proletarian state," by removing "undesirable and incorrigible 'resisters' " and forcibly employing them in the service of the new state.[12] By 1918, when the Cheka began to assume the dimensions of a state within a state, a predilection for arbitrary administrative measures, unchecked by any constitutional or moral constraints, quickly developed into an operational imperative.

Compulsory labor aimed at the bourgeoisie expanded dramatically as the Civil War got under way. Cheka press gangs, responding to state and military demands, began rounding up hundreds and then thousands of men and women for work on military fortifications and other labors on the various fronts against first the Germans, and then the various White and Allied armies. As regional Chekas proliferated, so too did forced labor roundups. Similarly, forced labor or concentration camps quickly spread throughout Bolshevik areas to house and guard the thousands caught in these dragnets, or the thousands charged with counterrevolutionary activities, black marketeering, and anti-Soviet agitation. Most of these camps from the start were under Cheka control because their inmates were thrown into them by Cheka administrative fiat. But two other agencies were also involved: the People's Commissariat of Justice (NKYu), which in late December 1917 (NS) established the Administration of Prisons (later renamed several times); and the People's Commissariat of Internal Affairs (NKVD), which shared with the Cheka a vast network of concentration camps formally introduced by VTsIK decree in 1919. A kind of cooperative fusion began in March 1919 when Dzerzhinskiy became NKVD chief concurrent with his Cheka post; places of detention were put under the NKVD, which shortly thereafter also had attached to it the Cheka's successor, the GPU. Thus, for a short period, all prisons and concentration camps were nominally under a single administration. By July 1923, with the creation of the OGPU, a bifurcation once again occurred when the OGPU separated from the NKVD. But, state security was the driving force behind the harsh regimen in all places of detention, whether prisons or concentration camps.

State terror, then, embraced more than hostage taking and mass executions. The determination to bend the population to the party's will flew in the face of economics and even the physical self-interest of the new party–state. However, class war, which is what the party and Cheka were conducting, was not intended to induce harmonious social relations so as to foster a generalized prosperity. The very elements of Russian society that could generate social and economic prosperity were incarcerated, eliminated, or driven into exile precisely because of that talent. Hate theories do not traffic with economic rationalism or Judeo-Christian moral inhibitions and are impervious to evidence. They can be put into practice on a national level only through the unconstrained operations of a police regime committed to smashing enemies invented by theories.

The actual dispensing of justice in the new revolutionary state was to have been shared by two successors to the destroyed tsarist courts and judicial organs. The local or People's Courts were established to handle less important violations of Soviet decrees and laws. The more important criminal offenses and crimes against the new state were assigned to the Revolutionary Tribunals. Both bodies were operated by the People's Commissariat of Justice (NKYu), initially headed by the Left SR, I. Z. Steinberg, and were promulgated by a decree of the Sovnarkom on 5 December 1917 (NS).[13] The charge given to the Revolutionary Tribunals read as follows:

> For the struggle against the counter-revolutionary forces through protecting the revolution and its achievements from them and also for deciding cases involving the struggle against profiteering, speculation, sabotage, and other misdeeds of merchants, manufacturers, officials, and other persons, workers' and peasants' revolutionary tribunals are established, consisting of a chairman and six assessors who serve in turn, and are elected by gubernia or city soviets of workers', soldiers', and peasant deputies.[14]

On 1 January 1918 (NS) Steinberg, the commissar of justice, signed an instruction on the Revolutionary Tribunal that amplified the earlier decree, including such items as penalties—no death sentence, as yet—and the stipulation of public tribunal sessions. Steinberg included an article that allowed the commissar of justice to request the Central Executive Committee of the Soviets to order a second and last trial if an injustice in the verdict was discovered.[15] Although the death penalty was added in June 1918, its absence, and the second trial article in the original instruction, were indicators of the slight braking effect the Left SRs exercised on the new regime in its early months. One might also argue that Left SR presence in the Cheka collegium and other high Cheka positions may havę had a similar restraining influence. However, it should be remembered that the Left SRs in the regime tempered its violence only as regards other socialists. Moderation was not applied to the nonsocialist enemies of the revolution and the Left SRs were as bloody in their persecution of them as the Bolsheviks.

Legally speaking then, the Revolutionary Tribunals and the Commissariat of Justice should have been the final determinants in crimes against the state. In practice the Cheka almost immediately began encroaching, dispensing its own justice—including summary executions. Though Steinberg did prevail in a few clashes with the Cheka, the departure of the Left SRs from the coalition government (March 1918) removed the Steinberg irritant. But Lenin and Dzerzhinskiy still had trouble with Steinberg's Bolshevik successors who, along with other Bolshevik Party and government officials, raised serious questions about the arbitrary and capricious operations of the central and regional Chekas. It was precisely fears and complaints of this order from within the party that ultimately produced the Kronstadt uprising in 1921. In any event, in early July 1918, following the assassination in Moscow of the German ambassador, Count W. von Mirbach, by Left SR Chekists, and the seizure of Cheka headquarters and Dzerzhinskiy himself by SR Chekist insurgents during the Left SR uprising, the last remnant of Bolshevik–SR collaboration collapsed. The Sovnarkom dissolved the Cheka collegium and replaced it with one filled exclusively with Bolsheviks. There followed a systematic extirpation of right and center parties and freedom of the press. Now, even the Left SRs were pasted with the dangerous label of "counterrevolutionary." Any restraints on the Cheka would now have to come from within the ruling Bolshevik circle. But its leader, Lenin, was himself intent on goading the party and the Cheka to even bloodier actions.

At first the Cheka was required to hand over state criminals, such as saboteurs and counterrevolutionaries, to the Revolutionary Tribunals for trial. Actually, the Cheka did not receive the power of arrest until 29 December 1917 (NS) in a Sovnarkom decree (signed by Steinberg). But that did not really matter, because there were several other bodies with such authority. Also, in its first days and weeks the Cheka was absorbed with getting itself organized. But organize it did on a national and regional scale and it was not long before it was doing much more than arresting "subversives"—which it did not necessarily hand over to the Revolutionary Tribunals.

It is generally held that the "Red Terror" was not unleashed by the Cheka until the summer–fall of 1918 in the wake of the Left SR uprising, the assassination of Propaganda Commissar V. Volodarskiy in June, of Petrograd Cheka Chief M. S. Uritskiy on 30 August, and the shooting and wounding of Lenin in Moscow the same day by the socialist revolutionary Fanny Kaplan. In spirit and practice the terror really began much sooner; the Sovnarkom Decree on Red Terror of 5 September 1918 merely gave "legal" sanction to state-directed homicide already under way since the previous December. Peasants and others had begun resisting Bolshevik requisition squads, and Lenin wasted little time in exhorting both mob and state violence against them. His solution to the spreading famine generated by Bolshevik policies was to brutally enforce such policies: "We can't expect to get anywhere unless we resort to terrorism: speculators must be shot on the spot"; or "[grain] speculators who are caught and fully exposed as such shall be shot by the groups [requisition squads] on the spot. The same penalty shall be meted out to members of the groups who are exposed as dishonest"; and "adapt the most extreme revolutionary measures to fight speculators and to requisition grain stocks."[16] When Steinberg, the Left SR commissar of justice, protested that they might as well rename his organization the "Commissariat for Social Extermination," Lenin happily allowed that that is what it should be but it would be impolitic to say it.[17]

The following month, on 21 February 1918, the Sovnarkom issued the decree, "The Socialist Fatherland Is in Danger," in response to the resumption of the German offensive. Point eight of the decree stated: "*Enemy agents, profiteers, marauders, hooligans, counter-revolutionary agitators and German spies are to be shot on the spot.*" Immediately thereafter a supplement was issued that declared death by shooting for possession of arms without government permission and for concealing food.[18] Again, Steinberg, who was still in the government at that moment, crossed swords with Lenin over the decree, especially point eight. He later concluded that its incitement to summary executions set the pattern for Cheka terror.[19] In this view he is more than seconded by a more recent Soviet source who saw the government's behavior in January 1918 as the beginning of the terror and the February Sovnarkom decree as its legalizing instrument.[20] What followed later that year and during the Civil War was the unbridled response to such base appeals to hatred.

The arbitrary arrests, mass shootings, torture, and imprisonment were an integral element of Bolshevik policy, well ahead of the formation of the White armies. There was considerable opposition even within Bolshevik circles to such a bloody tendency and to the independence and arrogance of Dzerzhinskiy and his Chekists. In June 1918, before the fury of the summer events, Dzerzhinskiy gave an interview to the Moscow correspondent of Maxim Gorky's newspaper, *Novaya zhizn'* (*New Life*). He was accompanied by Cheka Deputy Chairman G. D. Zaks, a Left SR. Both men evidently were responding to the building criticism, fear, and hatred of the Cheka and felt compelled to justify what they were doing. Yet, they gave a telling and prophetic insight into the direction the new Soviet state would take and the structure of the leaders' thinking. The latter is characterized by a counterintelligence mania driven by a fanatical certitude in the course chosen:

> Society and the press fail to understand correctly the character and task of our Commission. They think of the struggle with counter-revolution and speculation on the level of normal state existence and for that reason they scream of courts, of guarantees, of inquiry, of investigation, etc. We have nothing in common with the military revolutionary tribunal.[21]

Dzerzhinskiy then issued his famous statement on terror:

> We represent in ourselves organized terror—this must be said very clearly—such terror is now very necessary in the conditions we are living through in a time of revolution.
>
> Our task is the struggle with the enemies of Soviet power. We are terrorizing the enemies of Soviet power in order to strangle crimes in their germ.[22]

This last item might be labeled preemptive counterintelligence. Later refined by Stalin, it gave state security the precedent for targeting those who had the *potential* for opposition. Dzerzhinskiy then allowed as how a decision whether or not to execute a victim was a democratic one:

> It is useless to blame us for anonymous killings. Our commission consists of 18 experienced revolutionaries representing the Central Committee of the Party and representing the Central Executive Committee [of the Soviets]. An execution is possible only with the unanimous decision of all members of the commission at a plenary meeting. It is sufficient for a single member to express himself against execution by shooting and the life of the accused is saved.[23]

Of course, the latter was palpable nonsense. The VCheka (the central Cheka) simply did not operate with such parliamentary regard, let alone the wilder provincial and local Chekas.

Then Dzerzhinskiy made a very frank and ominous statement, one that portended the unrestrained operational style of state security for years to come:

> We decide matters quickly. In the majority of cases from the time of arrest of the criminal to the time of decision only 24 hours elapse. But this does not mean that our decision is not well founded. Of course, we may make mistakes, but up till now there have been no mistakes. This is proved by the minutes of our meetings. In almost all cases the criminals, when pressed against the wall by evidence, admit their crimes. And what argument would have more weight than the confession of the accused himself.[24]

There it was, efficient revolutionary justice: twenty-four hours from arrest to the decision to shoot. Dzerzhinskiy was, after all, speaking of executions here. The import of this interview cannot be exaggerated. New relationships of state to society with no restraints of the former and its police sword; state-directed terror; the infallibility not merely of the party but of state security as well; and the arrogant certitude that forced confession was the determinant of guilt—these were the legacies that found their fulfillment in the Stalinist era.

On 5 September 1918 the Sovnarkom, responding to Bolshevik and Chekist cries for blood, received Dzerzhinskiy's report on the growing opposition, peasant risings, and hostility to the burgeoning Cheka repressions. A resolution passed on Dzerzhinskiy's report was the formal Decree on Red Terror, signed by the commissars for justice and internal affairs:

> The Council of People's Commissars, having heard the report of the Chairman [Dzerzhinskiy] . . . finds that in the present circumstances it is of utmost importance to safeguard the rear through terror; that in order to improve the work of the [Cheka] . . . and give it a more systematic character, it must be reinforced with as many responsible Party comrades as possible; that it is important to secure the Soviet Republic from its class enemies by isolating them in concentration camps; that all persons involved in White Guard organizations, plots and uprisings shall be executed; and that it is necessary to publish the names of all those executed along with the reasons for their executions.[25]

If the Cheka had felt any restraints on its summary actions, they were now removed and an intensified orgy of arrests, torture, and executions ensued. Red terror begat White counterterror; however, the ferocity of the Red crusade, driven by a programmatic ideology preaching class hatred, far outpaced the reactive White impulse. The Cheka operated under an all-embracing plan, simple though it was: the bourgeoisie were to be exterminated. That this mass extermination was premeditated and not merely, as Soviets claim, a response to White reaction and foreign intervention, is seen by its continuance well after the defeat of the Whites and the withdrawal of foreign forces, that is, well into the 1920s.

The numbers of victims of Cheka–party terror during the Civil War are still debated, ranging from the Chekist M. I. Latsis's figure of 12,733, to about 500,000 estimated by Robert Conquest, although his figure is for the period 1917–23.[26] Others run the numbers far higher. Though Latsis's figures are patently absurd, Conquest's do not account for those shot immediately following the suppression of various rebellions, and those deaths caused by concentration camp and prison treatment. Not factored in are the battle casualties of the Civil War and deaths from famine and epidemics. The millions who fled or were exiled from Russia are not treated here as casualties, though indeed they were victims.

The Cheka is frequently compared with its tsarist counterpart, the Okhrana. The modus operandi of each, in a narrow counterintelligence sense, was similar, but symmetry evaporates on the facts of repression. Appendix A contrasts death and prison statistics for the last ninety years of tsarist rule with Lenin's sway from 1917 to his death in 1924. The figures for the tsarist and Soviet periods include Soviet estimates. Interestingly, these Soviet figures are not overstated for the tsarist years. But they are contradictory and inadequate for the Soviet period in question, as we would expect.

Certainly, both clusters of statistics are inadequate for absolutely definitive comparisons. However, the tsarist figures were more accessible because there was less to hide, as evidenced by the ease with which opponents accessed and used them. For the Soviet period the government had cause to be secretive and to dissemble, given the magnitude of the terror it had unleashed. Also, with the exception of Latsis's numbers, the bulk of the Soviet figures came from the Commissariat of Justice or its organs, the Revolutionary Tribunals and the People's Courts. Yet the Cheka bore a far larger share of the repressions than they had. It is doubtful that even party and state security archives have surviving or reliable documentation as to the true scope of the casualties experienced.[27] Such documents also would had to have made it unscathed through Stalin's long tenure, an unlikely probability.

What seems clear is that an unbroken patrimony between tsarist repression and Soviet terror cannot be claimed. Even at the height of tsarist repression following the Revolution of 1905 when the Gendarmes and Okhrana were responding to left-wing terrorism, nothing faintly approached the intensity and scope of Cheka ferocity. The conditions of imprisonment or exile contrasted sharply as well. While in prison Lenin composed and smuggled leaflets to industrial strikers and began work on his massive *The Development of Capitalism in Russia*, for which he received considerable assistance from prison officials. In Siberian exile Lenin was quartered with a peasant family of moderate means. He completed his book, did other writing, visited other exiles, traveled locally, hunted and fished, and regained his health. Escapes of political prisoners and exiles were fairly routine.

The difference in repression between the two systems was not only in degree but also in kind. It simply was not tsarist policy or practice to exterminate whole categories of people. Even at the height of its repressions against revolutionaries, tsarist courts offset Okhrana and Gendarme actions, thereby exercising a restraining hand. In Lenin's system the courts were either ignored or became creatures of the Cheka. This rather novel notion set the conditions for the bizarre, judicial circuses of the 1930s purge trials. Soviet jurisprudence has yet to sever itself from state security prerogatives and has never acquired the independence and legitimacy of the tsarist model.

The statistics hold other tales as well. Sergey Mel'gunov gives weight to the following categorization of Red Terror victims presented in a series of articles for an Edinburgh publication:

> Bishops, 28; ecclesiastics, 1,219; professors and teachers, 6,000; medical men, 9,000; naval and military officers, 54,000; naval and military men of the ranks, 260,000; police officials, 70,000; intellectuals and members of the professional classes, 355,250; industrial workers, 193,290; peasants, 815,000.[28]

One would expect to see sizable numbers of the clergy, police, officer corps, and educated portions of the population on such a list. What is significant are the extremely large numbers of peasants, which exceeded the next most numerous group of victims by a factor of more than two. Together with workers and military enlisted ranks (who would have come from among the peasantry and workers), the peasants comprised roughly 72 percent of the victims according to this account. Lest it be argued that Mel'gunov was a prominent Socialist Revolutionary whose peasant bias colored his statistics, Soviet statistics point in the same direction. For example, of the announced 40,913 NKVD camp inmates for December 1921, almost 80 percent were illiterate or had marginal schooling and were therefore peasants and workers.[29] The Cheka's class war certainly was an "aristocide" of the leading sectors of tsarist society, but its most numerous victims were the very classes it claimed to represent and serve. Leninist rhetoric and Chekist justifications for the savaging of the peasantry invariably centered on the nefarious intrigues of the kulaks, those smallholding, enterprising peasant elements. But this was a dodge to hide the real state of affairs. Growing peasant rebellion against the

Bolsheviks throughout the Civil War demonstrated the real loyalties of Russia's masses. The Kronstadt rebellion of Red sailors in 1921 was intimately related to peasant unrest and worker opposition. The Cheka knew who the internal enemy was; hence those statistics. From the state security perspective the kulak (read peasant) problem would not be resolved until collectivization a decade later eliminated them by the millions.

A comparison of the sizes of the Okhrana and the Cheka further highlights the fundamental differences between the two services. Richard Pipes observes that in 1895 the Department of Police (the correct title for what is generally known as the Okhrana) had but 161 full-time personnel, backed by the Corps of Gendarmes, which numbered less than 10,000.[30] Immediately before World War I (1911–13), Okhrana headquarters in St. Petersburg is reported to have had 400 officials and employees.[31] Its operational arms, the Security Divisions (Okhrannoye Otdeleniye or OOs), numbered 75 and technically were part of the Gendarme Administration of the empire. The OOs accounted for less than 13,000 permanent staff and officers on detached duty from other Gendarme positions.[32] By October 1916 (OS) these had increased to 15,000.[33] The St. Petersburg and other OOs controlled and ran the agents, double agents, and provocateurs used to penetrate the various revolutionary parties and groups. The only external, or foreign, operational capability of the Okhrana was the Foreign Agency (Zagranichnaya Agentura) located in the Russian Embassy in Paris. It was an outpost of the Department of Police in St. Petersburg, or more precisely the Special Section (Osobiy Otdel) of Department of Police Headquarters. The Foreign Agency was really tsarist external counterintelligence.[34]

The Cheka, on the other hand, grew from 23 men in December 1917 (OS)[35] to a minimum of 37,000 in January 1919.[36] By mid-1921, the Cheka accounted for approximately 262,400 effectives organized as follows: 31,000 "civilian" staff (it was really a quasi-military force); 137,106 Cheka (Internal) Troops; and 94,288 Frontier Troops.[37] The 31,000 figure, Latsis's number, is probably understated, given Latsis's tendency at this point to play down Cheka excesses. Even at that, 262,400 is an impressive number, as it is separate from Red Army, NKVD, and militia totals. Comparing it to the 15,000 plus of the Okhrana and its OOs, it is hard to argue a symmetry between the two services, either organizationally or in numbers.

Though the major fronts of the Civil War were secured by the Red Army by fall 1920, the requirement for Cheka "extraordinary measures" did not necessarily abate. However, there were strong internal party pressures to limit the scope of the Cheka's authority. There also were persistent rebellious movements among the peasantry and various national minorities, which picked up strength in the winter of 1920–21. These were abetted by the demobilization of the Red Army, itself a peasant conscript force, which pumped large numbers of men back into the restive countryside. But the party had little choice in view of the raging famine and a thoroughly wrecked economy. In some respects internal ferment in 1921 was far more threatening to the survival of Bolshevism than the Whites, Poles, and foreign armies had been collectively.

The depth of this anti-Bolshevik and anti-Cheka bitterness (in the eyes of many, the party and police were viewed as a singular criminal entity) was signaled by the uprising at the Kronstadt fortress on Kotlin Island, twenty-five miles west of Petrograd, in March 1921. These were the hero-sailors of the October Revolution, the leading edge of Bolshevik radicalism, and the scourge of the Provisional Government. Lenin had called them the "pride and beauty of the Russian Revolution." Yet they turned on the very system they helped to power, and the party was traumatized by the psychological and ideological impact of the event. The uprising struck at the very legitimacy of the system more profoundly than White propaganda could ever have hoped for. The published grievances of the communist sailors were volatile stuff:

> The power of the police and gendarme Monarchy passed into the hands of Communist usurpers, who, instead of giving the people freedoms, instituted in them the constant fear of falling into the torture chambers of the Cheka, which in their horrors far exceed the gendarme administration of the tsarist regime. The bayonets, bullets, and gruff commands of the Cheka *oprichniki*—these are what the workingman of Soviet Russia has won after so much struggle and suffering. . . . To the protests of the peasants, expressed in spontaneous uprisings . . . they answer with mass executions and bloodletting. . . .[38]

For the Kronstadt rebels the Cheka represented the Okhrana and the *oprichniki* (Ivan the Terrible's secret police) of the party.[39] In exchange for requisitional grain and confiscated livestock the peasants received "Cheka raids and firing squads."[40]

The rebels were subdued as viciously as any losing White Army in the Civil War. Selected party cadres, Red Army units, and special Cheka forces, with Cheka machine gunners at their backs to stiffen resolve, made several unsuccessful assaults across the ice before the rebels were smashed. Survivors were either shot outright or perished later in northern camps. Several thousand had escaped to Finland. Many of these, in response to a Bolshevik offer of amnesty, returned to Russia only to be shipped off to Cheka camps and death. Lenin did not want any of these people around to give witness to what October 1917 meant for dissenting Bolsheviks.

Heretofore, savage repressions were justified on the basis of the requirements of defending the revolution. Although recipients of Cheka bullets represented all shades of the political spectrum during the Civil War, certainly Bolsheviks were not among them. The decision to crush this protest of the Red sailors had far-reaching implications and consequences. For one it demonstrated the totalitarian bent of the leadership, justifying all the earlier fears of the Mensheviks, SRs, anarchists, and an earlier, pre-Bolshevik Trotsky. It exposed the arrogant cynicism of a leadership that would tolerate not the slightest inkling of dissent among the faithful, and established a precedent for later widespread suppression within the party itself. More importantly, it morally compromised a whole generation of party, military, and state security cadres who, acquiescing in the suppression of the Kronstadt rebels, deprived themselves of any moral anchors for standing fast against later atrocities on themselves and the country at large.

But Kronstadt did give the leadership cause to reflect on the need for tactical adjustments in state policy. Economic exhaustion, famine, and peasant rebellions linked to a widespread resentment against the Cheka still had to be dealt with. The suppression of Kronstadt may have spiked an immediate popular explosion, but disastrous conditions still threatened the party's exclusive claims to monopoly rule. The party's tenth congress in March 1921 coincided with the Kronstadt rebellion and was the occasion for some major policy shifts. The biggest tactical compromise was the New Economic Policy (NEP), which allowed a modicum of economic freedom to foster some sort of reconstruction, and political reconciliation with the bourgeois West. But at the same time Lenin proscribed opposition within the ranks of the party itself and initiated Cheka suppression of Mensheviks and SRs in a manner exceeding even earlier nastiness. Indeed, in the political realm a reversal of economic liberalization and international détente became the standard and was to be repeated periodically throughout Soviet history. The late-twentieth-century variant of this would be the ideological vigilance campaigns accompanying détente and other forms of increased foreign contact.

The next tactical adjustment came on 6 February 1922, when the Politburo had the All-Russian Central Executive Committee (VTsIK) pass a decree abolishing the Cheka and replacing it with the State Political Directorate (Gosudarstvennoye Politicheskoye Upravleniye, or GPU).[41] The GPU was subordinated to the NKVD, but because the latter was also headed by Dzerzhinskiy, no real structural or leadership shocks occurred. This was a bit of bureaucratic legerdemain. Theoretically the GPU under the NKVD was answerable to the Sovnarkom and was therefore a state agency. But, in political reality, nothing changed; state security, in practice, answered to the Politburo. If anything, the tenuousness implicit in the Cheka's official title was eliminated with the permanence conferred by the new designation as part of the image-building effort; the Commissariat of Justice (NKYu) and the Revolutionary Tribunals were to play greater roles in an atmosphere of enhanced "legality." In practice, subsequent decrees in the same year reconferred the bulk of the Cheka's old powers on the GPU while Lenin badgered Dmitriy Kurskiy, the commissar of justice, with the need for more shootings and terror against Mensheviks, SRs, and those seeking to take the NEP a little too seriously. The NEP and the redesignation of state security may have assuaged some timorous Bolsheviks and credulous foreigners, but Lenin, Dzerzhinskiy, and their Chekists knew otherwise.

However, the nominal subordination of the GPU to the NKVD lasted only a little over a year. In July 1923 the second Soviet constitution, which "created" the USSR (ratified in 1924), lifted state security out of the NKVD and established it as a separate commissariat under the Sovnarkom. It was retitled the United State Political Directorate (Obyedinennoye Gosudarstvennoye Politicheskoye Upravleniye or OGPU), a name it retained for eleven years. Dzerzhinskiy continued as its chief, but gave up his lesser NKVD post. His first and second deputy chairmen, Vyacheslav Menzhinskiy and Genrikh Yagoda, were to be successor chairmen over the next ten years, ensuring a continuity of personal service to Stalin's personal rule.

This period of conjoining events and name changes is critical in that it refined the relationship between the party and police in a manner that resonates into the late twentieth century. But central to this relationship was the role of Stalin. The 1923 constitution was Stalin's "first" constitution; as general secretary he played a critical role in its drafting and therefore in "legalizing" the position of state security in the party–state system. In addition to Lenin's growing friction with Stalin, there was a cooling of relations between Lenin and Dzerzhinskiy. Leggett observes that Dzerzhinskiy apparently resented Lenin's lack of confidence in his political and economic acumen.[42] It was not until after Lenin's death on 21 January 1924 that Dzerzhinskiy was named chairman of the Supreme Council of National Economy (or VSNKh; 2 February 1924) and candidate member of the Politburo (2 June 1924). Stalin's position and power made these appointments possible. Earlier (July 1923), he had evidently assisted Dzerzhinskiy in acquiring membership on the powerful and prestigious Defense Council.

These were important, but time-consuming positions, especially the chairmanship of VSNKh, which ran the national economy. This meant that the OGPU would, for all practical purposes, be run by Dzerzhinskiy's two deputies, Menzhinskiy and Yagoda. The former, partially disabled by health or hypochondria, was pliant and deferential to Stalin. The latter, for all practical purposes, was already Stalin's man. When Dzerzhinskiy died in July 1926, Stalin was in a position to control the OGPU.

It was also at this time (1923) that Stalin began using state security to target higher-level opposition within the party, signaling his drive to unitary rule. Kronstadt had set the precedent with the full blessing of Lenin and other senior Bolsheviks. In 1923, with Lenin gravely ill following a stroke, Stalin personally ordered the arrest of Mirza Sultan-Galiyev, a prominent Tatar party official in the Commissariat of Nationality Affairs, who had pushed for a Soviet Moslem republic and reestablishment of the Moslem Communist Party. Charged by Stalin with supporting the Basmachi insurgents, he "confessed" his guilt but was nonetheless purged. Lev Kamenev, who acquiesced in the arrest, is quoted by Trotsky as stating that Sultan-Galiyev was the first important party member cashiered in Stalin's personal order.[43] Wolin and Slusser state that Stalin accomplished this through the use of secret data (whether real or spurious is unknown) provided by state security.[44] It could be argued that this case set the OGPU above the party with the party collaborating in its own pending demise. But the potential and tendency in this direction had already been determined by the extralegal powers enjoyed from the Cheka's earliest days. Dzerzhinskiy always argued for special status for his organization with the invariable support of Lenin. Stalin had the cunning to perceive the implications and the will to act upon them. A state-within-a-state was about to be realized.

3

The Counterintelligence–
Active Measures Tradition

P ENETRATION, provocation, deception, and other related operational counterintelligence initiatives were not unknown to the Cheka and its early successors. As was seen in chapter 1, the leaders of the new state had themselves been victims of and matched wits with the Okhrana in the latter's various maneuvers to disable the revolutionary underground. Comparatively speaking, Soviet state security turns out to have been much more adept at these counterintelligence schemes. What had been a proclivity of the Okhrana became an operational imperative, and thus a tradition, of its Bolshevik successors. Penetration, provocation, and large-scale deception operations from the very start characterized party-directed state security activity in its foreign and internal dimensions. They were of such an all-embracing and persistent nature that the new regime quickly took on the characteristics of a counterintelligence state. Counterintelligence was not the mere province of a security service; it denominated the features of the whole party–state system.

What are now known variously as active measures (*aktivnyye meropriyatiya*), disinformation, and *maskirovka* (roughly speaking, military deception in its totality) are only the latest items in a stylized Russian and Soviet operational vocabulary used in the integration of varied state security operational initiatives. Such initiatives include among others:

provocation (*provokatsiya*)

penetration (*proniknoveniye*)

fabrication (*fabrikatsiya*)

diversion (*diversiya*)

agent of influence (*agent vliyaniya* or *agent po vliyaniyu*)

clandestine work (*konspiratsiya*)

disinformation (*dezinformatsiya*)

wet affairs (*mokrye dela*)

direct action (*aktivnyye akty*)

combination (*kombinatsiya*)

The first six terms evoke recognizable images from seven decades of Soviet state security practices. "Wet affairs" became part of the operational argot for assassinations, kidnappings, sabotage, and the like, especially after the creation in 1936 of Yezhov's Administration for Special Tasks, which set mobile killer teams loose against White officers, defectors, Trotsky, and other enemies outside of the USSR. "Direct action" appears to be of more recent vintage within state security and denotes the same types of action as wet affairs. "Combination," the last term, is indicative of Soviet fixation with complex operations analogous to intricate chess moves. It is an insider's term for relating, linking, or combining operational undertakings in different times and places to enhance overall operational results.

Organizationally, the Soviets did not find it expedient to centralize strategic political deception and *maskirovka* in highly bureaucratized structures until the Khrushchev era (about 1959). Given the nature of the Lenin–Dzerzhinskiy period and then the unique, personalized style of Stalin's leadership, a large centralized deception bureaucracy was neither necessary nor desired. Only after Stalin's death—which brought about an evolution of political leadership and which was followed by dramatic advances in military technology—did large-scale and continuous bureaucratic centralization emerge.

But this does not mean that centrally conceived and controlled deception operations did not occur during the Cheka–GPU–OGPU era. Indeed they did, but under the auspices of senior party and state security leaders, beginning with Lenin and Dzerzhinskiy and continuing with Stalin himself. Operations apparently were developed and executed through coordination among such seniors with operational oversight, first within state security, and later within Stalin's personal secretariat or chancellery, also known as the Secret Department (Sekretnyy Otdel) and later as the Special Sector (Osobyy Sektor).

Dzerzhinskiy brought a number of his fellow Poles into the Cheka, including at least two or three he personally converted following their capture in the Russo-Polish War of 1920. These were a Polish Army officer later known variously as V. Stetskevich, V. Kiyakovskiy, Kossinskiy, and Kolesnikov; an officer of Polish Intelligence named Ignace Dobrzynskiy; and the latter's fiancée, M. Navroska. Dobrzynskiy later worked under the alias of Sosnowskiy as a trusted member of the Cheka–OGPU.[1]

Other personalities who played key roles in directing Soviet provocation and deception schemes included Artur Kh. Artuzov (originally Fraucci or possibly Renucci, son of an Italo-Swiss émigré), chief of the Cheka Special Department (OO) in the Russo-Polish War and then chief of Cheka Counterintelligence (KRO, later KRU), where he ran the "Sindikat" and "Trust" legends (more on these later). He later directed the NKVD's Foreign Administration under Yagoda in 1934. Artuzov worked closely with Yakov S. Agranov, a senior Chekist who was later linked with Stalin's secretariat and was first deputy chairman of the NKVD under Yagoda. Both Artuzov and Agranov were arrested and executed, probably in 1937.[2]

Information on identifiable deception components within Soviet intelligence and security apparently first appeared in Western sources in the mid-1920s. A former tsarist intelligence officer, Colonel A. Rezanov, wrote that organizations in the Cheka, the Intelligence Directorate of the Red Army, and the Communist International were responsible for the circulation of propaganda and spurious information.[3] Concurrently, an English journal identified the Foreign Department of the GPU as bearing the responsibility for disinformation. Two bureaus of this department, a press section and a document section, respectively, "spread false news in the foreign press," and falsified "all kinds of documents of a financial, governmental, and political nature."[4] The journal further added that still another "special foreign section [of the Foreign Department of the GPU] was kept busy . . . issuing false banknotes of foreign countries in order to change them for good ones and use these later in the respective countries for Soviet propaganda."[5] It also identified one of the Trilliser brothers as responsible for "the so-called 'disinformation' of foreign countries against which the Soviet policy is now working with the idea of worldwide social revolution."[6] Most observers had long believed that there was only one Trilliser, Mikhail Abramovich, who headed the Foreign Department (INO) of the Cheka/GPU/OGPU and later was transferred to the Comintern. He had used at least one pseudonym, M. A. Moskvin, which some felt contributed to the story of two brothers. But the Soviets themselves later confirmed the existence of a brother, David Abramovich, who did underground party work and later held positions in the Red Army, the party, and economic organizations, thereby lending support to the early British report.[7] This report, then, not only identifies two important brothers involved in foreign intelligence and early active measures (somewhat in the tradition of the Bonch-Bruyevich brothers), but is among the earliest in English to employ the term "disinformation" in the context of state security foreign operations.

A Russian language newspaper from Riga, in 1927, states that the passing of disinformation ("dezinformatsiya") to foreign counterintelligence was a major GPU objective.[8] A few days later it connected a "Disinformation Bureau" to Soviet intelligence, but then incorrectly fused the GPU and military intelligence (Razvedupr).[9] This confusion was repeated years later in an article by White General Baron Pëtr Wrangel's political advisor, N. Chebyshev, who also subordinated a Disinformation Bureau to the Razvedupr (Intelligence Administration) of the GPU.[10] That both the GPU and Soviet Military Intelligence had been running sophisticated deception games is concluded by George Leggett, and it is probable that the sources of the Riga and Chebyshev information mixed the two services, wittingly or otherwise.[11] But Chebyshev was strikingly clear on what this Disinformation Bureau was to accomplish:

> Like all agencies involved in the defense of Soviet power, it was engaged in the fabrication of falsehoods to deceive European counterintelligence agencies. The Soviet bureau prepared false information about the Red Army and Navy. However, this was done carefully—with false documents and fabricated data, with an admixture of genuinely true but innocuous material. For example, the "Razvedupr" released information that was not of the secret type or that had lost its

importance, such as the mobilization of industry in the recent period, etc.[12]

This was a timeless recipe for military deception, notwithstanding improvements in technology and communications. What Chebyshev outlined still finds pertinence for Soviet state security and the GRU in the late twentieth century.

Little information has surfaced about the role of the People's Commissariat of Foreign Affairs (NKID) in early deception operations, although it has been demonstrated that as early as 1921–22, the NKID circulated spurious documents and otherwise supported state security in its deception actions.[13] The Comintern, a subservient Soviet creation carefully linked to the Cheka, likewise performed its part in Soviet active measures up to its dissolution in 1943.[14]

Though the information on Soviet organizational focal points for early strategic deception is somewhat fragmentary and a bit confusing, the operations show that many things were indeed going on and that some very senior party and state security personnel were heavily involved. Focusing precisely on such senior leadership involvement, a style of operation had emerged and carried on through the Stalin years. A personalized centralization characterized this operational style. Lenin is alleged to have instructed Dzerzhinskiy to "tell them what they want to hear" in constructing the Trust legend against the emigration and Western intelligence. Dzerzhinskiy himself took a personal interest in Sindikat I and II, the operations targeted against Boris Savinkov. Stalin made the decision to wrap up the Trust legend in 1927 and, during World War II, personally oversaw the major deceptions associated with key offensives against the Germans. Deception is a key ingredient of the counterintelligence state and the command leadership manipulates this ingredient on an unbroken continuum unfettered by Western distinctions of peace and war.

Among the first provocational operations, by Soviet account, was the so-called "Lockhart" or "Ambassadors'" Plot of August 1918. As with other Soviet intelligence-related actions, this story has more than one Soviet version. The British diplomatic agent, R. H. Bruce Lockhart, was claimed by the Soviets to have been central to a plot to overthrow the Bolshevik government and assassinate its leaders in the summer of 1918. Lockhart, working with Sidney Reilly and the French consul general in Moscow, is alleged in a 1924 Soviet account to have attempted to suborn the Latvian rifle regiments protecting the new Soviet government.[15] In much later accounts the Soviets escalated the affair into a conspiracy of Western ambassadors, renaming it the "Ambassadors' Plot" and adding to the scheme the U. S. consul general, the French military attaché, and a U. S. businessman with U. S. diplomatic ties, one Xenophon B. Kalamatiano.[16] But, they then also claimed that the affair was controlled by Dzerzhinskiy from start to finish—a conspiracy invented by the Cheka which, using two of its men, Shmidken and Bredis (real names Buykis and Sprogis), floated the scheme before Lockhart with the intent of entrapping him.[17] Lockhart, who was arrested, vehemently denied any part in a conspiracy to his interrogator, the Chekist Deputy Chief Ya. Peters (who authored one of the first Soviet versions of the story), and challenged him with the charge that Peters knew very well the conspiracy was a fake.[18] Lockhart also evinced a suspicion in his memoirs that while he was clean, he was not so sure of Reilly's part and intentions in the "alleged" conspiracy.[19] Thus we have an indignant Soviet charge, Lockhart's equally indignant denial and still another Soviet tale proudly hailing Dzerzhinskiy's provocational talents. Lockhart may have, and Reilly most certainly did, play at conspiracy. But they apparently were the unwitting tools of Dzerzhinskiy who called the events of August 1918 into existence and terminated them when his objectives had been reached or when conditions dictated—Lockhart and other arrested British and French personnel were exchanged for Maxim Litvinov and other Soviets who had been detained in London in retaliation. Finally, there are those who think Reilly was a Cheka agent from 1918 onwards, a Bolshevik provocateur thrust upon Lockhart and then insinuated into British intelligence after his escape from Russia.[20] A derivative refinement of this legend has Reilly as a loyal British intelligence operative but one who was "turned" by Dzerzhinskiy "to become one of the principal architects of Soviet penetration of Western intelligence . . . the creator of 'agents of influence.' "[21]

The Lockhart case then, appears to be the first of a Soviet genre of spurious dissident movements designed to surface and entrap opponents and their Western sympathizers. These provocations quickly assumed strong deceptive dimensions, which operated, and apparently still operate, with remarkable resonance among persistently credulous targets, especially in the West.

Lenin seemed to take a special delight in exploiting such gullibility among Western elites. A Soviet artist in 1924 was able to copy a set of Lenin's notes at the Lenin Institute, where the artist was working, which included the following:

From my own observations during my years as an emigre, I must say that the so-called educated strata in Western Europe and America are incapable of comprehending the present state of affairs, the real balance of power. Those elements should be regarded as deaf mutes and treated accordingly. . . . First, to soothe the fears of the deaf mutes, we must proclaim a separation . . . of our government . . . from the Party and Politburo and especially from the Comintern. We must declare that the latter entities are independent political organizations merely tolerated on Soviet soil. Mark my word, the deaf mutes will swallow it.[22]

Local opponents and those in the emigration were no less susceptible to these old Okhrana-proven techniques.[23] Two of the most successful and bizarre provocations involved Boris Savinkov, former SR terrorist, war minister in Aleksandr Kerenskiy's government, and bitter opponent of the Bolsheviks. In the latter capacity Savinkov organized and captained anti-Bolshevik uprisings, guerrilla movements, and terrorist forays as early as 1918. He had attracted the attention of the world's powerful, Churchill considering him important enough to be included in his *Great Contemporaries*.[24] The first Soviet operation against Savinkov, Sindikat I, began with probable penetrations of his immediate entourage during his Yaroslavl, Nurom, and Rybinsk uprisings of July 1918. The Sindikat I "legend" (an artful, provocational story) was designed to penetrate and spike Savinkov's networks and plans. Savinkov retreated into Poland where, with support from his old friend Marshal Józef K. Piłsudski, he set about organizing a substantial force for operations into the western USSR. In late 1920 and early 1921 Savinkov was visited from the USSR by one Selyaninov-Opperput, a self-professed anticommunist who convinced Savinkov to revive his old Union for the Defense of the Motherland and Freedom and to collaborate in a new round of uprisings against the Bolsheviks. The union expanded considerably, Selyaninov-Opperput meanwhile gaining access to the structure and names of the underground network in the USSR. In the summer of 1921 disaster struck with the arrest, imprisonment, and execution of hundreds of bona fide union members. Selyaninov-Opperput disappeared, but was to surface again shortly in another provocational entrapment. So ended Sindikat I, the first of a two-part Cheka provocation aimed at declawing and then capturing Boris Savinkov.[25] The Sindikat II would lure Savinkov back into the USSR and wrap him up for good while leaving a legacy of controversy over his true loyalties.

After Sindikat I, Savinkov retreated to Paris, where he continued to mobilize Western support for his activities against Moscow. The USSR had pressured Warsaw to put a stop to Savinkov's activities. Despite the disaster to his organization in Russia, he still commanded certain residual networks in the USSR and still ran forays from Poland. In 1924, Savinkov received two visitors from the USSR, Pavlov (first name unknown) and A. A. Fedorov (also known as A. A. Yakushev, an OGPU principal in the Trust) with letters from one Colonel Sergey Pavlovskiy, an associate and agent of Savinkov who insisted that Savinkov come to Russia to help guide a new liberal movement. Vladimir Burtsev, the one-man counterintelligence agency of prerevolutionary fame, warned Savinkov that this was a trap and that Fedorov–Yakushev was an OGPU agent. Burtsev later learned that Colonel Pavlovskiy had been apprehended and turned by the OGPU and was thus a party to the deception.[26] Savinkov would not be stayed. Accompanied by Pavlov, Fedorov–Yakushev, and two friends also believed to be OGPU agents, Aleksandr and Lyubov Dikgov-Derental, he entered Russia in mid-August 1924. On 29 August 1924 Moscow announced Savinkov's arrest by the OGPU.[27] The next day the Soviet press stated that Savinkov was tried before the Military Collegium of the Supreme Court of the Soviet Union on 27–28 August 1924, confessed his guilt, disavowed his anti-Soviet activities and associates and pledged himself to the recognition of and service to Soviet power.[28] Not only that, he called on his fellow Russians to "bow before the power of the workers and peasants and recognize it without reservations."[29] Sindikat II was concluded.

The effect on the emigration and Western governments was one of stupefaction. Many attributed the speedy volte-face of Savinkov to OGPU interrogation techniques coupled with a kangaroo court. The presiding judge, V. V. Ul'rikh, would earn similar notoriety thirteen years later for his role in the infamous show trials. Others drew the arguable conclusion that Savinkov turned traitor and may have been in Soviet service for some time before his arrest. This suspicion still resonates, fueled by the recent discovery of a letter from Savinkov to Marshal Piłsudski in December 1921 in which Savinkov informed the latter of a meeting he had earlier that month in London with the Soviet diplomatic representative L. Krasin, and during which meeting Savinkov set forth certain conditions for recognition of the Soviet government.[30] Some adduce from this that with the introduction of the NEP and the "elimination" of the Cheka, Savinkov's conditions were met in part, hence the suspicion that he was already Moscow's when he unaccountably left for Russia in 1924.

But was Savinkov really theirs? This may never be known definitively, barring an unlikely look at KGB archives. But it should be noted the bulk of the stories on Savinkov's demise originated with Soviet sources. Demoralization of the emigration clearly was in their interest.

Roughly concurrent with Sindikat I and II was the Trust (Trest) operation, one of forty or more legends initiated or run by state security during the interwar period. Where no genuine internal opposition organization exists, state security will invent one—both to infiltrate the more dangerous émigré organizations abroad in order to blunt or channel their actions, and to surface real or potential internal dissidents. If an internal opposition already exists, it will be infiltrated in an attempt to control it, to provoke opponents into exposing themselves, and to cause the movement to serve state interests. Fortuitous circumstances at times will allow counterintelligence to target the legend at internal dissidents, the emigration, *and* foreign governments or intelligence services. The Trust legend was one such example.[31]

The Trust may be viewed as the prototypical strategic deception and provocation operation in the Soviet repertoire. The Trust involved the creation of a notional opposition organization within the USSR by state security and was targeted against the anti-Soviet emigration in the West and Western intelligence services. It also comprised counterintelligence operations against opponents within the USSR, who were induced into surfacing themselves through Trust provocations.

Planning began in 1921, and the operation was orchestrated by state security until fall 1927. In addition to disinformation and prov-

ocation, the Trust simultaneously employed other techniques mentioned earlier: penetration, diversion, fabrication, agents of influence, and combination.

The official title given by state security to this bogus operation
was the Monarchist Association of Central Russia (MOTsR). Its
cover title was the Moscow Municipal Credit Association (hence the
Trust) operating under NEP dispensation. The direction of the
Trust was provided by the highest echelons of state security.

Through the Trust, the Soviets were able to identify, expose, and
neutralize opponents within the USSR. Many were allowed to operate for several years, not knowing that their activities were completely controlled by state security. It became possible, through
Trust channels, for the secret police to prevent the establishment of
a genuine anti-Communist underground in the USSR. Outside the
Soviet Union, state security was able to penetrate the White paramilitary groups, who were then used to funnel disinformation to unsuspecting Western intelligence services and governments.

It was through Trust channels that Boris Savinkov and Sidney
Reilly, connected with British intelligence, were lured back into the
USSR and eliminated (Savinkov in spring–summer 1924, Reilly in
August–September 1925). Another well-known émigré, V. V. Shul-
gin, undertook a lengthy "underground" trip (September 1925 to
April 1926) through European Russia, handled all of the time by
Trust (OGPU) operatives. His manuscript account of the trip, *Three
Capitals*, was read and approved by the Trust leadership and pub-
lished in Berlin in 1927—the year the Trust was folded by the
OGPU. Its disinforming message focused on how communism was
fading in Russia, how the Soviet leaders were really nationalists–
monarchists of a new stripe, and why any direct action by the West,
military or otherwise, would be undesirable.

Strikingly similar themes were advanced by the "returnism" (*voz-
vrashchentsvo*), and "change of landmarks" (*smenavekhovtsvo*) movements among certain émigré circles in the diaspora of the early
1920s. The latter tendency, the Smena Vekh movement, had its own
newspaper, *Nakanune* (On the Eve), in Berlin and journals in Riga,
Helsinki, Sofia, and Harbin. Also, several Smena Vekh journals
were allowed by the Soviet government to appear in Russia, Lenin
having acknowledged that the movement was "very useful" in gar-
nering non-Bolshevik support for his regime while allowing him to

keep an eye on such "candid enemies."[32] *Nakanune* faithfully reflected the Soviet party line and was of immense value to Moscow as an émigré instrument of conversion to the Soviet cause. It was backed by Soviet subsidies until it was closed in June 1924. The Soviets allowed Smena Vekh inside the USSR to continue for another year and a half before they suppressed it.[33] Like the Trust, when it had served its purpose it was terminated.

Polish intelligence was among the first to suspect the Trust. When Marshal Piłsudski became Polish minister of war in 1926, he devised a test of Trust sources. Yakushev, one of the principal characters in the Trust hierarchy, was tasked with providing the Poles with Soviet mobilization plans. Visibly disconcerted, he eventually produced something—which was promptly labeled counterfeit by Piłsudski, who had calculated his own figures on Soviet railroad capacity. Piłsudski apparently was able to check his own calculations against information coming from a Polish penetration of the Soviet government.[34] Suspicions in several other quarters had also surfaced, probably causing Menzhinskiy (Dzerzhinskiy had died in 1926) and Stalin to conclude that it was no longer wise to continue the fiction. In 1927, Moscow folded the operation. The ensuing exposé was shattering to the émigrés.

From Moscow's perspective, the Trust legend was a striking, yet continuing success. Some of its penetration operatives continued working among the very same groups that had been gulled. The Trust had disorganized the emigration, atomized further groups that were inclined to distrust each other to begin with, ruined their reputations as experts on Soviet affairs, and compromised them in the eyes of Western intelligence. Western intelligence was likewise duped but was destined to learn little from the affair and indeed succumbed to similar legends over the subsequent decades.

Finally, the Trust operation fostered the feeling in many circles in the West that, though no internal resistance to the new order in Moscow was possible, the new regime was tempering its actions and was amenable to doing business with Western governments and commercial enterprises. Indeed, the disinformation fostered through the Trust reinforced the initiatives of the NEP, which was also overseen by Dzerzhinskiy in his dual capacity as chief of state security and chief of the Supreme Council of National Economy. From this perspective, the NEP itself served a deception purpose in that it helped to refinance Soviet industry at Western political and economic expense.

But the NEP, by 1927, was finished and so too the need for the Trust. Stalin's first five-year plan was about to commence; new domestic and international goals were to be supported. State security simply could not continue the same provocation in a changed milieu that required different operations and objectives. It seems also that with Stalin's victory over Trotsky, the left and finally the right opposition, no more underground groups, even notional ones, would be tolerated on Soviet soil. This did not mean that OGPU provocations came to an end; their focus shifted primarily to foreign soil.

Nor was the OGPU completely finished with the émigrés. The Trust was finished in 1927, but numerous other provocations against the émigrés worked along parallel lines—as seen earlier in this chapter, numerous other legends were coterminous with the Trust. One of these was the penetration of the White Russian officers' organization, the Russian General Military Union or ROVS (Russkiy Obshche-Voyenskiy Soyuz), already affected by the Trust provocation. To counter the effects of the Trust and prevent future OGPU penetrations, the ROVS leadership under General Kutyepov approved the creation of the "Inner Line" as an active counterintelligence cell.[35] From its inception, however, the Inner Line itself was penetrated, principally through the OGPU's agents, General Skoblin and his wife, the popular singer Nadezhda Plevitskaya. Throughout the 1930s the OGPU used the Inner Line to take advantage of the internal bickering within the émigré community and to place more of its agents into important positions. Hence, as with the Trust, Moscow was able to systematically feed spurious information into ROVS, émigré, and Western government networks. Tragically, the Inner Line, and Skoblin's key position therein, facilitated the kidnappings of General Kutyepov in 1930 and General Miller in 1937, both of whom disappeared. Finally, the penetrations facilitated through the Inner Line carried into World War II operations (see the case of the MAX network in chapter 6) and over into postwar émigré politics.

4

The Second Revolution: Armageddon at Home

T HE COUNTERINTELLIGENCE STATE cannot prosper in non-crisis circumstances. Conspiracies presuppose enemies, and a conspiracy come to power must perpetually justify itself by exposing threats to its own exclusive claims. Comparatively speaking, the NEP years were rather tranquil, especially compared to what preceded them and what was to come. It was during these "quiet" years that a modicum of peace and prosperity had returned to the countryside, and to small artisans and traders in the urban centers. However, even such modest levels of socioeconomic harmony were unacceptable, not only to Stalin, the Trotskyites, and the Left Opposition, but even to still-vocal Mensheviks who carped about the presence of a new peasant–capitalist economy. The so-called kulak, or "prosperous" peasant, was therefore soon transformed from propaganda caricature into a flesh-and-blood enemy. The kulak became an abstraction of party demonology, subjected to irrational attacks by a state itself structured on the basis of further irrational abstractions. In reality it was the peasantry as a class that the party was after, for even in 1925, Stalin's henchman Mikhail Kalinin saw the kulak as merely a myth comprising, at most, a few individuals who were fast dying off.[1] It was precisely because of their initiative and independence (they were the largest and most productive segment of the population, and still somewhat free of the party's compulsive desire to smother all of society) that the peasantry was labeled a class enemy. The only element of the party–state that seemed to work with the same efficiency and dedication as the peasantry was state security, the OGPU, but its mission was destruction not production. It was fitting therefore that the OGPU should be the party's principal sword for striking this freshly reminted internal enemy. (The kulaks had earlier been declared an enemy during the Civil War.)

Although the NEP was not officially terminated until late 1929, socioeconomic harmony was vigorously assaulted considerably earlier. Food sales to the state had begun dropping in 1926 (production had never reached pre–World War I levels) and major shortages in all categories were registered by mid- to late 1927. Trotsky and Zinoviev, Stalin's most potent challengers, were expelled from the Central Committee in October 1927. Then in January 1928, Trotsky was exiled to Alma Ata in Kazakhstan and thirteen months later was deported to Turkey. From May to July 1928 the first of a series of drumhead show trials, the Shakhty trial, involving over fifty engineers and managers, including several German engineers assisting in Soviet industrialization, served as a precursor for the blood spectacles of the late 1930s. In 1927, a Stalin-manufactured war scare further unhinged civil stability and was no doubt connected to moves against Trotsky and the opposition. It was also a means to psychologically prepare the population for the coming dislocations associated with collectivization and industrialization. The OGPU, at Stalin's bidding, had a central role in all of these interconnected events.

The OGPU had, if anything, grown in power since the days of the Cheka. For a short period between February 1922 and July 1923 it had been nominally subordinated as the GPU to the People's Commissariat of Internal Affairs (NKVD). As the OGPU (United State Political Directorate), state security once more operated as a commissariat titularly under the Council of People's Commissars. In practice it answered only to the party and more specifically to Stalin as he consolidated his control. Dzerzhinskiy remained in charge of the OGPU until his death on 20 July 1926. Stalin had helped Dzerzhinskiy politically and it was through their collaboration that state security actually came to be placed above the party apparatus.[2] Stalin knew what he was about. As Dzerzhinskiy became more prominent in both party and government—candidate member of the Politburo, Commissar of Communications Means, chairman of the Supreme Council of National Economy, among others—he likewise became busier. This allowed Stalin to work Dzerzhinskiy's deputies, especially Second Deputy Chairman Genrikh Yagoda, permitting Stalin several access points and levers to manipulate the service, a

technique he employed up to his death. Still, Stalin and Dzerzhinskiy saw eye-to-eye on the most critical issues such as the struggle against the opposition, industrialization, the expanding labor
camp empire, and operations against the émigrés and Western
governments.

Thus, when Dzerzhinskiy died (the circumstances of which had
raised suspicions of a Stalin role), things proceeded much as they
had been. Vyacheslav Menzhinskiy, another Pole (though Russified)
of bourgeois intellectual origins, was named OGPU chairman, with
Yagoda as his principal deputy. A gifted linguist and intellectual dab-
bler, Menzhinskiy was either sickly or a hypochondriac, all of which
made, in his case, for a weak leader. This suited Stalin's technique,
because Menzhinskiy's deputy Yagoda already was one of Stalin's
henchmen.

The "Second Revolution" had two aspects, industrial and agricultural, accommodated by the party's first five-year plan, which covered the years 1928–32. It resulted in the transformation of Soviet
society and the economy at a human and financial cost of such magnitude that the effects are still being felt. The persistent debilities of
late-twentieth-century Soviet agriculture can be traced directly to
the collectivization and the ensconced ruinous policies of Stalin's successors. The OGPU played a key part in enforcing industrialization,
but it was with collectivization that its punitive powers had the most
telling effect. The drive to expropriate the peasants began in 1928,
although there were many instances of earlier actions. Because the
peasantry still comprised the overwhelming majority of the population, this might have appeared to be a large order for a regular police
force. But the OGPU was no ordinary state police; it had its own
army or, more correctly, armies, dating back to the Civil War. They
were also independent of Red Army control. Indeed, control worked
the other way around via the party-sanctioned OGPU Special Departments (Osobye Otdely or OOs), which penetrated the regular
armed forces for counterintelligence and internal security purposes.[3]
Additionally, OGPU military formations performed border troop
duties, comprised elite internal security divisions, guarded the prisons and labor camp empire, and provided leadership protection and
guard functions for senior party and state leaders.[4] Such troops had
fought not only in the Civil War but were used to suppress the Kronstadt sailors in 1921, the countless peasant uprisings of the 1920s,

and fought the long campaign against the Basmachi, or more correctly Beklar Hareketi (Freeman's Movement) of Moslem Turks in Central Asia until the 1930s. They were in many respects a party praetorian guard and had more in common with the SA, SS, and Waffen-SS formations in Nazi Germany than they did with the regular Red Army. Totalitarian regimes have need of such forces to perform tasks for which conscript armies and officer castes are either ill-suited or unreliable.

I cannot go into detail on the numerous search-and-destroy operations (to use late-twentieth-century military parlance) of the OGPU against the peasantry during collectivization, but the scope of the undertaking was of monumental proportions. At first, party cadres (stiffened by levies of factory workers) were dispatched to the countryside to confiscate grain, livestock, and other foodstuffs and to force peasant households into the new slapdash collectives. Spontaneous peasant opposition blossomed into uprisings and the killings of party activists. The OGPU was quickly called in with brutal and telling effect.

This was one of those several periods in the history of the Soviet state where Western intellectuals, politicians, and journalists shamelessly contributed to the horror by naively or wittingly hailing the "noble" Soviet experiment and filing flawed, deceptive, or dishonest accounts of the disasters.[5] However, some observers, even those sympathetic to the USSR, did report the truth. From one of these we get an insight into the morally degrading effects that state-commanded genocide had on even some state security officers. Isaac Deutscher, biographer of both Stalin and Trotsky, described his 1929 encounter with an OGPU colonel on a train trip from Moscow to Kharkov, in the Ukraine:

> The colonel was completely broken in spirit by his recent experiences in the countryside. "I am an old Bolshevik," he said, almost sobbing, "I worked in the underground against the Tsar and then I fought in the civil war. Did I do all that in order that I should now surround villages with machine-guns and order my men to fire indiscriminately into crowds of peasants? Oh, no, no!"[6]

The OGPU colonel's account was not an isolated, discrete event. Similar state security operations occurred throughout the land and with particular severity against the Ukraine. Although the Soviets normally eschew discussions of the frightful costs of collectivization, the literature of state security carries laudatory accounts of the war against the "kulaks." For instance, a unit history of the OGPU's Dzerzhinskiy Division sees its combat actions against "kulak gangs" as a heroic chapter.[7] Other categories of state security troops, such as the Border Troops, participated in similar punitive operations against the peasantry.

The party was not content merely to break peasant resistance; it was intent on eliminating every vestige of peasant independence. It meant to demonstrate that its second revolution honored no moral or international boundaries. Ismail Akhmedov, a former GRU officer who was serving in the Caucasus during collectivization, read intelligence reports describing how Azerbaidzhani peasants who had fled to the mountains were hunted down by combined Red Army, Border Troops, and OGPU forces.

> In my hands were the daily situation reports sent by these punitive forces to my department. One I remember indelibly said: "Whole villages are offering desperate resistance. Our units are forced to burn the villages, to put to the sword not only men, but also the women and children. When the men were killed fighting our forces, their women, instead of surrendering, threw themselves to death on the bayonets of the Red soldiers." Some of these people, other reports said, had managed to escape across the border to Iran but to no avail. The Soviet troops reported that they crossed the border in pursuit and wiped them out.[8]

Akhmedov further described a bizarre fusion of OGPU punitive operations and a GRU agent infiltration action, a unique example of a dual service *kombinatsiya* (combination). The OGPU in Armenia had learned that a group of about eighty men, women, and children were preparing to flee the USSR for Turkey. Rather than simply arrest the group beforehand, the OGPU chose to lay an ambush at the border crossing site. The local GRU commander simultaneously was looking for a means of infiltrating one of his agents back into Turkey and was invited by the OGPU to have the man join the group planning to flee, as they would provide an excellent cover for the agent. The latter was given careful instructions on how to identify himself during the ambush to keep from being shot. The OGPU operational group (*operativnaya gruppa*) ambushed the people on the appointed night, firing indiscriminately into the defecting peasant families. As arranged, the GRU's agent got through unscathed, one of the very few of the ambushed group to make it into Turkey. When asked why the OGPU had not simply arrested the peasants before their attempted escape, Akhmedov observed that this would not have had the same dramatic effect on further peasant resistance to collectivization. Widespread bloodshed was the preferred OGPU way to break the peasantry.[9]

These Caucasian killings were far from unique. As just mentioned, the Ukraine was particularly hard hit during the collectivization drive from 1930 to 1932 and its aftermath, the terror-famine of 1932–33. In 1932, Eugene Lyons, a U. S. correspondent in the USSR at the time, reported hundreds of corpses of peasants shot daily by Soviet border troops as these starving masses tried to escape into Romania. Moscow of course made the requisite denials but then sent its representatives from Bucharest to a joint Romanian-Soviet commission to identify and bury the dead.[10] Lyons reported similar occurrences from Poland and other countries bordering the USSR.[11]

Not only were peasants prevented from escaping Soviet territory, but Robert Conquest, in his seminal work on collectivization and the state-induced famine of 1932–33, points out that the state security organs actually sealed off the famine's center, the Ukraine, from the rest of the USSR where conditions were moderately or marginally better.[12] Peasants attempting to cross into contiguous Soviet areas from the Ukraine were turned back by the OGPU; if they were successful in getting through, purchasing food and attempting to return to their villages, the food was confiscated and the peasants frequently arrested or shot.

Thus, in addition to breaking the peasantry as a class in general, Stalin and his OGPU had targeted the Ukraine for special treatment and the man-made famine of 1932–33 was the means. Again, the most definitive evidence is that adduced by Conquest. Conservative death totals for both collectivization (dekulakization) and the terror-famine for the years 1930–33 come to approximately 14,500,000 for all of the USSR. (This includes peasants arrested during 1930–33 but dying in labor camps as late as 1937.)[13] Of this figure the terror-famine accounted for about 7,000,000, broken down as follows: 5,000,000 in the Ukraine; 1,000,000 in the North Caucasus; and 1,000,000 elsewhere.[14]

The party was able to keep a rather tight lid on such monstrous news through its own censorship and, in no small part, through collaboration of Western sympathizers and inadequate and tendentious reporting by the Western media (examples abound with George Bernard Shaw, Beatrice and Sidney Webb, Sir John Maynard, Anna Louise Strong, Walter Duranty, among others). Honest reporting of the events and the terror tactics of the OGPU by such writers as Eugene Lyons, William Henry Chamberlin, and Malcolm Muggeridge (and by Western diplomatic establishments) simply could not offset the falsification, deceptions, and the dogged will to disbelieve that seemed to prevail among Western establishments. An "apologia pro Sovietica," an early McCarthyism-of-the-left, seemed to have prevented the development of a sensitivity, let alone outraged indignation, among the admirers of OGPU methods for advancing the cause of socialism.

The OGPU did not have things all its own way, however. Alexander Orlov, a high state security official, reports that opposition to collectivization and the famine went well beyond isolated peasant acts of violence. Such information is highly compartmented, but Orlov was well informed (he had been chief of Border Troops in the Caucasus) about what went on in the North Caucasus, next to the Ukraine one of the hardest hit areas during collectivization and the famine. Peasant rebellion spread to the Red Army, a number of small detachments of which went over to rebel peasant groups. A whole Air Force squadron refused to attack cossack villages. OGPU deputy and rival of Yagoda, I. S. Akulov, was sacked by Stalin for not getting help to an OGPU regiment that was surrounded and destroyed by cossack rebels. Mikhail Frinovskiy, chief of the OGPU's Border Troops at the time, was charged by Stalin with suppressing these insurgencies. His scorched-earth methods resulted, as he reported to the Politburo, in thousands of bodies washing down North Caucasus rivers.[15] Orlov claims that the OGPU reported to Stalin that the man-made famine cost between 3,300,000 and 3,500,000 deaths, but he states that even sympathetic (to the USSR) foreign journalists counted between 5,000,000 and 7,000,000 victims.[16] Interestingly, this latter range comes remarkably close to Conquest's much later estimates, which rely on subsequently available census figures and numerous other confirmatory, but later, sources of information. The upshot of all this is that the truth was available at the time but suppressed, manipulated, or ignored.

As is so often the case in the seven-decade history of the Soviet state, such draconian examples of the counterintelligence state in action have a way of resonating in later periods. Frinovskiy's scorched-earth counterinsurgency sweeps against the peasantry originally drew on the experiences from the suppression of such peasant uprisings as the Makhno and Tambov insurgencies of the 1920s and the more-than-decade-long Freeman's (Basmachi) insurgency in Central Asia. In the immediate post–World War II era, Baltic and Ukrainian insurgents were finally crushed by combined state-security special designation troops and Red Army units whose techniques included mass executions and deportations and the laying waste of huge tracts of agricultural regions so as to physically eliminate the rebels' human and material base. Viewed against this tradition, Soviet actions in Afghanistan since 1979 are neither unique nor should they be surprising. KGB, MVD, and GRU special designation units employ techniques that combine intelligence, provocation, and small-unit actions against the rebel Mujahedin infrastructure, with the use of superior fire power and scorched-earth capabilities of the regular Soviet air and ground forces to savage a traditional agricultural society. In one respect the Soviets give away the game by referring to the Afghan insurgents as Basmachi, an opprobrious designation originally invented to besmirch the smallholding peasants of a traditional Moslem culture. Coupled with the massive export of thousands of Afghan children to the USSR for years of indoctrination and training, these actions portend the Soviet intention to make over Afghan society in a manner reminiscent of what they did in the early 1930s in their own rebellious countryside.

The weight of the state-enforced famine on the Ukraine and the Kuban–North Caucasus regions was due, no doubt, to nationality considerations—Stalin did not trust the Ukraine. Through the combination of collectivization and famine the OGPU broke the back of actual or potential peasant resistance. The Ukrainian party, state, and other leading cadres were left to the OGPU's successor, the NKVD, which would handle them in the 1936–38 terror purges.

But still there was no nationalist conspiracy either among the peasantry or the Ukrainian party, state, and security chieftains.

In certain critical ways the collectivization and famine prepared
the police, party, and state cadres for the more generalized terror a
few years later. The events of 1929–33 should have been the eye-
opening "Kronstadt" for the more principled among them. Instead,
all too many became further morally compromised and degraded by
their participation or acquiescence. Those military commanders who
collaborated with OGPU counterparts in shooting starving peasants
later had no moral alternative than to collaborate in the denunciation
of their comrades-in-arms, and then themselves, in the purges. As
for the state security cadres themselves, their bestial enforcement of
the famine was but another step in the sequenced psychological and
moral degradation of these men and women as they advanced to
ever-increasing heights of criminality in enforcing party directives.
They carried a greater guilt than their military colleagues, for they
knew more of the true state of events and played a far greater and
sinister role in them. Imprisoned by the sufferings they inflicted
upon millions of simple peasants, they proved to be a more-than-
willing enforcer of increasingly bizarre party writs against the cream
of the party and state itself.

But state security still was only a partner to the Stalinist cadres in
the famine enterprise. State security ranks repeatedly were replen-
ished and stiffened by infusions of young communist cadres. For the
party bureaucrats the widening gap between ideal and reality was
filled by terror routinized as an administrative weapon during collectivization and the famine. Terror became the normal bureaucratic
means for the pursuit of hideous yet unattainable objectives. Some,
like Nikolay Bukharin, admitted to the dehumanization of the party
apparatus as a result of the war on the peasant.[17] But compromised
by his own role in the creation of such a regime, he was powerless
to offer real moral or physical resistance when his turn as victim
came, notwithstanding a spirited performance that embarrassed the
state prosecutor, Andrey Vyshinsky, at Bukharin's 1938 show trial.
In short, no meaningful numbers of the party–state phalanx emerged
unsullied from the events of 1929–33. When Stalin unleashed the
police on them in 1936–38, there were few prominent party people
who could make a stand on the basis of party principle, because they
were compromised and implicated by their loyalty to it. Service to

the party meant participation or acquiescence in genocidal activity. They simply had no moral defenses left when state security came after them.

In the wake of the 1932-33 famine Stalin began making preliminary moves leading to the "Great Terror" of 1936–38. The first five-year plan was declared a success in late 1932 and a second five-year plan was immediately launched for 1933–37 and formally announced at the Seventeenth Party Congress in January 1934. Termed the "Victor's Congress," in part for the victories over the millions of peasants and workers who were killed or terrorized into submission, the Seventeenth Party Congress was also a celebration of Stalin's successes over the various factional tendencies—Trotskyites, the Left Opposition, the Right Opposition—some of whose members were allowed to crawl back to party service following degrading recantations. During the congress, Stalin declared, "there is nothing more to prove and, it seems, nobody to beat," a statement at once ironic and portentous.[18] Stalin's counterintelligence state could not prosper without enemies and the next round of these he would declare within the party itself. Of the 1,966 delegates to this "Victor's Congress," 1,108 were to be arrested or executed during the 1936–38 purges. Of the 139 members and candidates of the Central Committee elected at this congress, 98 would be executed.

At the Seventeenth Party Congress a further refinement of the powers of the Osobyy Sektor (or Special Sector; also known as the Secret Chancellery or Secret Department—Sekretnyy Otdel) of the Central Committee's secretariat, placed that element at the heart of Stalin's control over state security.[19] It became the secret link between Stalin and the organs and from about 1928 to 1952 was headed by the shadowy personal secretary of Stalin, Aleksandr Poskrebyshev. Dating to about 1922, the Special Sector had already controlled the flow of the most important categories of information essential to the functioning of the whole system. With its new role as Stalin's portal to the organs it achieved effective control over all elements of the party–state amalgam on Stalin's behalf.

Over the years membership in the Special Sector (in addition to Stalin and Poskrebyshev) included the successive chiefs of secret police, the chiefs of the principal party and state control agencies and related Central Committee secretariat personalities and offices. Personalities fluctuated with Stalin's favor but the sinister Poskrebyshev remained central to the operation up to the last months of Stalin's reign. The Special Sector, along with Stalin's moves against the opposition in the party, helped him consolidate his dictatorship and render the rest of the Politburo and the Central Committee superfluous in the decision-making process. Another Central Committee element, the Organization–Assignment Department, gave Stalin control over cadre appointments in critical party and state positions. Later in Soviet history the Administrative Organs Department would perform that function in its oversight of all punitive organs.

In May 1934, the OGPU chief, Menzhinskiy, died and was replaced by his deputy, Genrikh Yagoda. Immediately (July 1934) the OGPU was abolished and absorbed as the Main Administration of State Security (GUGB) within the People's Commissariat of Internal Affairs (NKVD). As happened before and since, all state security internal and foreign elements, border troops, internal troops, firemen, concentration camps, and militia (regular police) were again under one administrative center with an enormous concentration of power.

Despite these and other centralizing moves, Stalin still lacked the unitary control he sought while such popular figures as Leningrad party boss Sergey Kirov enjoyed wide support among party cadres. The Kirov problem became a solution when he was assassinated on 1 December 1934 by an allegedly disgruntled party cadre who acquired easy access, while armed, to the NKVD-guarded offices of Kirov on two occasions, murdering him on the second try. It is generally accepted that this was an NKVD operation under Yagoda's direction and Stalin's orders. Stalin used the event to launch a third revolution: the blood purges of 1936–38. More immediately, mass executions of imprisoned "Whites" occurred in Leningrad and other cities, and thousands were arrested. Stalin rushed to Leningrad with NKVD chief Yagoda to personally oversee the investigation. After a private session with Stalin, the assassin, one Leonid Nikolayev, was shot on 29 December 1934, along with thirteen others following a secret trial (and still secret!). The chief of the Leningrad NKVD, F. D. Medved', and his deputy, I. V. Zaporozhets, were given exceptionally light (and comfortable) prison sentences for failure to take adequate measures to protect Kirov. This confirmed to experienced insiders that Stalin was behind the affair.[20] Neither man, however, made it through the purges. It is doubtful that Medved', who

had been close to Kirov, had been part of the conspiracy; Zaparo-
zhets, however, certainly was.

The contrived stories of culprits and culpability in the Kirov case
went through several stages. The first charged, aside from Nikolayev, were alleged "White Guardists" who were executed in the
hundreds by the NKVD. Then Zinoviev and Kamenev were alleged
to have inspired Nikolayev to commit the act and in a secret January
1935 trial were affixed with "the political and moral responsibility"
for the murder and given ten- and five-year sentences, respectively.
Yagoda personally oversaw this business on Stalin's behalf. According to Orlov they were to have been charged with the actual operation but Zaporozhets had botched the affair and was not able to
safely run a public trial of Nikolayev, who knew that he had been
set up.[21] The next stage came in 1936, when Zinoviev was accused
of actually having ordered Kirov's murder. Then, in 1938, Trotsky
was included among the accused, with the claim that it had all been
physically orchestrated by NKVD chief Yagoda working through
his on-scene henchman, Zaporozhets. Such contradictory madness
was duly reported in the Soviet state-controlled press and uncriti-
cally repeated by foreign observers.

The NKVD, under Stalin's oversight via his Special Sector, now
mobilized for the assault on the party. Both the police and Stalin
appear to have been keenly affected by Hitler's June 1934 lightning
extermination of Ernst Röhm and his SA, and elements of the German military. The instrument of Hitler was Himmler's SS. Walter
Krivitsky, a former NKVD officer, stated that Stalin carefully read
every secret report from Soviet intelligence in Germany relating to
Hitler's purge.[22] Krivitsky had observed that mounting opposition
within the party—in 1932 M. N. Ryutin, of the Moscow party organization, had circulated a secret dissident party program that labeled Stalin as the "great agent provocateur"—convinced Stalin that
mere humiliation of the Old Bolsheviks was not enough and he had
to get rid of these men.[23] Hitler had shown how to do it.

During the Ryutin business Stalin had clamored for the death penalty for these party opponents, a reversal of Lenin's policy of ex-
empting Bolsheviks from such punishments. Kirov, it should be
noted, had successfully opposed Stalin on this issue. Now with the
Kirov murder Stalin had his excuse; he modified the penal code with
a new decree providing for secret trial and speedy execution in all

political assassination cases. He then proceeded in a manner similar to Hitler's, except on a far greater scale and over a longer period of time. The mutual impact these two totalitarian dictators had on each other and their respective state security establishments is often overlooked and seldom noted. There was much more in common between them than Soviet historiography could ever allow. As Krivitsky observed at the time, Stalin read the Nazi purge not only as a model for his own actions, but concluded at that early point (1934) that he had to cut a deal with Hitler.[24] There is more to this particular aspect of the affair that will be examined in chapter 5.

Yagoda's NKVD prepared all the groundwork for the first two of the three showcase trials. By this time, state security had become a well-established subculture, so to speak, within the party–state structure. Somewhat like Himmler's SS in Germany, the "Chekisty" thought of themselves not only apart from most of the rest of the system, but rather above it. Of course, both Lenin and Dzerzhinskiy encouraged this state of mind. Stalin carefully cultivated Dzerzhinskiy, but at the same time groomed Dzerzhinskiy's deputies, thus reinforcing this tendency to arrogant aloofness. This aloof professional identity, if that is what it could be called, was precisely what Stalin needed to go after elements as venerable as the old Leninist elite. Stalin would have had no trouble unleashing these Chekists against Ryutin, just as he certainly had been able to count on them earlier to hunt and harass Trotskyite sympathizers. Rather like Old Bolsheviks themselves, these Chekists were a stable, long-serving, interconnected bunch with the potential for advancing their own agenda which, in Stalin's eyes, could entail connections to his opponents in the party and real or perceived disagreements with his policies. Indeed, most of the NKVD's central leadership were themselves Old Bolsheviks.[25] This meant two things: state security itself would ultimately become a target, and Stalin had to start grooming new cadres for the top layers of the organs, drawn from outside the central state security echelons or even external to the organs themselves.

On the other hand the institutional cohesiveness of state security was crucial to Stalin in his war on the peasantry, and then for the early stages of his attack on the party. By implicating state security in such inhuman excesses he honed a reliable instrument that was free of any moderating ties external to itself or Stalin. As it turned out later, even this was not enough, as thousands of NKVD personnel would feel the ax of Yezhov in 1937 and then of Beria beginning in mid-1938.

It was this cohesiveness, which entailed lateral movement among various directorates of the NKVD, that has afforded the outside world at least a partial inside view of these bizarre and bloody events. Among the primary sources in the study of the Soviet counterintelligence state are the defector accounts. Two of the most crucial of these were Alexander Orlov (Feldbin) and Walter Krivitsky (Ginsberg). Orlov was active in the Red Army (guerrilla warfare and counterintelligence) during the Civil War; was a law graduate of Moscow University and assistant prosecutor under Nikolay Krylenko; served under Dzerzhinskiy as deputy chief of the Economic Directorate of the OGPU; and was brigade commander of Border Troops in Transcaucasia. He also saw tours of duty in the Foreign Department (INO) of the OGPU/NKVD that took him to Paris, Berlin, Switzerland, the United States, Austria, Czechoslovakia and, finally, Spain, whence he defected in 1938. Orlov enjoyed an access that spanned the commanding intersections of party, state, and state security and the personal linkages thus afforded. He represented a breed that combined internal security service with foreign espionage and direct action. Such cross-experience and access are highly unlikely in today's KGB, but in those early years of the system there were many men like Orlov. Foreign operations in those days seemed to be the external manifestation of internal state security writ large. Professional revolutionaries like Orlov were expected to be capable across a broad axis as called for by a universal ideology.

Like Orlov, Walter Krivitsky ended his Soviet career in intelligence work with state security. He began, however, with military intelligence; he was transferred to the OGPU in the 1930s. Krivitsky was not a general in military intelligence, as claimed by his Western publishers; Orlov was of general officer equivalence in the NKVD. Krivitsky was operating as NKVD illegal *rezident* in the Netherlands in the fall of 1937 when he received the ominous order to return to Moscow. When his lifelong friend from both the GRU and NKVD, Ignace Reiss, was assassinated by one of Yezhov's killer squads in Switzerland following Reiss's defection, Krivitsky decided he had had enough and also defected. Orlov's information on the purges and the workings of state security really did not surface until the early

1950s. But Krivitsky's revelations began shortly after his defection, with debriefings to the French and British security services; articles in France; testimony to the House Un-American Activities Committee in 1939; articles in the *Saturday Evening Post* in 1939; and then a book, *In Stalin's Secret Service,* the same year.

The connections both Orlov and Krivitsky had made during their long years of service to the Soviet security organs have provided the fundamental basis for our understanding of the first twenty years of the service and Stalin's accretion of power. By and large they have withstood the test of time with some minor exceptions.[26] Orlov's accounts dealt mostly with the internal dynamics of the party and state security and were especially incisive on the great purges of the 1930s. He also was an excellent witness for the operations of the NKVD in Spain during the Civil War and for Stalin's campaign against Trotsky through the NKVD provocateur, Mark Zborowskiy. Most of Krivitsky's career had been in external GRU and NKVD operations. These offered him key vantage points for assessing Stalin's foreign policy and attendant state security operations. Both men's testimony have held surprisingly well and few later revelations of the Stalin era of the 1920s and 1930s deviate from their witness.[27] It is from such men and from superb Western analysts as Conquest and Slusser that we derive our understanding of how Stalin and state security savaged the USSR in the late 1930s.[28]

Returning now to the purges, Stalin carried out a more complex and prolonged variant of Hitler's "Night of the Long Knives" violence against the SA and the military. Whereas Hitler struck in lightning fashion, Stalin choreographed his attack in keeping with Soviet conditions (for example, the enormous prestige of his Old Bolshevik victims) and for maximum psychological effect on the country as a whole. The three major Moscow show trials were his centerpiece. The trials wiped out the Left Opposition, then the remnants of an alleged Trotskyite center, and finally the so-called Right Opposition (with recently fired NKVD chief Yagoda thrown in for good measure).

The first public trial, in August 1936, was of Zinoviev, Kamenev, and fourteen other Old Bolsheviks. Though both men had been charged in the secret January 1935 trial with the "political and moral responsibility" for the death of Kirov, they were now forced to confess the actual deed *and* the intent to murder Stalin as well. By agreeing to confess to this and to being in league with Trotsky, and to implicate others, they had nothing left to bargain with and Stalin reneged on his promise to spare their lives. They were executed in the NKVD cellars.

At the second showcase trial, in January 1937, seventeen oppositionists of the alleged "Anti-Soviet Trotskyite Center" were convicted. Among the convicted were Grigoriy Pyatakov and Karl Radek. With the exception of Radek, these men were Old Bolsheviks and ex-Trotskyites from the period of struggle in the 1920s. They were charged with espionage for Germany and Japan, sabotage, and terrorism; Trotsky was the ringleader from afar. All except Radek, Grigoriy Sokol'nikov, and two others received the death sentence. Radek was reported by two KGB defectors to have been murdered in 1938 in a Siberian prison during a violent encounter with a fellow convict.[29]

The third and most notorious trial was in March 1938, and was aimed at the alleged "Anti-Soviet Bloc of Rights and Trotskyites." This was a gala performance, and featured some of the most lionized figures of the revolution and other leading lights of the Soviet state:[30] M. P. Tomskiy killed himself before the trial; Bukharin, Aleksey Rykov, and Nikolay Krestinskiy were members of Lenin's Politburo; Yagoda (replaced by Yezhov in September 1936 and arrested in April 1937) had been NKVD chief and he himself had launched this butchery; Christo Rakovskiy of revolutionary fame; and about sixteen others ranging from people's commissars to several medical doctors. Bukharin turned in a stellar performance: he refuted the charges in detail but confessed to them in general. The court sentenced all but three to death. Bukharin was among those executed.

Note that Yagoda was one of the principals in the third trial. His downfall marked the beginning of a period of severe instability and casualties among NKVD cadres that lasted into the first months of Beria's tenure—purgers' justice, so to speak. Even earlier, Stalin had made Nikolay Yezhov a party secretary and placed him in charge of the party's purge machinery. As a secretary he was already in a position to oversee the organs.

Yezhov did have, however, a serious and dangerous skeleton in his own political closet of which we are aware. In the early 1930s he had been a deputy people's commissar for agriculture and had been an intimate friend of a certain Konar, a Polish penetration agent who himself became a high Soviet agricultural official. Konar, whose real name was Poleshchuk, had infiltrated the USSR with the party card of the real Konar, who was shot in the Russo-Polish war of 1920. He then rose high in agricultural and party circles. He was exposed in 1931–32 by a chance meeting with a party official who knew the original Konar.[31] Because Yezhov reportedly had helped him get the agricultural post, Yezhov had to be tainted. For once a bona fide spy had penetrated high in the Soviet structure. No doubt Stalin marked this serious breach of security but it is unclear why Stalin did not make Yezhov pay the supreme penalty at the time. What is clear is that Yezhov moved to the top of state security. Was Yezhov's ferociousness in the purges a consequence of the incriminating evidence that Stalin had on Yezhov? It is curious that when Yezhov was dismissed in 1938 there were no trial and ritual denunciations as had occurred with his predecessor, Yagoda.

Yagoda's fall was preceded by a telegram to the Politburo from Sochi on 25 September 1936, signed by Stalin and Andrey Zhdanov. It stipulated the urgent need to place Yezhov in charge of the NKVD, in view of Yagoda's poor performance in "unmasking the Trotskyite-Zinovievite bloc" and complained about the police being "four years behind in this matter."[32] On 27 September Yagoda's removal and his replacement by Yezhov was announced.[33] The following April Yagoda was arrested,[34] and a lengthy interrogation/prepping ensued preparatory to the third show trial in March 1938.

There then followed the "Yezhovshchina," or Yezhov phase of the purges, in which the military and state security cadres themselves joined the growing list of party and other victims. This phase lasted from September 1936 to Beria's appointment as Yezhov's deputy in July 1938 (he officially took over as NKVD chief in December 1938). The purges continued under Beria into about 1941 but with a diminished ferocity; the numbers of arrested and executed lessened somewhat, and in 1939 some two hundred thousand framed "enemies" were actually freed.[35]

Under Yezhov the intensity of the cycle of denunciation, arrest, imprisonment, and exile took on dimensions that challenged the holocaust of collectivization and famine. Throughout the country, state security officials were given factory-like production norms for ferreting out and arresting "enemies" and "spies." Vladimir Petrov, an NKVD communications officer at the time, processed hundreds of

NKVD signals to all parts of the USSR that contained fixed extermination quotas: "To NKVD Frunze. You are charged with the task
of exterminating 10,000 enemies of the people. Report results by
signal—Yezhov." And the reply would come back: "In reply to yours
of such-and-such a date, the following enemies of the Soviet people
have been shot. . . ."[36]

Yezhov's headquarters compiled specific lists for each district and
even specific towns—Sverdlovsk was ordered to exterminate 15,000
"enemies of the people"[37]—that were approved by Stalin before
being wired to the pertinent NKVD office. The local officials would
then scour their files for the most arcane items that could be used to
incriminate people so as to fulfill the quotas. NKVD cadres themselves were terrorized into "production" frenzies by surprise visits
from NKVD headquarters officials. In an unannounced visit to the
Rostov NKVD office, Genrikh Lyushkov, a high-ranking state security officer, charged the gathered officials with laxness in pursuing
enemies and immediately fingered three of their own number as enemies; the intimidated district chief quickly prepared the charges and
had his accused men shot.[38]

To process such increasing workloads the number of NKVD interrogators had to be expanded, frequently with infusions of new
party levies. One important memoir on the production-line quality
of the interrogations during Yezhov's tenure counts about three thousand NKVD interrogators just for Moscow.[39] The total for the country had to have been many times greater. If Moscow, with a population of 4,137,000 in 1939 had three thousand interrogators, such a
ratio applied to a population of 170,557,000 (1939 census) could yield
123,680 interrogators. Given the detailed extermination quotas
wired out to regional NKVD offices, such workloads would make
such a figure conceivable. Numerous officers were assigned to such
duties even if they were not involved in internal security or counterintelligence functions. This applied to very senior officials and included those from the Foreign Department (INO). These comprised, among others, M. Shpigelglas, F. Gurskiy, Boris Berman,
Abram Slutskiy, and Igor Kedrov, several of whom were assigned
interrogation duties in the Zinoviev trial preliminaries. Stalin and
Yezhov no doubt intended to implicate as many senior NKVD officials in these atrocities as possible, so as to morally and psychologically isolate them. However, we have also seen that an institutional

cohesiveness and exclusivity was by this time a hallmark of the service. There were far fewer intrabureaucratic fences than in today's KGB; such cross-directorate assignments were not that uncommon. It was this cross-fertilization and the personal networks thus established that allowed broad access to participants like Orlov, Krivitsky, Petrov, and, later, Deriabin, all of whose testimony proved so incisive and reliable.

When Yezhov took over, most of the senior NKVD cadres had been in state security since Dzerzhinskiy's days. By the time he himself was purged in 1938 he had already replaced most of these central cadres with new blood brought in from the party and from regional and other functional departments of the NKVD. The process was again repeated when Beria arrived in late 1938, but this time many Georgians and others from Beria's Transcaucasian NKVD apparat were the new replacements.

Regardless of services performed, these old Chekists proved as vulnerable as their victims. The names of those executed or who vanished constitute a roster of the leading figures from the Civil War, the Trust operation, collectivization and famine, foreign operations, and the Spanish Civil War: Ya. S. Agranov, A. Kh. Artuzov, V. A. Balitskiy, L. N. Bel'skiy, the Berman brothers (Boris and Matvey), G. I. Bokiy, L. I. Chertok, T. D. Deribas, G. E. Evdokimov, M. P. Frinovskiy, K. V. Gay, K. M. Karlson, Zinoviy Katsnel'son, I. M. Kedrov, L. G. Mironov, G. A. Molchanov, K. V. Pauker, R. A. Pilyar, G. Prokofiev, S. Redens, A. M. Shanin, M. Shpigelglas, A. A. Slutskiy, M. Trilliser (his brother, David, died in 1934), A. I. Volovich, and L. M. Zakovskiy.

Foreign Department operatives, as well as GRU officers, also suffered heavily following summons from Moscow. Those who defected, or attempted to, on foreign territory, were hunted by mobile groups from Yezhov's Administration for Special Tasks. NKVD officer Ignace Reiss was murdered in Switzerland in 1937 following his declared break with Stalin. Alexander Orlov was spared this fate by going underground in the United States after escaping Spain in 1938. There seems to be little doubt that his threat to publish damaging information on Stalin's crimes if he or his family were harmed, indeed worked. In 1940, Trotsky was murdered in Mexico by Ramón Mercader, the son of a Spanish communist who was the lover of Naum (Leonid) Eitingon (also known as General Kotov), the

NKVD officer who oversaw the operation. Earlier, Trotsky's son Lev Sedov died in France under suspicious circumstances. Yezhov's killers were also responsible for the kidnapping of the White Russian General Miller in Paris in 1937.

As a department the INO (Foreign Department) suffered particularly because it was smaller by comparison with the large domestic elements of the NKVD. Whereas INO men were required to be able to perform in the internal departments—for example, as interrogators—it was not possible the other way around. Hence, the INO and the GRU were especially hurt by the purges and it was not until the war that recovery began. (It should be noted that for a time in 1937–38, Yezhov headed both the NKVD and the GRU—a precedent for the KI [Committee of Information], which fused the MGB and GRU for foreign intelligence activities.) The recall, imprisonment, and execution of scores of intelligence personnel contributed directly to the debacle of 1941. GRU officer Richard Sorge in Japan was one of the fortunate exceptions, but his warnings of Germany's intentions were received with suspicion. Stalin wanted the pact with Hitler; bad news was unwelcome.

The most bizarre feature of Yezhov's tenure was the seemingly senseless attack on the Soviet military. I say "seemingly" because of the objective result—the butchering of talent in the Soviet officer corps. The fruits of this operation were demonstrated by poor Soviet performance in the Winter War of 1939–40 against Finland and the smashing German successes of 1941 and 1942. A common early estimate is that about 15,000–35,000 officers, or upwards of 50 percent of the Soviet officer corps, were executed or dispatched to prisons and concentration camps during the period 1937–38.[40] However, killings and imprisonments actually began in 1935 before Yezhov's ascendancy and continued up to the German invasion in 1941. Later studies by émigré and resident dissident researchers place the losses at 50,000–60,000 officers out of an officer corps of 100,000–130,000 men.[41] Added to this casualty figure would be at least another 20,000 political officers.

The earlier and lower casualty figures would roughly compare to the rates in the party at large; that is, approximately one-half. The later and higher figures exceed this ratio. If the latter are more representative, then the military was a special target of Stalin and state security. A Soviet source published in the early 1960s states that the number of communists in the army during the purges was cut from

250,000 to 125,000.[42] Because most military party men would have been in the officer corps, then these state-sanctioned figures bear out our belief that the military was a special target. Interestingly, it also posits a larger officer corps and therefore a greater total casualty figure than either of the two ranges of estimates cited above.

Why should the military have been singled out? The conventional wisdom seems to be that Stalin was merely doing a "Sherman's March" through all of the major Soviet institutions to ensure that even the *potential* for opposition to his singular rule would be excised. Others, such as Krivitsky and V. A. Antonov-Ovseyenko have observed that Stalin already, by the mid-1930s, had his sights on a deal with Hitler and that the military would have stood in his way.[43] Orlov, in addition, revealed in 1956 that there indeed had been a conspiracy against Stalin involving both military (Marshall M. N. Tukhachevskiy, for one) and NKVD elements following the discovery of Stalin's Okhrana dossier, which allegedly proved Stalin's background as an Okhrana agent-cum-provocateur prior to the Bolshevik revolution.[44] Both Orlov and Krivitsky refer to the panicky suddenness with which Tukhachevskiy and eight commanders were arrested and executed in June 1937. Krivitsky quotes Mikhail Frinovskiy, one of Yezhov's NKVD deputies: "We've just uncovered a gigantic conspiracy in the army, such a conspiracy as history has never known."[45] Orlov confirms this from a discussion with another high NKVD official, M. Shpigelglas, in Spain the following October: "There was panic at the very top. All passes to the Kremlin were suddenly declared invalid. Our NKVD troops were held in a state of alarm. It must have been quite a conspiracy."[46]

Krivitsky and Orlov appear never to have been in touch with each other following their defections and prior to Krivitsky's death in 1941. Their reports of high-level panic are drawn from separate high-ranking NKVD officials who appear to confirm each other. Krivitsky's account has no information of a military conspiracy but his book gives the impression of an incomplete story on this point. On another level he and Orlov provide parallel accounts of forged documents passed from the Germans to the NKVD via the offices of the apparently unwitting President Eduard Beneš of Czechoslovakia. These papers purported to show collusion between the Red Army chiefs and German military intelligence (more on this in chapter 5).

In several interviews with the FBI in early 1954 Orlov provided a running critique of Krivitsky's book, of which he was pointedly critical in a number of particulars. Orlov made no comment on Krivitsky's recounting of Frinovskiy's statement about a gigantic military conspiracy, yet he reacted strongly and negatively to several other claims by Krivitsky.[47] It must be presumed that Orlov took no issue with the alleged Frinovskiy statement. We have, then, two important testaments, one oblique and the other direct, to some sort of move against Stalin by the military and elements of the NKVD, by two old and well-connected Chekists. However, beyond these two witnesses little evidence has ever surfaced of either a preemptive or reactive military–state security move against Stalin.

We are left, then, with the *possibility* of a bona fide conspiracy; and the *probability* that Stalin expected something from that quarter, real or not. The question of an Okhrana file is still to be resolved and remains for the day, if ever, when party and KGB archives yield the facts. But there *was* a Hitler–Stalin Pact and there is strong evidence that Stalin had his sights on such a rapprochement as early as 1934. He was keenly sensitive that the Red Army chiefs would not share his cynical strategic rationale for cutting such a deal. If he had no qualms about destroying the cream of the party, why should he hesitate to sacrifice the military leadership, especially if it meant becoming a partner in a combination that promised to broker power across Eurasia and beyond? The unleashing of Yezhov against the military was one of Stalin's last major internal moves before he got down to serious business with Hitler.

The final major internal move involved state security itself. Orlov observed that the NKVD men whom he claims were privy to Stalin's Okhrana dossier and were involved with the army men in the conspiracy against Stalin were either executed along with the army officers or committed suicide. These included the alleged discoverers of Stalin's file, one Stein, who shot himself; the head of the Ukrainian NKVD, Central Committee member and member of the Ukrainian Politburo, V. Balitskiy, who was shot; and Ukrainian NKVD official Z. Katsnel'son, cousin and informant of Orlov, also shot.[48] Stanislav Kossior, CPSU secretary, Politburo member boss of the Ukraine (and Khrushchev's superior in the Ukraine), who allegedly was also in on the secret, was executed.

While Yezhov had been busy eliminating half the army's officers and the still-surviving NKVD cadre of Yagoda's days, he had not quite gotten to the Transcaucasia NKVD stronghold of Lavrentiy Beria. By May 1938 he had started poking into Beria's domains, with the obvious intent of incriminating Beria. Beria countered with a visit and personal appeal to Stalin, who then made Beria deputy NKVD commissar in the summer of 1938. An intense struggle within the NKVD ensued in which Yezhov clearly was the target. Yezhov, though retaining his NKVD post, was given the added job of commissar of water transport in August. By the fall Beria had taken over the Chief Directorate of State Security (GUGB), the state security successor to the OGPU when it was folded into the NKVD in 1934. This gave Beria access to all national-level documentation on NKVD operations and investigations and enabled him to checkmate Yezhov's moves against him. It also provided Beria with ready access to Stalin. By early December 1938, Beria had prevailed. His men had been placed in all critical NKVD posts around the country and Yezhov was dropped from his NKVD position on 8 December. His fate was never officially announced but rumors of his end ranged from execution, to suicide, to madness, to having been murdered by a fellow inmate. It is highly unlikely that Stalin would have kept him alive.

5

The Second Revolution:
The External Dimension

T HE ASSAULT on the peasantry and then on Soviet institutions
themselves did not exclusively absorb the interests of state security. Invariably, the internal focus of the counterintelligence state
carries an external dimension. This portion of the book examines
several lines of the service's foreign activities, lines that highlight Stalin's fixation with Trotsky as his most dangerous enemy, Hitler as a
potential ally, and the active-measures–direct-action operations that
continued the service's tradition as the party's sword.

Trotsky and the Trotskyite movement in Europe before World
War II were perceived by Stalin and his secret police as the most
compelling challenge to Stalin's rule. Objectively speaking, neither
the man nor the movement had the resources or the clarity of purpose to constitute a meaningful danger to Stalin's position. Trotsky's
opposition to Stalin was hamstrung by an ambivalence stemming
from his own role in helping to create the system on the top of which
Stalin sat. He could not disassociate himself either from the system
or Stalin's methods because even in opposition he defended them.
He never saw the contradiction in his position.

Likewise, he was a defender of the OGPU and its methods. During the Civil War he effected an exceptionally close cooperation between the Red Army and the Cheka. As the organizer and commander of the Red Army it was he who arranged for the creation of
the political commissars whose job it was to keep an eye on the "military specialists," or former tsarist officers. To complement this incipient political security service, he worked closely with Dzerzhin-

skiy in establishing the Cheka's Special Departments (OOs), a penetration network within the military for ferreting out dissidence, malcontents, espionage, and politically unreliable elements. He was therefore very familiar with the ways of intelligence, espionage, counterintelligence, and provocation. Indeed, his many years in the underground before 1917 were excellent preparation for his collaboration with Dzerzhinskiy in the business of intelligence and counterintelligence.

Boris Nikolaevskiy had observed that Trotsky never attacked state security, even after he had been exiled and pilloried by Stalin and his clique.[1] In May 1930, Trotsky's *Byulleten' oppozitsii* (*Bulletin of the Opposition*) vigorously defended the OGPU, citing Soviet encirclement by a hostile world, and chastising liberals and Social Democrats for putting the question "on a formal basis." For Trotsky the issue of repression and terror was to be handled on a "class basis"— that is, in whose name was repression to be applied? As he put it, it was a "matter of revolutionary expediency, not one of supra-class justice."[2] Simply put, Trotsky defended terror and the extralegal actions of Stalin's secret police, as long as they were applied against the bourgeoisie. Their use against revolutionaries was another issue of course.

All of this made Trotsky something of a contradiction. He clearly had excellent experience in conspiracy, intelligence, and counterintelligence, yet he was a signal failure in protecting himself and his movement from Stalin–OGPU penetration and provocation. While in exile he took not even the most elementary measures of counterintelligence protection, a failure that negated the physical security arrangements about his person. He seemed incapable of making a causal connection between Stalin and the OGPU, going out of his way to defend OGPU actions, as witnessed by the 1930 *Byulleten'* piece.

When Yakov Blyumkin, an allegedly pro-Trotsky OGPU operative, visited Trotsky's Turkish exile residence in 1929, Trotsky entrusted him with a message to the Left Opposition in the Soviet Union. Victor Serge claims that Blyumkin had in fact been dispatched by the OGPU to spy on Trotsky and perhaps to run some sort of provocation against him.[3] (Blyumkin, it should be remembered, was the assassin of the German ambassador, Count Mirbach, in 1918.) The latter may indeed have been the case and the carrying of secret messages back into the Soviet Union the actual provocation. This would have allowed Stalin and the OGPU to actively hunt down the remaining Trotskyites and at the same time get rid of their own provocateur, Blyumkin. Blyumkin was arrested and executed within a month of his return. Orlov states that Blyumkin was betrayed by both Karl Radek and a female OGPU officer, Liza Gorskaya, assigned to sexually entrap him, and that Blyumkin yelled "long live Trotsky" immediately before he was shot.[4] Whether Blyumkin was witting or not, the visit certainly appears to have been primarily a provocation and not simply a surveillance mission. The OGPU had other penetrations of Trotsky's staff to handle the purely surveillance function. The elimination of Blyumkin was a harbinger of the fate that befell many other state security officers privy to too many details of Stalin–state security intrigues.

The Blyumkin affair was only one milestone in a series of provocations against Trotsky and his followers. Even prior to Trotsky's foreign exile Stalin had the OGPU arrange a provocation in a manner calculated to portray Trotsky and the Unified Opposition as renegade factionalists. Following Trotsky's ouster as commissar of war in 1925 and his expulsion from the Politburo in 1926, the Unified Opposition expanded its clandestine anti-Stalin activity. But at this point the opposition was already penetrated by the OGPU at many levels. One of these penetrations involved an OGPU operative by the name of Stroilov whose service dated back to the Cheka.

In 1927 an operation occurred reminiscent of the Avlabar press raid in 1906 near Tbilisi. The Okhrana raided an underground revolutionary press and were suspected of having the assistance of a provocateur/penetration agent—Josef Stalin. For the 1927 provocation, Yagoda had his man Stroilov supply a particular group of oppositionists with the printing materials for the preparation of a Trotskyite platform that Stalin had refused to allow at the forthcoming party congress. When the anti-Stalinist platform was printed and ready the OGPU struck. It was a classic provocation that Stalin then used to launch a major attack on Trotsky and the opposition. In a speech delivered before a combined Central Committee and Central Control Commission meeting in October 1927, Stalin announced that the OGPU raid on the "Trotskyists' illegal, anti-Party printing press" had been accomplished with the aid of a "former Wrangel officer" whom the opposition had enlisted but who really was an

OGPU agent helping to "unmask counter-revolutionary organizations."[5] Complicity with White officers was serious business and the
opposition leaders were at a loss, unable to mount a coherent counterattack against the charge. Trotsky's credibility was fatally compromised; he, Zinoviev, and almost a hundred others were expelled
from the party in November 1927.[6] The following month the Fifteenth Party Congress endorsed the expulsions. Then in January
1928, Trotsky and some thirty oppositionists were internally exiled.
No longer a member of the party and without the protection it afforded, Trotsky would now "legitimately" be subject to all variety of
attention from the OGPU.

Who was this "Wrangel officer" whom Stalin and the OGPU used
to "unmask" Trotsky's "counter-revolutionary conspiracies"? Orlov
tells us he was none other than Stroilov, the OGPU provocateur.[7]
When Yagoda reported the successful seizure of the printing press
and, hence, the success of Stroilov's provocation, Stalin is claimed to
have responded: "Good! Now promote your secret agent to the rank
of an officer of General Wrangel and indicate in your report that the
Trotskyites collaborated with a Wrangelian White Guardist."[8]

Trotsky does not seem to have known that the whole business was
a provocation and he therefore did not register its impact on his political fortunes. But it was not to be his last instance of political or
counterintelligence naïveté vis-à-vis Stalin and state security. More
was to come.

As for Stroilov, little is known about his fate though it may be
surmised. We do know that in 1937, one Mikhail Stroilov was tried
as both a German spy and a Trotskyite. His scripted confession to
the court has him reading Trotsky's *My Life*, at the recommendation
of an H. von Berg, an alleged German spy who supposedly recruited
Stroilov.[9]

Probably the most dramatic example of the OGPU's success
against Trotsky (other than his murder in 1940), and Trotsky's inability to recognize the game, was the repeated penetration of his
personal staff while in exile and the penetrations and manipulation
of the overall Trotskyite movement in the West. A favorite technique
was for certain OGPU operatives to gain the confidence of Trotsky
and poison Trotsky's attitude toward his bona fide supporters in the
movement, leading Trotsky to believe that the latter themselves were

OGPU agents. The Sobolevicius brothers, known better by their assumed names Jack Soble and Robert Soblen,[10] were especially adept at manipulating Trotsky's perception of his followers in Germany and disrupting the Trotskyite movement there. For example, they played Trotsky off against his loyal and influential supporter Kurt Landau so successfully that Landau and others were expelled from the movement; Landau then refused to have anything else to do with Trotsky.[11] Even after it became clear by late 1932 what they were up to, Trotsky still could not come to terms with the implications. Both Jack and Robert later surfaced in the United States in the 1950s when they were arrested and tried on charges of espionage for the Soviets.

If the OGPU considered itself satisfied with Soble/Soblen's work against Trotsky, it must have felt especially successful with the performance of Mark Zborowskiy.[12] Zborowskiy, born in Russia and raised in Poland, became a communist before he appeared in Paris in the late 1920s. In the early 1930s he was associated with the Union of Returnees, the Vozvrashchentsy, a notorious NKVD front for encouraging émigrés to return to the USSR. He befriended French Oppositionists in Paris, affecting Trotskyite sympathies, which brought him into contact with Russian Trotskyites around Lev Sedov, Trotsky's son, who ran the Fourth International and published the *Byulleten' oppozitsii*. Zborowskiy, known to Sedov as Etienne, worked his way into Sedov's confidence and from 1934 to 1940 was closely associated with the Fourth International and the *Byulleten'*, and even became a trusted correspondent with Trotsky himself.

During this time, Zborowskiy was a close associate of Lilia Estrin, later wife of David Dallin, who is known for his many books on the USSR.[13] Lilia Dallin was a secretary to Boris Nikolaevskiy at the International Institute of Social History and together she and Zborowskiy became indispensable helpers to Sedov in his work with the Fourth International and the *Byulleten'*. Orlov, who knew of Etienne from his own days in the NKVD, had an awkward meeting with Lilia and David Dallin in December 1954 in which they admitted to knowing Etienne for a number of years and to having helped bring him to the United States in 1941. Lilia Dallin seemed defensive and evasive about her relationship with Etienne, and Orlov suspected that she warned Etienne that Orlov was providing evidence on him to the FBI. Orlov states that Lilia Dallin attempted to blame Elsa Bernaut, the widow of assassinated NKVD officer Ignace Reiss, for the warning to Etienne.[14]

Trotsky repeatedly was warned about Etienne by a number of his (Trotsky's) followers, but to no avail. As in the case of the Soble/Soblen brothers, Etienne had a way of turning the charge of OGPU agent back on the accusers with the result that Trotsky lost true supporters while Etienne repeatedly received endorsements by his two targets, Trotsky and his son Sedov. Orlov, too, attempted to warn Trotsky in a letter and by telephone, after Orlov had defected and arrived in North America.[15] But this warning got nowhere either.

Etienne–Zborowskiy's damage to Trotsky, his son, and his followers was, quite literally, lethal. He handled Trotsky's correspondence from the Paris end, worked on the *Byulleten'*, and was involved with all manner of activities and persons associated with the Trotskyite movement. All of this information was passed to his NKVD case officer(s) either through the Union of Returnees or the Soviet Embassy itself. The NKVD could not ask for a better penetration.

Etienne was central to the 1936 NKVD burglary and theft of certain of Trotsky's papers sent to Nikolaevskiy's International Institute of Social History for safekeeping. It has been suggested, however, that the theft itself was a sham to cast Etienne in a favorable and even heroic light. Several accounts have it that the stolen documents were not that valuable. According to Deutscher, Etienne was guarding the most critical parts of the archive in his own home at the very moment of the burglary.[16] Etienne, Lilia Dallin, Sedov, and Nikolaevskiy were the only people who knew of the archival transfer. Etienne, therefore, looked not at all suspicious and indeed quite trustworthy. It can be argued that the theft was conceived precisely to enhance his reputation and keep the penetration going. As Deutscher remarks, with Etienne on the inside the NKVD was already seeing the most important material and did not have to steal anything.[17]

In 1938 Etienne had a hand in Lev Sedov's dispatch to a private clinic (staffed by émigré Russians of dubious repute) for a routine operation, and informed the KGB. Sedov died under highly suspicious circumstances. Etienne also played an informant's role in the murder of NKVD defector Ignace Reiss in 1937 in Lausanne, Switzerland, and would have succeeded in setting up Walter Krivitsky for assassination by one of Yezhov's killer squads had Krivitsky not had French police protection. At Sedov's request Etienne had served as companion and *bodyguard* to Krivitsky in Paris and admitted to reporting on this activity to his NKVD case officer![18] Krivitsky later was found shot to death in a Washington hotel room in 1941. The police ruled it a suicide. However, Etienne, in his testimony to a U.S. Senate subcommittee, quickly blurted out in response to the question "Who assassinated Krivitsky?"—the Soviet police. Moments later he reversed himself and claimed ignorance as to who did the assassination.[19]

After Sedov's death, Etienne and Lilia Dallin edited the *Byulleten'* and Etienne had his hand in other affairs of the movement. He was thus able to provide his NKVD superiors with vital intelligence on Trotsky and his followers. There may be reason to believe that he met on several occasions with Trotsky's murderer in Paris before the actual event, but this is not known for sure. Equally important, as an agent provocateur in the Trotskyite movement he was able to misdirect it from within. His close relationship with Trotsky allowed him to deflect or blunt the warnings that came from numerous prominent Trotsky supporters or well-wishers like Victor Serge and Henk Sneevliet, the Dutch Trotskyite, who declaimed: "This dirty little Pole is a Soviet agent."[20]

There were other targets, victims, and crimes attributable to Etienne. He admitted to reporting to the NKVD on Aleksandr Barmine, a Soviet defector from the Foreign Commissariat.[21] Dallin states that Etienne used his friendship with him and Lilia Dallin to get to Viktor Kravchenko, a Soviet defector whom Andrey Gromyko, Soviet ambassador to Washington, demanded be forcibly returned to the USSR.[22] Etienne's NKVD task was to keep Kravchenko from going underground by establishing a friendship with him through the Dallins. Despite Etienne's work, the NKVD did not get Kravchenko. Kravchenko subsequently wrote a book, *I Chose Freedom*, which was charged by a French communist weekly as having been written by U.S. intelligence. Kravchenko sued for libel in a French court and won in 1949.[23] In 1966, however, Kravchenko was found shot to death in his New York apartment. As with Krivitsky in 1941, the official finding was suicide. Finally, there is reason to believe that Etienne's service to the NKVD may have played a part in the 1937 execution of Trotsky's one-time secretary Erwin Wolf in Spain, and the probable murder of the secretary of the Fourth International, Rudolf Klement, in 1938 in France. A headless body believed to be Klement's was found floating in the River Seine.

Orlov's disclosures had finally led to Etienne's questioning by the FBI and a U.S. Senate subcommittee, but in the end Etienne received only a short term for perjury before a grand jury. Few provocateurs had achieved so much for state security. While Trotsky flailed ineffectually at Stalin, Stalin seems to have puppeteered precisely such a response. Etienne's admissions to the U.S. investigators were carefully calibrated to acknowledge limited service to the NKVD that involved only passing a small amount of information, while taking pains to exculpate himself from any role in Stalin's violence. He claimed that he intellectually broke with Stalin in 1938, but that, like his other claims, was clearly part of a dissembling pattern to frustrate charges of espionage or other crimes.

It may be that Stalin and the NKVD were pleased to assist Etienne to get to and establish himself in the United States with no more taxing duties to perform than surveillance jobs on émigré Mensheviks, Trotskyites, and defectors. This he did within the Soblen network, which in the case of Soblen and Zborowskiy was a reevocation of Stalin's anti-Trotsky squad.

His service against Trotsky and the Trotskyite movement was brilliantly executed. When Etienne arrived in the United States, Trotsky had been murdered; the movement was hopelessly fragmented and dispirited; and there was no surviving follower around with the stature, fortitude, or brilliance to rally the squabbling "tendencies" as the factions were and are still known. Trotskyism was interred with the "Old Man" thanks in no small part to Etienne–Zborowskiy.

Germany and the Soviet Union in the post–World War I era exercised a certain magnetic pull on each other, notwithstanding the fierce political and ideological struggles between them. Political schizophrenia seemed, on the surface at least, to characterize the relations between these two anti-Versailles, international political outcasts. It is a commonplace that the USSR, for one, conducted its affairs with Germany on two tiers: state-to-state, in which a modicum of good relations occurred; and on the covert level, Moscow seeking to bring about a communist revolution through political warfare.

This does not capture the spirit of what really occurred. For instance, even at the covert level (where state security and the Comintern operated), Soviet policy was contradictory. On the one hand Moscow's operatives and agents worked to bring down the Weimar Republic; on the other, Moscow clandestinely entered into a highly sensitive military collaboration with Berlin that lasted until Hitler's accession to power. The secret relationship between the Reichswehr—the postwar German army—and the Red Army was immensely beneficial to both military establishments, especially to the Germans, in view of the Versailles restrictions. Thus, though it was well known that there had always been an "Eastern" tendency among elements of the German military and state establishments, it is generally not appreciated that the German card had much more attraction for Stalin than deals with the principal Western democracies, Britain and France.

It is not my purpose to examine Soviet grand strategy and its tortuous foreign policy between the wars.[24] Stalin's Germany policy, however, had no small role in thrusting Europe and then the world into this century's second general war. Various forms of OGPU–NKVD covert action, or active measures, in keeping with the habits of the counterintelligence state, were hallmarks of this policy. I will explore some of these actions.

As was seen in chapter 4, Stalin was impressed by the decisiveness displayed by Hitler in handling real or imagined opponents. Hitler's June 1934 purge of Ernst Röhm, his SA lieutenants, and certain other troublesome elements served as both model and opportunity for Stalin. Krivitsky tells us that Stalin called an emergency meeting of the Politburo while Hitler's purge was under way. Also in attendance were Krivitsky's former boss, General Yan Berzin, chief of Military Intelligence (from whom Krivitsky learned of the meeting); Maxim Litvinov, commissar for foreign affairs; Karl Radek (who was to play an important role in the German business); and A. Kh. Artuzov of the OGPU's Foreign Department. (Krivitsky was transferred in 1934 to the NKVD, but he retained ties to his old GRU colleagues. And Artuzov was shifted to the GRU for a short period of time.) The purpose of this extraordinary session was to take stock of what was happening in Nazi Germany and what it portended for Soviet foreign policy. According to Krivitsky, Berzin reported Stalin's summing up of the Politburo's discussion as contrary to the conventional wisdom in the West: "The events in Germany do not at all indicate the collapse of the Nazi regime. On the contrary, they are bound to lead to the consolidation of that regime, and to the strengthening of Hitler himself."[25]

Stalin, according to Krivitsky, at that point determined that he would cut a deal with Hitler regardless of setbacks or rebuffs. This was not the standard contemporary Soviet, or Western, historiography and when it was articulated by Krivitsky in 1939 before the Hitler–Stalin Pact, it was well-nigh heretical. But it was the story brought out by an intelligence insider on whom history has smiled more benignly than on his detractors. Krivitsky and other Soviet insiders observed that Stalin began working secretly on the Germans through two prominent intermediaries, Karl Radek, and Stalin's trade representative in Berlin, David Kandelaki, not long after Hitler took power. Evgeniy Gnedin, the son of Alexander Helphand (Parvus), who had been with the Soviet Embassy in Berlin in 1935–36, states that Radek, while editor of *Izvestiya*, was involved in 1934 in secret diplomacy with German diplomats on Stalin's behalf.[26] Another Soviet diplomat had confidentially pointed out (like Krivitsky) that Stalin had been single-minded about an agreement with Hitler since 1933.[27] Radek told Krivitsky that the then-current press campaign Radek himself was directing against Nazi Germany was simply strategic eyewash for fools and that Soviet policy was in reality bound to Germany. Gnedin reported similar impressions given to Soviet officials in Germany by the Soviet deputy commissar for trade.[28] Kandelaki, though a trade representative, was used by Stalin in 1935–37 for sensitive political representations because Stalin was convinced the best way to get to Hitler was through the industrialists whom Stalin saw as the real power behind the new German leader. In May 1936 Kandelaki reached as high as Hermann Göring, who sympathetically promised to approach Hitler on the matter of improving Soviet–German relations. Two months later another Soviet official in Germany, Sergey Bessonov, outlined to the German Foreign Ministry the conditions necessary for a nonaggression pact.[29]

Up to Yezhov's appointment as NKVD chief in 1936, the NKVD seemed to be reporting in a manner seemingly at variance with Stalin's foreign policy. For instance, in 1934 the head of the OGPU's Foreign Department (INO), Artur Artuzov, disagreed with Stalin on the prospects for an accord with Poland, and Stalin charged that he was "misinforming the Politburo." A year later Artuzov produced a report from one of his best agents in Berlin, the essence of which held that Soviet appeasement of Hitler was doomed and that Hitler himself was the chief impediment to an understanding. Stalin's response was that the intelligence was wrong; Hitler had just granted the USSR a loan of 200 million gold marks, hence it was impossible for Hitler to make war on the Soviet Union. Besides, Stalin reasoned, big business was behind Hitler and they would not allow it.[30] In 1937 Artuzov perished in the purges.

If there had been any further inclinations for the NKVD to forward intelligence at variance with Stalin's German initiative, it is unreported. Artuzov seems to have represented that strain of state security officer whose roots were in the Cheka and who operated with a degree of professional aloofness incompatible with the horrific direction of the 1930s. With the ascendancy of Yezhov in 1936 and then the appearance of Beria and his gang of Georgians, the "sterling" old Chekists were violently rooted out of the service. Artuzov was of the Trust tradition and had a keen nose for the target and a sure sense for the psychology of the opponent. No doubt he perceived in Hitler the reflected Western variant of Stalin and smelled trouble.[31]

This is not to say that state security did not support Stalin's initiatives with Hitler or that after Yezhov finished working over the service all the intelligence reaching Stalin was cooked. Despite their aloofness they were still the elite action arm of the party and a disciplined lot. The NKVD's role in the assassination of Kirov demonstrates that point. As for supporting the Hitler card there is other evidence, albeit more tenuous, that state security was providing Stalin what he needed. What about quality intelligence after Yezhov and Beria finished trashing both the NKVD and Military Intelligence? At the senior levels a case can be made that Stalin was told what he wanted to hear. At the operational levels the purges took their tolls but, surprisingly, a respectable degree of performance still occurred.

Let us begin with Stalin's Hitler initiative. We have seen how Stalin's desire for a deal had him employing Radek and Kandelaki in recurring secret contacts while one of them, Radek, ran a hostile public diplomacy against Berlin. Typical of the Soviet system and Stalin the man, the covert dimension was the one through which meaningful attitudes and messages were portrayed and passed. Also typical was the practice of employing more than one channel through which to communicate these messages. One favorite and successful channel was a disinformational one, demonstrated so adroitly in the Trust legend of the 1920s. Recall that the Trust utilized not only provocation to achieve its counterintelligence goals, but trafficked heavily in forged and other spurious documents and intelligence reports against the émigrés and Western intelligence services.

In the 1930s a series of documents purporting to be minutes of Soviet Politburo meetings began appearing in Europe. With Hitler's rise to power these materials made their way to Berlin, where some were read by high Nazi officials including Joachim von Ribbentrop (the foreign minister) and Hitler himself. They covered the years 1934, 1935, and 1936.[32] The documents focused mostly on foreign policy items although a few did deal with internal Soviet matters. Most of the few Western specialists who reviewed the documents were convinced they were forgeries, on the basis of style (for example, prerevolutionary orthography), the realities of the Soviet way of rule (Politburo resolutions are state secrets and are not disseminated to Soviet embassies overseas as these were), and the bizarre quality of the substance of some of the documents.[33] Interestingly, whenever the resolutions took up the German question they tended to deal with the need for a Soviet–German understanding to prevent hostilities from developing.

A useful question to ask would be, Whose forgeries? The initial (1950s–1960s) response from Western academic investigators was that they were probably done by White Russian émigrés in Europe with the intent of selling them to Western governments. A declassified OSS memorandum from late 1945 concludes that White Russians sponsored by the Germans prepared the documents "to arouse other powers against the USSR, or to convince them of the weakness of the USSR so as to persuade them (e.g. Japan) not to hesitate to attack it."[34] A core assumption of this conclusion was that because the Politburo resolutions were found among the captured German documents at the end of World War II, they were probably German-inspired in the first place. A major problem with this is that the

Politburo papers were intended to reach German officialdom in the first place.

Still, it was not unreasonable to suspect Russian émigré or defector authorship because the interwar period witnessed a lively business in émigré-inspired forgeries motivated by profit and political warfare. Paris, for instance, was famous as a forgery mill during that time and after World War II. Grigoriy Bessedovskiy, a former Soviet diplomat who defected from the Soviet Embassy in Paris in 1929, is frequently associated with the Paris operations. He was one of those controversial defectors whose heavy volume of literary activities prompted many charges ranging from fabrication for profit to outright disinformation on Moscow's behalf.[35] Bessedovskiy was suspected of having become an OGPU provocateur within a year of his defection but he could have been one from the start. Because of his notoriety with other literary fabrications (usually favorable to Moscow's purposes) he is not unreasonably suspected of authorship of the Politburo resolutions. Bertram Wolfe felt that the Paris forgeries, with which Bessedovskiy was associated, had three motives: to raise money; to defend the Soviet Union; and to drive out of circulation serious studies of the real nature of the USSR with sensational and bemusing revelations.[36] The Politburo resolutions certainly were sympathetic to the USSR and evinced a preoccupation with Soviet security vis-à-vis Germany and Poland; the latter was clearly the object to be acted upon by the other two powers. Bessedovskiy also was suspected of having been connected to Hitler's intelligence by 1938; the oddity of such congruent connections led to the suspicions of his role in the Politburo affair. These are reinforced by his reported service in the French communist resistance during the war, which prompted an alleged "pardon" by Moscow for his Nazi connections.[37] The whole business smacks of an NKVD legend.

Had the 1934–36 documents been the only items of this genre, émigré fabricators would certainly be the leading suspects. But the titillating subject of Politburo-derived materials predates the "resolution" documents by about ten years. As early as January 1924 the U. S. Legation in Riga, Latvia, began dispatching resolutions and minutes of Politburo meetings acquired from a "confidential source (IS/1)" to Washington.[38] Over the next several years periodic reports of Politburo minutes, Central Committee meetings and minutes, and Sovnarkom meetings were acquired from the same source and forwarded to Washington. They dealt with such items as internal economic matters, the powers of the new GPU, mundane procedural issues of Politburo meetings, and even the problem of forgeries (a purported letter from the chief of the Secret Section of the Central Committee of the Russian Communist Party).[39]

There clearly was, then, a precedent for channeling "inside" information on high-level party deliberations to foreign governments. Interestingly enough, these included minutes of the most inner sanctum of the party—the Politburo.

Then, in 1929, the British Mission in Riga was approached directly by the OGPU *rezident* there, one Gaidouk, who offered to sell the British government copies of the minutes of Politburo meetings![40] Both the price asked and the contents of the documents were breathtaking and the British took the bait. Apparently, several deliveries of minutes of different Politburo meetings occurred and the British were impressed by both their timeliness and content. Public Soviet announcements of each of the Politburo meetings occurred some time after British receipt of their clandestine gems. Therefore, the British were duly impressed and the credibility of the documents was enhanced. Positive reinforcement, as it were.

For whatever reason, the British decided to run a check on their find and approached Boris Bajanov, a Soviet defector who had been Stalin's secretary, for an independent judgment. Bajanov immediately branded the materials forgeries.[41] He pointed out an important feature of the Soviet system that had been forgotten by later recipients and assessors of alleged Politburo minutes. A state security *rezident* simply did not receive such materials. Classified as highly sensitive state secrets, Politburo minutes did not go beyond or below members and candidate members of the Central Committee. They did not reach beyond the highest central authorities in Moscow, let alone to a *rezident* abroad. Sloppy security procedures were never an affliction of the Soviet counterintelligence state.

It is worth noting that in this case a known OGPU officer made the actual approach, which itself may be construed as an attempt to portray disaffection among state security elites. This should have raised some warning flags, especially if the man showed no inclination to actually defect or evinced no palpable disillusionment with the Soviet system. These 1920s cases suggest that state security was still employing some rather direct techniques in the tradition of the recently terminated Trust case. On the other hand, the 1930s offerings of Politburo minutes were more indirect but that may have been because of the singularity of the target—Germany.

Offhand, it would appear that a gap of several years lapsed between the OGPU offering of 1929 and the 1934–36 Politburo minutes held in the Hoover Archives and referenced in the OSS memorandum of September 1945. However, the continuity really was not broken, as was discovered by a Czech émigré scholar, Mikhaíl Reyman, writing recently from West Germany.[42] Reyman came across numerous documents in the German Foreign Ministry files acquired by West German military intelligence for the years 1932–33. Based on their numbering system he concluded that the materials actually began arriving in 1931 and maybe earlier, although documents for 1931 were not present in the Foreign Ministry archive. He concluded that about 120 documents a year were passed and that the last file was numbered 291.[43] The Hoover documents number approximately 136 for 1934 and 1935 and the OSS memorandum counts about 1,500 pages for 1934–36.[44] Thus, at least for the 1930s, there was a very large volume of allegedly intimate inside information on high Soviet policy circulating in the West.

Reyman concludes that the documents he found were bona fide materials from the highest organs of the USSR: the Politburo, the government, and the Presidium of the Central Executive Committee. The most sensitive of this collection was a file under the heading of "Stoyko Informatsii" (stoic information) dealing with Politburo meetings, and documents for February 1932 to February 1933. He judges that a member of Stalin's personal staff was the source of the information. Although an OGPU fabrication could not be ruled out, the goal of such an effort was obscure. Reyman gives no indication that he was aware of either earlier or subsequent materials of a similar nature. He clearly credits the authenticity of the materials and, as the title of his two-part article suggests ("Agent in the Politburo"), the inner sanctum of the Soviet leadership was penetrated by a disaffected insider.

What we seem to have here, then, is the discovery of the final link in a run of apparent forgeries spanning more than a decade and purporting to give an inside view of top-level thinking and policy of the Soviet leadership. What kind of information did the materials contain? From among the earliest available (the IS reports from the

U. S. Legation in Riga) we find such bizarre things as resolutions of the Central Committee to approve the foreign policy of the Commissariat of Foreign Affairs—as if the foreign commissariat developed its own foreign policy subject only to Central Committee rubber stamping.[45] This same tendency recurs in the 1934–36 Politburo documents, suggesting that someone was trying to portray the party as having less power than it actually did. The same benign presentation of the Soviet system was a feature of the Trust materials as well.

It is not known publicly what substance the Gaidouk (the OGPU *rezident* in Riga) documents had because these were received by British intelligence. But if the precursor and subsequent materials are any guide, similar themes most likely were propagated. With the Stoyko and the 1934–36 materials, changes in the international scene clearly influenced the substance and tone of the messages. Amid the clutter of trivia were persistent signals of a desire for improved relations with Germany at Poland's expense. In the Stoyko materials an elaborate charade is worked around the March 1932 attack in Moscow on F. von Tvardovsky, advisor to the German Ambassador von Dirksen. The alleged assailants, I. M. Stern and S. S. Vasiliev, were claimed by the OGPU to have been working for Poland. Such a story was bound to sour Polish–German relations but enhance Moscow–Berlin ties. That this was all staged to begin with is reinforced by what followed. Stoyko has a report of a 2 April 1932 Politburo meeting—from which Stalin is absent—in which Nikolay Krestinskiy, a Central Committee secretary and an Old Bolshevik, voiced a strong suspicion that the assassins were "OGPU undercover agents" but that he hoped that the OGPU would turn up something to convince the German government that Polish and French secret agents were responsible.[46] Sure enough, several days later, the Military Collegium of the Supreme Court of the Soviet Union confirmed that Poland was responsible for the attack!

The whole business smacked of an OGPU provocation with Krestinskiy's suspicions part of the charade. The very act of raising the issue of an OGPU role would ensure that it would be disproven and not believed—a favorite disinformation technique. This was reminiscent of the machinations with the Trust and Bessedovskiy's later fabrications.

Another piece of bizarre material in the Stoyko documents has Marshals Voroshilov, Blücher, and Tukhachevskiy attacking the authority of the Politburo, demonstrating that a major split existed between the party and the military. In a raging counterattack in a surprise appearance at a 21 April 1932 Politburo meeting, Stalin threatened all three officers with charges of Bonapartism; however, Voroshilov was forgiven on the condition that he submit to the unconditional authority of the Politburo.[47] This all would seem the height of absurdity had it not been for subsequent provocatory fabrications concerning the military and then the smashing of the Soviet officer corps a few years later. It is worth noting that Voroshilov, in the Stoyko material, is excused and forgiven. He survived the purges. Blücher and Tukhachevskiy were shot.

As events progressed closer to Hitler's accession to power the German card was given special attention by Stoyko. In a May 1932 Politburo meeting, Molotov presented a letter from Krestinskiy that insisted that Moscow could not sustain a war on two fronts. It went on: "Polish–German relations are such that (here much depends on us) a conflict between Poland and Germany is more likely than one between Poland and the USSR. . . . Let's lay out our cards with Germany and restore international cooperation with them. . . . And even more: open Soviet markets—informally, of course—to the Germans and use their expertise for the practical reform of the USSR economy. . . ." Reyman makes the observation that this pro-German tilt of Soviet policy enjoyed the strong support of the Soviet military.[48] On Hitler's assumption of power, Stoyko offered another Politburo session in which Krestinskiy, on 6 February 1933, again addressed Germany and the USSR: "the interests of the USSR are not served by entering into any kind of adventure with France and Poland aimed against Germany." Krestinskiy also saw a coming conflict in the Far East, first between Japan and China, and then between Japan and the United States; Japan's break with the League of Nations created favorable conditions for a treaty between Japan and Moscow.[49] All very prophetic.

Reyman, a former Czech official, is persuaded that the Stoyko documents were authentic notes of Politburo meetings by an intrusive presence. They appear, however, to be authentic forgeries, that is, their point of origin was probably the USSR and more specifically the OGPU. But they were not Politburo resolutions. Their purpose, as with the precursor documents, was to proffer a false image of the USSR. However, there was an added twist—a subtle plea for an understanding with Germany. The fact that the Stoyko materials and the follow-on 1934–36 materials were found in impressive numbers in German Foreign Ministry holdings, some of which originated from German military intelligence, points to the German government as the specific target audience.

The 1934–36 materials appear to be a logical progression from the Stoyko materials. Despite the presence of assorted trivial concerns, a preoccupying theme involved Soviet policy vis-à-vis Germany, and to a lesser extent Poland, in the West, and Japan in the East.[50] Other important themes from among these materials involve discontent among the Soviet military (as in Stoyko) and a tactical retreat by Stalin from Soviet ideology![51] But the "driving of a wedge between Berlin and Warsaw" and the necessity of getting Berlin to drop its Polish orientation in exchange for a more "realistic combination" that would "give Germany immediate and tangible advantages" was presented by one of the Politburo resolutions as one of the essential tasks of Soviet foreign policy.[52]

Were the Germans receptive? It is hard to say. Milton Loventhal, one of the few researchers who systematically evaluated the materials and who was a believer in their authenticity, queried two former Nazi and German government officials and received contradictory responses. The former Nazi official, whose name appeared in the back of several of the Politburo documents, wrote to Loventhal on 9 May 1956:

> The reading of the pages . . . impressed me with the fact that it was a question of a positively expert report which in diction, terminology and contents gave an impression of a genuine nature. Nevertheless, I was skeptical from the first. I considered it as the work of a well-versed and intelligent man or of many such persons who wanted to attain a definite political goal with it. . . . I considered it possible that it could be a question of a Soviet source which would . . . hand over correct reports in order to smuggle in misleading information and eventually create, by this means, a dangerous effect. In short I considered it, *if anything* as "framed material" which, in the beginning probably would transmit useful information in order to introduce itself, but then it would become an instrument of some provocation or other.[53]

This man appears to suspect the materials as probably Soviet-inspired forgeries.

The other German, a former Soviet researcher in the Foreign Policy Office of the Nazi Party provided two responses on 11 July 1960 and 2 December 1960, respectively:

> The reports of the Politburo had been brought to me in those days through intelligence service channels. At first I had doubts about their authenticity. . . . I had the Soviet press and the Soviet periodicals as well as the foreign press. . . . and from this received the impression that the reports represented a valuable source of information, and even if they were perhaps not genuine, nevertheless they dealt with problems which according to other information, came up for discussion in the sessions of the Politburo and essentially included the contents of the resolutions of the Politburo.[54]

This December response provided the level of German readership: "[Alfred] Rosenberg [of the Nazi Party's Foreign Policy Office] believed that the contents of the Politburo reports were genuine. . . . So far as I remember, the reports served as general information on Soviet policy."[55] Additionally, according to Loventhal, Rosenberg's diary entry for 11 June 1934 notes that Hitler read at least one of the resolutions and responded in a manner indicating that he accepted it as authentic.[56]

A long-time student of Soviet forgeries and other disinformation, Natalie Grant took issue with Loventhal and concluded that the 1934–36 materials were Soviet forgeries. She feels they were intended to foster a distorted image of the USSR and hint to Nazi Germany that an accommodation between the two dictatorships was possible and desirable.[57] She also notes an intriguing item missed by other students of this topic. Soon after David Kandelaki arrived in Berlin in 1935 as Stalin's trade representative and made secret approaches to the German government, the Politburo resolutions ceased coming.[58] Had Stalin chosen to halt the OGPU's indirect approach in favor of direct, but covert, contact?

Barring the opening of KGB and party archives, we cannot know the definitive story of the Politburo documents and their role, if any, in propelling the Soviet–German rapprochement and pact of August 1939. But they definitely have the substantive marks of authentic Soviet-inspired forgeries, and they do fit into the general mosaic of Soviet foreign policy of that period. Likewise, they bear the demeanor of OGPU–NKVD-inspired provocations in keeping with the state security–active measures tradition with its numerous legends of the interwar period. That much, at the very least, may be said.

Before leaving the Politburo resolutions let us return to a related topic: the possible role of Bessedovskiy in the fabrication of the 1934–36 materials. By German accounts the documents were acquired from a Soviet Embassy source in Vienna.[59] Bessedovskiy was operating out of Paris at that time but this posed no great geographic problem. Bertram Wolfe, in his correspondence with Milton Loventhal, at first felt that the Politburo minutes were "quieter in tone and less sensational than the forgeries put out by the forgery mill in Paris"—in the context of his other correspondence he clearly has Bessedovskiy in mind here.[60] A month later in another letter to Loventhal, Wolfe decides to take the plunge: "Strange to say, I think we are contemplating the earliest of Bessedovskiy's forgeries, when he was desperately looking for a way of making a living without becoming a chauffeur, and the style is explained by the fact that it is not to be sold to boulevard journals but to governments."[61] Though allowing that some of the material in the Politburo minutes is more in keeping with the later Bessedovskiy (1940–1950s), he does come down hard for Bessedovskiy as the culprit. In answer to the Politburo document that speaks of the USSR "ceasing to be communist in its acts and measures," Wolfe declares: "If this is not pure Bessedovskiy, then he has a superior of whose existence I am not yet aware."[62]

These are plausible conclusions—but only at the time they were voiced. Neither Wolfe nor Loventhal appeared to know of the Politburo documents from the U. S. Legation in Riga in the mid 1920s, the Gaidouk Politburo documents in 1929, or the Stoyko information for 1932–33. Two of these three predated Bessedovskiy's operations in Paris.

On the other hand, an argument for Bessedovskiy's role in forging the 1934–36 Politburo documents might still be adduced *if he were under OGPU control from the start of his defection or soon after.* That may be a reasonable proposition. The closest thing to a biography of Bessedovskiy, Brook-Shepherd's *The Storm Petrels*, raises doubts about the man's bona fides, hinting at Soviet control. More recently, Mikhail Agursky, a Soviet émigré scholar in Israel, concludes that Bessedovskiy's defection was a deception to begin with, a "faked defection." He was under control from the start and was dispatched precisely to execute a disinformation mission.[63] But Agursky does not address the Politburo documents, rather he focuses on Bessedovskiy's later heavy output of fabricated books (these didn't begin until 1945/46), all of which subtly advanced Stalin's and Moscow's image while appearing to be critical of the USSR. As for the believability of such material—and this may apply to the Politburo resolutions as well—Agursky concludes: "It should also be noted that the Soviet trials of 1936–38 used the same quality of evidence as the above mentioned forgeries [Bessedovskiy's and another fake defector's works], and were received with the same credence by Western observers."[64]

Soviet active measures during the 1930s comprised considerably more than forgeries aimed at influencing Germany's behavior. NKVD provocations and forgeries figured in the smashing of the Red Army leadership in 1937.

We have already seen that Tukhachevskiy's and Blücher's names appeared in one of the Stoyko Politburo documents in 1932. They, with Voroshilov, were alleged to have attacked the party's authority. Of the three, only Voroshilov was "exonerated." This was an ominous portent. In the Soviet pressure cooker of the 1930s such a negative flag invariably proved to be extremely dangerous. During the purges, for instance, even the benign mention of someone's name in the course of an interrogation or a trial signaled that that person's turn was next.

Tukhachevskiy had earlier run afoul of Stalin during the Russo-Polish War of 1920. Stalin, a vengeful grudge-bearer, never forgot. When Tukhachevskiy was executed in 1937, one of the charges against him was alleged collusion with the German military. If Stalin were building a dossier to work his vengeance, it would not have been difficult to fabricate a case. Tukhachevskiy naturally worked with the Germans during the Reichswehr–Red Army secret collaboration that ran until Hitler came to power. At the termination of the military accommodation Tukhachevskiy is claimed to have told one of his German guests: "Don't forget that it is your policy which separates us, but not our feelings—the feelings of friendship which the Red Army has for the Reichswehr. And always remember this: you and we, Germany and the Soviet Union, can dictate world peace, if we march together."[65]

This clearly was not treason, for even Commissar of Defense Voroshilov, in hosting some high-ranking German officers in Moscow, stressed the Red Army's desire to continue the close relationship with the Reichswehr.[66] But it was a potent theme that could be woven by the secret police into a broader fabrication. And weave they did, actually creating several different fabrications to get Tukhachevskiy and the Red Army leadership. Czechoslovakia appeared to play an unusual middleman role in this business.

First, from December 1935 until April 1936 an anticommunist Russian émigré monthly published in Prague, *Znamya Rossii* (Banner of Russia), ran a series of articles about an opposition movement in the Soviet Union involving the military in a plot against Stalin. The editors claimed to have acquired the information a year earlier, that is, in late 1934. Other émigrés attacked the publication of a Red commanders' conspiracy as a legend of Soviet state security.[67]

Next, according to Alexander Orlov, an NKVD officer by the name of Israelovich had been arrested in Prague in 1936 following a meeting with two German General Staff officers. The Czechs thought the Soviet an agent of the Germans but Israelovich blurted out that it was the other way around and he produced the films he had just received from the Germans as proof. They contained photos of secret German General Staff documents. Israelovich was released but only after he signed a deposition. President Beneš, in a goodwill gesture to Stalin, passed the police report and deposition to the USSR. Stalin later used this incident to intimate to Beneš that Israelovich was the contact man to the German military for Tukhachevskiy.[68] The Czechs, though they knew better, circulated the fabrication.

Next, in late 1936–early 1937, General Nikolay Skoblin, chief of the Inner Line of ROVS, the White Russian veterans organization in Paris, and an aide to ROVS Chief General Yevgeniy Miller, approached Reinhard Heydrich ("The Hangman"), chief of the Nazi security service, the SD. Skoblin was a penetration agent of the NKVD within the White organization and concurrently an agent of the SD.[69] Skoblin's wife, Nadezhda Plevitskaya, a popular singer, was also a Soviet agent and may have been the source of Skoblin's recruitment. Skoblin informed Heydrich of a "conspiracy" between the Red Army and the German General Staff. Heydrich, with Hitler's approval, manufactured a dossier of fabricated materials that implicated Tukhachevskiy and other senior Red Army officers in a plot against Stalin. The so-called "Red Folder" was passed in April–May 1937 by the SD to the NKVD, which in turn slipped a copy to President Beneš, so that Stalin could receive it from "clean" hands.[70] The initiative for the folder originated with the NKVD and Stalin, even though Heydrich actually concocted the material with an eye towards emasculating the Red Army high command.

Some accounts attribute the execution of Tukhachevskiy and other Red Army leaders in early June 1937 to the evidence of treason set forth in the Red Folder.[71] Actually, there was no way of knowing or ensuring that when Skoblin passed his bogus information the Germans would forge an incriminating dossier. There is even some argument over whether the idea of the dossier was Heydrich's or Hitler's. Neither Stalin nor Yezhov had any way of manipulating that level of response. Second, it seems certain in view of the foregoing information about Tukhachevskiy that he was a marked man well before the Skoblin initiative. Krivitsky and others feel that Stalin needed to get such men out of the way to secure his deal with Hitler.[72] Finally, as seen in chapter 4, Orlov strongly asserts and Krivitsky vaguely hints that a real coup involving the military had been in preparation and prompted the lightning arrests in late May 1937 by the NKVD. There was never a public trial, only a drumhead tribunal and postexecution press releases. In that event, Heydrich's Red Folder would have been irrelevant because its value would have been in its publicity.

Tukhachevskiy has since been rehabilitated but the party has said precious little about the affair other than point to the German forgery effort; nothing about the NKVD's and Skoblin's parts in the drama is hinted at.

Related to NKVD active measures during the 1920s and 1930s was a direct-action dimension, that is assassinations and kidnappings. Extraordinary measures had fallen within the purview of state security since the days of the Cheka and had become a key feature of the counterintelligence state. If state security had few constraints on what it could do to Soviet citizens at home, it follows that defectors, apostates, and the occasional foreigner were fair game, subject only to the degree of alertness of foreign governments and security services.

From early on defectors, declared opponents, and selected others were targeted by state security operatives who could rely upon local communists or sympathizers to assist in kidnappings or assassinations. Generalized terror was a common feature of the counterintelligence state—the Red Terror of the Civil War; collectivization; liquidation of the "kulaks"; the terror-famine; the 1930s purges—but external direct action was carefully crafted for high-value targets deemed particularly dangerous to Soviet interests. However, in the first two decades of the regime there was a congruence of sorts between direct-action operations and other state security activities. Also, it was not until 1936, with the appearance of Yezhov's Administration for Special Tasks within the NKVD, that an institutional bureaucratic focal point was specifically identified. Thereafter an element of state security specifically charged with the "wet affairs" (*mokrye dela*) aspect of Soviet active measures has remained in operation, under different names, to current times.

In my estimate, one of the first such actions was Blyumkin's 1918 assassination of German Ambassador Count von Mirbach. As discussed earlier, the standard view is that Blyumkin committed that crime as a Left SR. Yet, as we know, he was never really punished and later served as a senior OGPU officer before being executed in 1929 as an alleged Trotskyite. He would seem to have gone through several extreme ideological personas in such a relatively short career (he was only thirty when executed). One of the final results of von Mirbach's murder was the suppression of the SRs and their elimination as partners of the Bolsheviks, both in the government and in the Cheka. The Bolsheviks then had a pure monopoly of power. As with the so-called Lockhart or Ambassadors' Plot the same year, this too was probably one of Dzerzhinskiy's provocations.

Blyumkin was involved in an unsuccessful assassination attempt in 1928 in Paris on the first major Soviet defector, Boris Bajanov, from Stalin's secretariat. The man who was to have done the actual murder, another OGPU defector by the name of Arkady Maximov who had accompanied Bajanov in his escape, himself died in mysterious circumstances in a fall from the Eiffel Tower in 1937.[73]

In May 1926, General S. Petlyura, Ukrainian nationalist leader in exile in Paris, was assassinated by the OGPU. The same year Ado Birk, Estonian envoy to Moscow, was kidnapped by the OGPU in a bizarre provocation associated with the Trust operation. He escaped from OGPU custody and made his way back to Estonia where he had to face OGPU-inspired charges of treason.[74]

One of the most publicized cases was that of General P. A. Kutyepov, chief of ROVS (Russkiy Obshche-Voyenskiy Soyuz), the Russian General Military Union, in Paris. Kutyepov was kidnapped on 26 January 1930 by the OGPU. General Skoblin, also of ROVS and later implicated in the kidnapping of Kutyepov's successor, General Miller, and involved in the Tukhachevskiy affair, was part of this operation as one of the OGPU's inside penetration agents. The Soviets heatedly denied any knowledge of the affair. Thirty-five years later, however, they not only admitted the action but bragged about it and gave other information:

> Commissar of State Security Second Rank S. V. Puzitskiy took part in the Civil War, was an ardent Bolshevik-Leninist, and a pupil of F. E. Dzerzhinskiy. Not only did he participate in the capture of the bandit Savinkov and in the destruction of . . . the "Trust," *but he carried out a brilliant operation in the arrest of Kutyepov and a number of White Guard organizers and inspirers of foreign military intervention and the Civil War.* S. V. Puzitskiy was twice awarded the Order of the Red Banner and received honorary decorations of a Chekist.[75]

This is an unusual and candid admission by the Soviets. It would be intriguing to have the names of the other Whites they admit "arresting."

Numerous murders and kidnappings were carried out by the clandestine German apparat of the OGPU, which was especially active on the German waterfront, facilitating the shipment of victims to the USSR. Actually, these were "international" in character. For instance, George Mink, an OGPU chieftain on the U. S. waterfront, and Hugo Marx, resident OGPU agent in Hamburg, cooperated in a number of murders and abductions.[76] Mink later gained notoriety as an NKVD executioner in Republican Spain in 1937 under the name Alfred Herz and was involved in arrangements in Mexico for Trotsky's assassination.[77] He may also have been connected to the disappearance of dissident U. S. communist Juliet Poyntz.

On 5 September 1937, Ignace Reiss, a disaffected GRU officer and friend of Walter Krivitsky, was shot to death in Switzerland by an NKVD-led execution team, some of whom were drawn from a penetrated group of Whites in Paris. Mark Zborowskiy (Etienne) is believed to have played a role in this action.

Zborowskiy's association with NKVD direct action spanned the burglary of Trotsky's papers at Nikolaevskiy's International Institute of Social History, to the death of Trotsky's son Lev Sedov and the disappearances and murders of Erwin Wolf and Rudolf Klement, the former an ex-secretary of Trotsky, the latter a secretary of Trotsky's Fourth International.

Spain during the Civil War was a veritable NKVD killing field—but *behind* Republican lines, not against the Nationalists. Whether against Trotskyite, anarchist, socialist, or communist, Yezhov's killers (who, like Mink, were not all Soviets) carried out Stalin's wishes. The victims included, among scores of others: Kurt Landau, against whom Soble–Soblen turned Trotsky; Henri Maulin, French Trotskyite; Andrés Nin, leader of the POUM (Workers' Party of Marxist Unification); Marc Rein, son of exiled Menshevik leader, Raphael Abramovich; and José Robles, a professor from Johns Hopkins University. Andre Marty, French communist and commander-in-chief of the International Brigades, played a key role in many of the NKVD atrocities in Spain. Also prominent in these actions was Naum (Leonid) Eitingon, the organizing spirit behind Trotsky's assassination. The Eitingon name also figured in General Miller's kidnapping. Communists and others not caught in Spain were ordered back or lured into the Soviet Union.

The murder of Leon Trotsky in Mexico in 1940 was the culmination of Stalin's long vendetta against his chief ideological opponent and claimant to Lenin's mantle. Eitingon, known as General Kotov, recruited a son (Ramón Mercader, also known as Frank Jacson) of his mistress in Spain, Caridad Mercader. Mercader completed the deed on 20 August 1940, served twenty years in a Mexican prison whence he was whisked to Czechoslovakia, on a diplomatic passport, via Cuba. He received his Hero of the Soviet Union medal in a different era and from a different Soviet leadership—one that refused him membership in the Communist Party of the Soviet Union.[78] But his NKVD mentor, Naum Eitingon, fared even worse.

Eitingon was one of the more enigmatic figures of Stalin's state security. His father and brother were doctors in Europe, the brother Mark a psychiatrist and student of Sigmund Freud.[79] Mark apparently was linked to General Skoblin and his wife Plevitskaya; he moved to Jerusalem two days before the kidnapping of General Miller. Naum Eitingon's biggest success was the Trotsky assassination for which he received the Order of Lenin and the warm appreciation of Stalin, who is alleged to have said that as long as Stalin lived, no harm would come to Eitingon.[80] When Stalin died, Eitingon and General Pavel Sudoplatov, commander of partisan operations in World War II and known as the "master of special detachments," were thrown into prison. Eitingon received twelve years; Sudoplatov got fifteen, going blind during imprisonment. When Rudolf Abel was exchanged for Francis Gary Powers in 1962 and learned of Eitingon's and Sudoplatov's fate, Abel allegedly organized a petition on their behalf.[81] It did not work. A shabby reward for the man who led the operation against Stalin's most personal enemy.

The General Miller kidnapping is one of those vivid examples of the confluence of a number of NKVD operations, resulting in a classic example of a *kombinatsiya*, whether intended or not. Miller had succeeded to the leadership of the ROVS upon the kidnapping of General Kutyepov in 1930. General Skoblin, an NKVD agent involved in Kutyepov's kidnapping, became a friend and protégé of Miller. He was also chief of the Inner Line (Vnutrennaya Liniya), an internal security–counterintelligence element of ROVS designed specifically to frustrate OGPU provocation and penetration operations such as the Trust. Because the Inner Line was so seriously penetrated itself, it figured prominently in both Kutyepov's and Miller's kidnappings, and was a source of systematic disinformation to both ROVS and Western intelligence sources.

The Inner Line was never really abolished, even after the notoriety of Miller's kidnapping and the penetrations associated with it. Though it suffered some realignments and shifts, it continued serving Soviet state security throughout the late 1930s and into World War II. Even though the experience of the Trust legend and Kutyepov's kidnapping had shown the vulnerability of both ROVS and the Inner Line, inadequate defensive security allowed the likes of Skoblin and Plevitskaya to continue operating. Miller made virtually little or no changes and it was because of this that the NKVD was able to use the Inner Line to kidnap Miller.[82]

Plevitskaya's connection to Mark Eitingon apparently involved significant financial support, but whether the money came from the Eitingon family or from Soviet sources is unclear. (The Eitingon family at one time had been well-off but apparently lost much of its wealth in the depression.)

The actual kidnapping of General Miller occurred on 22 September 1937. Had Miller not left a letter warning that he was meeting with Skoblin and two alleged German diplomats, he would have simply vanished. When confronted with the incriminating letter, Skoblin became visibly nervous but quickly made himself scarce.[83] Plevitskaya was tried and sentenced by a French court to twenty years for complicity in Miller's disappearance. She died in a French prison in 1944, taking her secret with her.[84]

Mark Eitingon's name came up in the trial but not Naum's. Yet a Soviet dissident source claims it was Naum who organized and ran the Miller abduction.[85]

Why did Stalin and Yezhov risk the notoriety of such an operation if Miller and the ROVS were so ineffectual? The Soviets no doubt wanted their man Skoblin as Miller's ROVS successor. Another reason offered is that Skoblin feared that Miller suspected, and was about to destroy, the Inner Line, thus ruining a more than decade-long NKVD penetration.[86] Krivitsky however, feels that Stalin wanted everyone silenced who knew anything about the German–Soviet provocation to frame Tukhachevskiy and the Red Army leadership.[87] This would presume that Miller knew that Skoblin was involved with the fabrications against the Red Army commander. This then might suggest that he was aware of Skoblin's service to the NKVD. It may simply be that Stalin and Yezhov were taking no chances. Miller's prestige in émigré circles was such that public doubt uttered about Skoblin and the Inner Line could have led to the unraveling of too many connections.

In a certain sense Krivitsky may have been close to the truth of Stalin's motivations. But Miller was only a small element in a broader skein of NKVD atrocities. The overall matrix of murders and kidnappings during the mid- to late 1930s constituted an external manifestation of what was happening in the USSR. After all, the Administration for Special Tasks, which carried out the actions just discussed, was set up under Yezhov precisely to handle the more sensitive features of the purges. Whatever else Stalin had in mind with such bloodletting, he was clearing the scene for a major new initiative that was bound to be shocking and potentially disruptive:

the agreement with Hitler. Krivitsky sensed that this was coming, but he keyed only on a few singular events (such as the Miller kidnapping) as harbingers of the event.

Despite Hitler's early 1937 rebuff to the last of Kandelaki's proposals for a Soviet–German rapprochement, it is clear that Stalin did not lose hope. In the meantime he completed his housecleaning with a change of command at the top levels of state security. In late summer 1938 Beria was brought in as Yezhov's deputy but for all practical purposes, Yezhov was on ice. Then in December 1938, Yezhov was whisked away and Beria officially became the new NKVD chief. At this point the system literally had been reworked from top to bottom through the unrestrained use of the security organs, which were then turned in on themselves. Anyone who knew anything about Stalin's provocations, and most of those who were used to contact the Germans (Kandelaki, Radek, Krivitsky, Gnedin, Bessenov, and others), were eliminated or imprisoned. It was through survivors such as Gnedin (son of Parvus-Helphand) that we learned the specifics of what Krivitsky understood in outline.

By March 1939 Stalin appeared ready to roll the dice again, spurred on by Hitler's success at Munich the previous fall and his preparations for the attack on Poland. A former Soviet diplomatic historian, Aleksandr Nekrich, observes that Stalin's speech at the Eighteenth Party Congress that month was both a warning to France and England that their strategy vis-à-vis Germany was doomed to fail, and an indirect approach to Germany for a resumption of talks.[88] After the signing of the Hitler–Stalin Non-Aggression Pact on 23 August 1939, Molotov on two occasions referred to Stalin's March speech as having been clearly understood in Berlin.[89]

Stalin was jubilant and took the pact seriously, adhering faithfully to its provisions. It was the culmination of a process begun in the early 1930s. By his lights it would not have occurred without his second revolution at home and abroad. And that could not have been accomplished without an extralegal action arm ensconced between the party–state apparatus and the person of Stalin. The year 1939 was one of the counterintelligence state triumphant.

6

War and Expansion

THE HITLER–STALIN ALLIANCE and the beginning of the official Beria phase of Soviet state security history occurred within a year of each other. From December 1938 to early February 1941 Beria served concurrently as commissar for internal affairs (NKVD) and head of the Main Administration of State Security (GUGB). The latter organ had been subordinated to the NKVD with the name change from OGPU in 1934. For a brief period from February to July 1941, Stalin had separated the two organs once again, this time creating a People's Commissariat of State Security (NKGB) under Vsevolod N. Merkulov while leaving the NKVD under Beria. NKGB Chief Merkulov, a member of Beria's Georgian Mafia and, hence, a subordinate, controlled the traditional state security and the Foreign Directorate (INU); Beria retained general responsibility for internal affairs, including the vast camp and prison empire. The shock of the German invasion propelled a fusion in July 1941 and the two organs were united once again as the NKVD under Beria. This arrangement lasted until April 1943.

In the realm of foreign operations the last of the pre-Beria holdovers, Aleksandr (Mikhail) Shpigelglas, was acting chief of the Foreign Department until around mid-1938, following which he was arrested and shot. It is unclear who followed him; possibly one Sergey Passov until 1939. The veteran Chekist and crony of Beria, Vladimir Dekanozov, may have run the INU before becoming a deputy commissar of foreign affairs; in 1940 he became a "special envoy" to Lithuania, in effect to prepare that hapless country for Soviet takeover. His colleagues with similar portfolios in Latvia and Estonia were Andrey Vyshinskiy and A. A. Zhdanov. Following his Lithuanian mission Dekanozov became Soviet ambassador to Germany, a post he held until the German invasion of June 1941. His service in the INU, his ambassadorship to Berlin, and his membership in the Beria clique coincided with the poor appreciation of German plans for the attack on the Soviet Union. Dekanozov, together with Beria, General F. I. Golikov of the GRU, and Stalin himself bore responsibility for the military disasters spawned by the German surprise attack.

Other organizational changes in the police empire occurred as the war dragged on. On 14 April 1943, the NKVD was again split into the NKGB under Merkulov and the NKVD under Beria. This nomenclature lasted until March 1946. As Merkulov was a Beria man, the latter's oversight and control continued. These particular organizational changes (February 1941 and April 1943) were never fully explained but they may have had something to do with digesting captive lands and peoples.[1] The February 1941 reorganization followed the war with Finland, the Soviet invasion of Poland from the East, the takeover of Latvia, Lithuania, and Estonia, and the extraction of Bessarabia and Northern Bukovina from Romania. Population increases from these territorial acquisitions exceeded 10 million.[2] Arrests, deportations, executions, and prison camps increased, mandating reorganized and expanded security forces. Likewise, the victory at Stalingrad and associated Soviet advances offered the prospect of reconquered lands and populations. Hence, the 1943 NKGB–NKVD separation once again.

As for military counterintelligence, it too was affected by changes in subordination. From the days of the Cheka, state security exercised exclusive responsibility in this sphere. Unlike Western systems, the Soviets (with only a couple of limited exceptions) never allowed the Red Army to have its own counterintelligence. From December 1918 the OOs or Special Departments of state security ran military counterintelligence. For a short period from February 1941 to July 1941, the military was in charge. The OO–GUGB of the NKVD was transferred to the regular armed forces as the Third Directorate of the People's Commissariat of Defense (NKO) and the Third Directorate of the People's Commissariat of the Navy (NKVMF). An OO was left behind in the NKGB to conduct security operations among the troops of the NKGB and the NKVD.

The disasters and massive surrenders following the German invasion spiked those changes. On 20 July 1941 the Third Directorates of the NKO and NKVMF were moved back under the Chief Administration for State Security (GUGB) of the NKVD and received their old nomenclature of OO–NKVD. This situation lasted until 14 April 1943.

On that date Stalin again placed military counterintelligence under the Commissariat of Defense—or at least it appeared that way. The Special Departments of the NKVD (OO–NKVD) became the Chief Directorate for Counterintelligence of the People's Commissariat of Defense (GUKR–NKO). It is better known by its popular (or notorious) acronym, SMERSH, from Smert' Shpionam or "Death to Spies."[3] Most of its officers came from the OO–NKVD, providing an unbroken continuity. Its chief, Viktor S. Abakumov, was the chief of OO–NKVD and he now became a deputy commissar of defense.

These personnel moves were critical to maintaining the state security orientation of the outfit.[4] Titularly, SMERSH was part of the military. In subordination, it answered directly to the State Committee of Defense (GKO, or Gosudarstvennyy Komitet Oborony) and its chief, Stalin. Stalin and the GKO were the supreme command authority during the war. Under it were the military, the party, state security, the economy, defense industry—the essence of the system. Through the GKO Stalin directly controlled the totality of the war effort; he therefore had direct authority over military counterintelligence without working down through the military *or* Beria. As a recent Soviet history of the OOs puts it, SMERSH was created "to unify the defense leadership of the country in the final stages of the war and insure the security of the armed forces, [and] to have the army command pay closer attention to the work of military chekists. . . ."[5]

Other reasons for the creation of SMERSH were psychological: to confuse German intelligence with still another security organ; to combat desertions and surrenders by evoking the image of an omniscient and brutal military security service; and, with the emphasis on military patriotism, it was in Stalin's interest to have such a repressive organ known as a *military* outfit reporting to him as the supreme *military* commander. Image was important; state security could officially have it back after the war. And in reality, SMERSH officers *were* from state security, with the result that at the operational level, military men knew where those people came from. If they did not, they soon learned, as Solzhenitsyn found to his sorrow. (Solzhenitsyn, an artillery captain in 1945, was arrested by SMERSH for criticizing Stalin in letters to a friend. He spent the next eleven years in prisons, camps, and finally exile in Kazakhstan.)

Deriabin observes that SMERSH had another role as well, one subsequently inflated by Soviet propagandists and state security itself: the protection of Stalin.[6] Indeed, Abakumov's deputy, Sergey Kruglov, ran Stalin's security detail at the Tehran Conference in 1943 when rumors (probably originated by SMERSH) talked of an attempt by Otto Skorzeny of the SS to kill Stalin. Whether or not SMERSH competed with the NKVD–NKGB's bodyguards department is beside the point. In elevating Abakumov and his deputy Kruglov to positions of direct access to Stalin, the dictator in effect bypassed both Beria (NKVD) and his crony Merkulov (NKGB) and set the pattern for the postwar diminution of Beria's power. Abakumov was not one of Beria's Georgians. Whatever may be said about Stalin, he cannot be accused of lacking strategic vision.

SMERSH lasted until 16 March 1946, when it was folded in its entirety into the newly created Ministry of State Security (MGB) as the Third Chief Directorate. The OOs were revived at the operational level throughout the newly renamed armed forces; the Ministry of Defense subsumed the Commissariat of Defense (NKO) and the Commissariat of the Navy (NKVMF).

The NKVD likewise became a ministry (MVD) at the same time. It and the MGB retained these organizational labels until immediately after Stalin's death. The war, then, propelled a great deal of organizational ferment in the organs. This time it was driven by external factors—a bona fide enemy—rather than by Stalin's purges and caprice.

Before Hitler invaded the Soviet Union, Stalin had done everything he could to keep the alliance going. This included cooperation between the NKVD and such Nazi security services as the Gestapo and SD. Such collusion derived from the secret clauses of the Hitler–Stalin Pact that provided for respective spheres of influence in Eastern Europe and established boundaries (as in jointly occupied Poland). According to the Polish General T. Bor-Komorowski, a joint NKVD–Gestapo mission in Cracow, Poland, met for several weeks in early 1940 to discuss joint methods for working against Polish resistance organizations.[7] Bor-Komorowski was of the opinion that the Germans were learning from the NKVD how to suppress the Polish underground and he concluded that the Soviets were far more experienced and dangerous in this respect.

Both Poles and Germans have testified to the exchanges of prisoners between the two partners. Jan Karski had been a young Polish officer when captured by Soviet forces in 1939. When he learned that enlisted Polish soldiers of German background were to be handed over to the Germans in exchange for Polish troops of Ukrainian and Belorussian nationality, he ditched his officer's tunic and passed himself off as a private. During the exchange he observed the close working arrangements between Soviet and German officers overseeing the massive flow of hapless Polish POWs.[8] Both groups ended up in prison camps. In Karski's case, however, had he retained his officer's identity he would not have been exchanged and would probably have been among the thousands of other Polish officers executed by the NKVD at Katyn Forest or other mass murder sites.

The depth of NKVD–Gestapo collaboration is best illustrated by the memoirs of a German-Jewish communist, Margarete Buber, wife of German Communist Party leader Heinz Neumann. Heinz, threatened with extradition to Nazi Germany from Switzerland, sought refuge in the Soviet Union in 1935. In 1937 he was arrested and disappeared. Margarete was arrested in 1938 and spent two years in various NKVD camps. In 1940, following the Hitler–Stalin Pact, she and other German communists were loaded aboard trains by the NKVD and shipped West. At the border, at Brest Litovsk, the NKVD turned them over to the SS, who then sent them to German concentration camps.[9] These were not Poles, but German communists, Jews among them, who were given over to the SS. Margarete was then incarcerated in SS concentration camps until the Nazi collapse in 1945.

Finally, there was the odd coincidence between the NKVD–Gestapo conference at Cracow in March 1940 and the mass extermination of the fifteen thousand Polish officers later that spring in Katyn Forest in Western USSR.[10] It is impossible to prove a causal link between these events, but the connections between the two services raise the suspicion that at the least there was a sharing of information on ways of handling the recalcitrant Poles.

There were other ways in which Stalin sought to demonstrate to the Germans his desire to continue the Non-Aggression Pact. Under Comintern and NKVD guidance, communist parties in the Allied Nations agitated against the war with the effect that they took the German side against their respective governments. The treasonous policy of the French CP contributed in no small way to the confusion, poor morale, and then collapse of France in the spring of 1940. In the United States the CPUSA agitated with slogans like "The Yanks are *not* coming." Following the German invasion of the USSR the CPUSA cynically revised its banners with a minimum of editing to, "The Yanks are not coming *too* late!"

On a more subtle level Beria's NKVD employed strategic political manipulation to get Stalin's message to Hitler. By early 1941 Soviet intelligence was collecting an increasing number of indicators that Hitler had the USSR on his list for invasion. It seems the more signals of this Stalin received, the harder he fought to keep the alliance going. A representative covert example of his faithful courting of Hitler to keep the marriage alive involved the German Consulate in Harbin, Manchukuo, from about March to May 1941. The German consul, Dr. August Ponschab, was forwarding to Berlin "intercepted" Soviet diplomatic communications to Soviet missions in the Far East. David Kahn suggests that this series of intercepts was an unusual exception to the established record of security of Soviet diplomatic communications channels.[11] State security—then as now—oversaw such communications channels and was not noted for weak cyphers or poor communications security practices.

Another analyst noted that the material seemed "designed for interception."[12] It included such items as the Soviet understanding of German interests in the Balkans; the need to maintain the Soviet-German treaty; and the maintenance of normal trade relations with Germany, should the latter start a conflict in the Balkans, even if the Danube (critical to German-Soviet trade) were closed as a result. Moscow would get its oil to Germany by rail. Certain messages specifically supported the German attack on Greece so as to threaten Suez, the British colonies, and British forces in Africa. Moscow definitely would not interfere with German interests in the Balkans. Above all, it was stressed, the Soviet–German treaty should not be jeopardized because it was central to the most critical objective, the destruction of the British Empire.[13] It seems that Moscow was bent on using this channel to manipulate German perceptions in the direction of Moscow's interests and desires to keep the German–Soviet "détente" going. The hostility to Great Britain was palpable. Britain, standing alone against Germany, was the clearly intended victim of this manipulative initiative. In all, the operation was not dissimilar to the strategic thrust of the Politburo forgeries. But in this case it did not succeed.

The war brought massive expansion in the size and missions of state security and increased prestige and authority to Beria. Beria's rising star had actually preceded the German invasion following the disappearance of Yezhov in late 1938. The ascendancy of Beria was due in no small part to his ability to stroke and flatter Stalin, playing on the latter's mania for identifying and ferreting out "enemies." Despite the drubbing the NKVD took during the latter phases of the purges under Beria himself, the organs had in effect become Stalin's most reliable instrument and Stalin lorded it over all other institutions of the Soviet state.

Following the turmoil of the late 1930s an NKVD leadership stability, of sorts, set in, a result of which was that Beria's cronies such as V. N. Merkulov, V. G. Dekanozov, Bogdan Kobulov, Mikhail Gvishiani,[14] L. F. Tsanava, Lev Vlodzimirsky, S. A. Goglidze, L. F. Raykhman, A. N. Rapava, Ivan Serov, and Stepan Mamulov all lasted into the early 1950s. Most were then arrested and/or executed upon Beria's fall in 1953. The depredations visited on Soviet citizens, the Soviet military, and the captive populations throughout the Baltic and Eastern Europe belong to the Beria phase of state security.

And brutally powerful it was. The war years comprised one of the peak periods of the counterintelligence state in Soviet history. The Polish General Władysław Anders had been captured by the Soviets in 1939 and was one of the lucky few who escaped the Katyn massacres (he had been wounded and was recovering in a hospital). His release was negotiated so he could lead a Polish army under the Western allies against the Germans. Anders observed that the NKVD was superior in every respect to the rest of Soviet society, especially the military: "The military . . . had no voice. In all facets of civilian and military life the all-powerful NKVD ruled."[15] With a very few exceptions the Soviet military carried the overwhelming burden of the fighting and casualties. The NKVD–NKGB were parasitical attachments whose savaging of the military and the populace ran a close second to that of the Germans.

Beria's good fortunes apparently rubbed off on his service. Even before the German invasion Beria had been promoted to commissar general of state security (*general'nyy komissar gosbezopasnosti*) (January 1941), a grade equivalent in those days to marshal of the Soviet Union. His "promotion" to marshal of the Soviet Union in July 1945 may therefore have had more to do with the formality of the NKVD–NKGB acquiring military rank across the board (which the KGB and MVD still have) than with an actual promotion. (Soviet leaders seem attracted to military titles.) Since 1939 Beria had been a candidate member of the Politburo, and received full membership right after the war (1946). Probably more important, given the emasculation of party power, was his membership in the State Defense Committee (GKO or Gosudarstvenny Komitet Oborony), established in June 1941 and the actual decision body running the totality of the war effort and *all* matters of state.[16] There originally were only five members on the GKO and Beria was one of them. He had broad internal responsibilities that made him a viceroy unfettered by any constraints save Stalin's disapproval. Stalin did little to stay Beria's hand. Beria's, and by extension the NKVD's, power and prestige were enhanced when he became deputy chairman of the GKO (Stalin was chairman) in May 1944.

Up until April 1943 the OOs of Beria's NKVD terrorized the armed forces through their military counterintelligence charter. Even after the creation of SMERSH under Viktor Abakumov—not one of Beria's creatures—Beria still was able to humble the military through his own troop formations and by virtue of his seat in the GKO, which sat above SMERSH, the Stavka (General Headquarters of the Supreme High Command) and the General Staff. The military roundly hated Beria, his lieutenants, and his Chekists; there was little they could do. But they could remember.

Beria's numerous awards (five Orders of Lenin, alone), accumulated positions of authority, and rank of marshal raised the prestige of state security higher even than it had been under Dzerzhinskiy. No state security boss before or since had risen so high in rank and honor. The Beria precedent was invariably invoked as an argument *against* a secret police chief achieving the position of party leader. It was automatically assumed that the party would never again allow the state security boss to collect so much authority, power, and prestige. Yuriy Andropov was the sole exception, but he really had spent most of his career in party and state posts and had never been granted the title of marshal of the Soviet Union. Beria was unique.

The activities of state security during the war were, by and large, punitive and partisan operations (not counting, of course, foreign intelligence operations that it shared with the GRU). But there were combat operations against the Germans from the very first day as NKVD Border Troops units attempted, in vain, to stem the German onslaught. The Border Troops, then and now, belonged to state security. Along with the Internal Troops (currently under the MVD) they comprise a praetorian guard, independent of the military, responsive to party–state security needs and direction. This independence of the military carried a price in 1941. There were little horizontal communications and coordination between the NKVD Border Troops and the regular military forces of colocated military districts. The disasters of 1941, stem, in part, from such independent command lines.

Both the Border Troops and the Internal Troops subordinated to the NKVD and NKGB expanded considerably during the war. Total numbers are difficult to adduce, as Soviet sources seldom give these—or when they do, accuracy is suspect. However, in a recent commentary on Internal Troops in World War II, a Soviet General Nekrasov stated there were a total of fifty-three divisions and twenty-eight brigades of NKVD troops, "not counting numerous other independent units and Border Troops."[17] This is a significant admission, and it moves Soviet figures closer to official German and U.S. figures from that time as well as to early and later defector estimates. U.S. War Department estimates in 1945, based in part on German intelligence, figured a range of 500,000 to 750,000 for Border, Internal, and NKVD Signal Troops.[18] A wartime figure of two million is given by former NKVD troop officers.[19] It has been concluded that MVD "operational troop" divisions at the end of World War II were organized along the lines of motorized or cavalry divisions and comprised 15,000 men,[20] or roughly 50 percent more than a comparable army division. A former KGB officer, who served in a special state security assault division under General Kobulov (one of Beria's principal deputies) beginning in 1944, stated that it was much larger than an army division and had between 20,000 and

25,000 men.[21] This was closer in size to a Red Army mechanized corps than to a division.

General Nekrasov's 1985 division tables may be reasonable figures. Even if NKVD Internal Troops divisions averaged only 10,000 men (roughly the size of army divisions) then we are dealing with at least a half million men for the Internal Troops alone, not counting Nekrasov's twenty-eight brigades, and the Border and Signal Troops. If these divisions were larger, say 15,000 to 20,000/25,000 as U.S. and defector sources state, then we get closer to the two million figure as claimed by former NKVD troop officers for all NKVD–NKGB troop forces. But even at the lower range of three quarters of a million men, that is a very respectable number of troops under Beria's control.

Besides the Border Troops, the most numerous state security forces apparently were the NKVD Troops of Special Purpose (Osnaz or Osobogo Naznacheniya). During the war two whole NKVD Armies of Special Purpose were formed. One of them, under NKVD General Ivan I. Maslennikov, had a major part in breaking the German lines in the Kuban and on the Taman Peninsula.[22] By and large, though, these forces had punitive missions behind their own lines. Their activities included acting as blocking detachments behind the regular military (to stiffen their resolve and prevent retreats); exercising mass repression in rear areas against recalcitrant or suspect peoples or repression in newly conquered territories; conducting counterinsurgency operations against anti-Soviet partisan units; and sometimes sending their own special purpose units (spetsnaz or diversionary) behind enemy lines. It was such forces that arrested, deported or exiled, and executed such non-Russian minority peoples as the Volga Germans in 1941 and the Chechens, Balkars, Ingushi, Kalmuks, Karachay, and the Crimean Tartars in 1943–45 after accusations of disloyalty. John Erickson observes that in late 1942 Beria built a parallel NKVD staff in the North Caucasus and, in addition to suppressing a local revolt, had his subordinates Kobulov and Rukhadze work over the military soviet there and threaten the commander of the "Don group," General Rodion Malinovskiy (later minister of defense), with arrest.[23] With Stalin's support Beria operated his NKVD armies and divisions with an independence similar to that of SS and Waffen-SS units relative to the regular German military.

One of the more important state security activities during the war had to do with partisan operations. At the end of the war and for several years thereafter this activity was transformed into antipartisan and counterinsurgency operations. These were the roots of contemporary Soviet special operations (spetsnaz) and direct-action activities. Because of the sensitive political nature of such operations, they have always come under the purview of the intelligence and security services of the USSR.

The experiences in Spain and Finland immediately before World War II strongly influenced Soviet partisan actions against the Germans. During the Spanish Civil War concurrent NKVD and Military Intelligence (after 1943 known as the GRU) terrorist and guerrilla activities were carried out on Stalin's direct orders behind Nationalist *and* Republican lines. Orlov had identified Ivan Konev (later Marshal Konev) as one of the principal military figures conducting terrorist training; actual NKVD sabotage and guerrilla operations behind Nationalist lines were controlled by Naum Eitingon (alias General Kotov), who was Orlov's assistant in Spain.[24] Eitingon then applied that experience in running partisan operations in the USSR during the war under General Pavel Sudoplatov. They were both imprisoned in the purge of Beria's lieutenants after Stalin's death.

Another intelligence officer, but from the GRU, who developed guerrilla experience in Spain was General Khadzhi-Umar Mamsurov.[25] He and other GRU officers led special units fighting with the Republican Fourteenth Corps, carrying out attacks on the transportation and communications networks in the Nationalist rear areas. Mamsurov later surfaced in Finland during the Winter War of 1939–40. He brought a special designation unit (spetsnaz) of about fifty men to the front in an effort to capture Finnish soldiers for intelligence purposes and thus gain a certain psychological redress for the severe defeats inflicted on the Soviet giant by the tiny Finnish army. As with overall Soviet military performance in this war, Mamsurov's operation was a failure. What is significant about this particular experience is that it represents the first prewar instance of an identified Soviet military entity with responsibility for diversionary (that is, special operations) activity. Mamsurov's unit was subordinated to the Fifth Department (Otdel) of the GRU and was openly referred to as the Otdel Diversii (Diversionary Department).[26] Penkovskiy in the

early 1960s revealed that the Fifth Department had been elevated to
the Fifth Directorate (diversion and sabotage) and that General
Mamsurov had risen to become one of two deputies to GRU Chief
Ivan Serov.[27] More recent information shows that the Fifth Directorate of the GRU still has line responsibility, through a dedicated
Spetsnaz Department, for controlling standing GRU Spetsnaz Brigades posted in the USSR, Eastern Europe, and Afghanistan.[28]

Soviet partisan operations served as the major formative laboratory for subsequent Soviet state security and military structures for
running or supporting postwar diversionary (including terrorist) and
guerrilla movements. Although a Central Staff of the Partisan Movement under the Supreme High Command (Stavka) had been organized under General P. K. Ponomarenko, party and state security
cadres were the actual controlling elements. The announced purpose
of the partisan movement was the harassment of the German rear
areas, but the real objective was to reintroduce party control in occupied territories. (Yuriy Andropov, for instance, worked closely
with state security in partisan, Gulag, and other security operations
in the Karelo–Finnish area from 1941 to 1945; apparently he never
worked behind enemy lines). Many of these actions involved deceptions and provocations to surface and eliminate real and potential
opponents to the reimposition of Soviet rule. They also involved the
neutralization and compromise of non-Soviet resistance and partisan
groups. A major means for accomplishing all this was the provocation of terror and German counterterror with the ultimate objective
of both intimidating and infuriating the local population.[29]

Organizationally, partisan operations were structured as follows.[30]

Central Staff of the Partisan Movement under the Supreme High Command
(also known as the Partisan Directorate). Technically, all partisan
units not directly under the control of the NKVD–NKGB or the
GRU—essentially "civilian" partisan units—were controlled and coordinated by the Partisan Directorate, itself subordinate to the party.
It was, however, heavily staffed by the NKVD–NKGB. From 1942
to 1944 it was directed by General P. K. Ponomarenko.

NKVD–NKGB. The following types of units have been identified in
Soviet, German, and U.S. accounts as being subordinated first to

the NKVD (until 1943), and then to the NKVD and NKGB (after 1943). After 1943 it is difficult to sort out the exact organizational subordination.

Partisan Units. These were specially organized units operating independently or in coordination with other partisan units; they also organized and trained additional partisan units. As the war progressed, these units operated in Eastern and Central Europe in advance of the Red Army. Men from these units operated with communist partisan detachments in German-occupied countries of northern and western Europe as well.

Spetsnaz Units. The term *spetsnaz (chasti spetsial'nogo naznacheniya)* is occasionally used to designate particular NKVD–NKGB units operating in the German rear. They appear to have been employed mainly for independent operations although on occasion they did work with other partisan units. Descriptions of their activities indicate that they were used to eliminate collaborators, propagandize the local population, conduct positive intelligence and counterintelligence operations, and generally serve as enforcers of party control. They also conducted operations against the Germans.

Extermination Battalions. These units were formed in the initial days of the war, and operated in both the German and Soviet rear areas. Operations included actions against German agents and German special units, Soviet deserters, dissidents, nationalists, and other persons or groups deemed as "anti-Soviet" or not behind the war effort. They may have come from the NKVD Osnaz divisions, but this is unclear.

Special Detachments. These units spanned a wide range of size and composition, and included such entities as radio intercept units, agent communications units, radio disinformation teams, parachutist "reception" committees, "hit" teams, and positive intelligence collection teams.

Hunter Units. These were designated to mop up nationalist and other anti-Soviet activities, as well as Nazi stragglers in recently occupied territory. These units may have been successor units to the early extermination battalions.

Special Assault Divisions. Such units were of very large, division-plus size, and were formed towards the end of the war to combat Ukrainian nationalists, and Polish, Lithuanian, and Latvian guerrillas. One of these was identified under General Kobulov's command

(Kobulov was one of Beria's lieutenants). Such divisions may have been formed from the large pool of state security Osnaz and Border Troops divisions.

Singleton Operations. Individual special detachment members—party and Komsomol personnel, and politically reliable local inhabitants—were used to carry out clandestine activities such as agent servicing, intelligence collection, and courier services. Additionally, hundreds of state security officer personnel were sent into the German rear to take over command and commissar positions in partisan units comprising non-NKVD–NKGB personnel. This was a means of strengthening party control over the partisan movement. Personnel from "uncontrolled" units frequently wound up in the Gulag when their regions were reoccupied by the Red Army. The system brooked no independence.

NKVD Internal Security (Osnaz) Divisions. These divisions operated mostly in the Soviet rear, but they did conduct counterinsurgency and counterguerrilla operations against anti-Soviet elements. However, they contributed thousands of snipers to the regular military and to partisan detachments.

GRU. The following units operated under military intelligence control and drew their personnel from the ground, naval, and air forces of the regular Soviet armed forces.

Partisan Units. These consisted of specially organized teams inserted to operate as partisans in the same fashion as the NKVD–NKGB partisan detachments. General Mamsurov, of Spanish and Finnish reputation, evidently continued his diversionary activities in this category of operations.

Special Detachments. As with state security, a variety of apparently GRU-subordinated special units appears in the literature. These often seemed to be specially configured teams for intelligence collection (including prisoner snatching) against specific targets or for surveillance of enemy activities in a narrowly defined geographic area. Such teams were landed from Soviet submarines in Norway and Poland to observe Nazi shipping in support of Soviet submarine operations from 1943 on. These were Soviet variants of "coastwatchers," so to speak.

Singleton Operations. GRU activities of this type tended to mirror those of state security; but they were more focused on military targets.

Coordination, command, and control over these diffuse entities were not easily accomplished. The confused Soviet response to the German invasion was reflected in the partisan movement. Units were slapped together and thrown in with little regard for standardization, efficacy of mission, redundancy, or human cost. The initial objective was to do something, anything, to stem the German advance and prevent the Soviet system from collapsing. Hence the need to foster the image of party presence in occupied areas.

Nominally, the party exercised control over all partisan operations. In practice, it seems to have been state security that provided the abiding presence. Feuds between the military and state security were not uncommon and it was to resolve these that the Central Staff of the Partisan Movement was created. This was a move not unlike the creation of SMERSH, that is, the joining of several organizations in a suprainstitutional body (in this case the Stavka) to rise above the fray in pursuit of broader national objectives. But as with SMERSH, state security still played the preeminent role. Throughout the war state security maintained tight control over its many partisan or related activities, even running them directly from Moscow Center, without coordinating with its own district or regional echelons. For instance there were cases of radio disinformation operations, based on turned German agents, run from Moscow Center. Their broadcasts were picked up by local NKVD radio intercept units that could not break the ciphers, unaware that the radio traffic came from Moscow in the first place.

As the tide of war on the Eastern front turned and the German retreat speeded up, Moscow increased the insertion of special units in the enemy rear. For instance, NKVD partisan units went into Czechoslovakia ahead of the Red Army, and played a major role in precipitating the Slovak uprising. When the uprising was smashed by the Germans, the Soviets had fewer potential opponents to worry them when they foisted a communist government on that country. Soviet-trained teams of Bulgarians and Romanians were inserted by submarine into both nations prior to the arrival of the Red Army and helped to coordinate the imposition of communist rule there. In Norway, special reconnaissance units involved in military operations there during the war were also laying the groundwork for subversive actions after the war, conducting recruitments for espionage and covert action agents.

At the end of the war, Moscow was busy with securing its newly seized territories and reestablishing Soviet rule in areas occupied by Germany. Violent nationalist guerrilla movements had risen throughout the Baltic republics, Western Belorussia, the Western Ukraine, and in Poland and Slovakia. Moscow made extensive use of NKVD–NKGB hunter/extermination units and the special counterguerrilla division of the NKVD created and commanded by Beria's associate, General Kobulov. A former KGB officer and member of this unit states that this division went directly from Yalta (where its members provided security for the Yalta Conference) to the Western Ukraine and Western Belorussia. Fighting continued for this division until 1947, when the division was disbanded. However, operations against Ukrainian guerrillas continued into the early 1950s.[31]

Prominent among state security officials involved in all aspects of the partisan–counterinsurgency experience during and immediately after the war were Merkulov (NKGB), Kobulov (NKVD), and Serov, who served under Kobulov. Sudoplatov, who worked for both Merkulov and Kubolov, was known as the "master of special detachments." Serving under him was the organizer of Trotsky's murder, Naum Eitingon, alias General Kotov. Sudoplatov and Eitingon had the task, under the newly minted MGB after the war, of setting up a covert state security diversionary infrastructure for operations against the new NATO alliance. All of these men were arrested following the downfall of Beria, Sudoplatov and Eitingon being fortunate enough to receive only prison terms. Their colleagues were executed. Despite their unceremonious exits, they were the men who built the organizational and operational framework for contemporary KGB and GRU direct-action, special operations capabilities. In a certain sense, the road to Afghanistan in the 1980s led from the partisan experience during World War II and ultimately the anti-Basmachi campaigns of the 1920s–30s.

Partisan operations run by state security, the GRU, and the Central Staff of the Partisan Movement were major contributors to the defeat of Germany and the securing of the Eastern European countries as satellites within Moscow's new sphere of influence. State security contributed in other critical ways, in keeping with its earlier established traditions of the counterintelligence state. These contributions involved political–military deception operations that encompassed a variety of time-tested and proven operations common to Soviet active measures. The linkages to one of these operations (the MAX case) date to penetrations, provocations, and Cheka–OGPU legends as far back as the 1920s.[32]

In a U.S. Army interrogation report, dated 24 June 1945, General Major Reinhard Gehlen, formerly chief of Foreign Armies East Department, talked freely of Soviet deception and propaganda efforts. While crediting the Soviets with effective deception through manipulation of the foreign press and through the careful use of POWs, he makes a negative declaration about Soviet "radio deception," but offers no supporting evidence:

> No major radio deception scheme has ever been attempted by the Russians, who realize that such a scheme is easily detected if it is not accompanied by thoroughly planned deceptive measures and in all other fields. Tactical radio deception has been employed, but was of only limited importance.[33]

On both counts, Gehlen is strongly contradicted by other evidence. The following examples are illustrative.

The MAX Case, 1941–45.[34] One of the important deception operations run by Soviet state security during World War II was the MAX case. This involved an agent network allegedly working in the USSR that supplied the German Abwehr with wireless transmissions (via Sofia to Berlin) from July 1941 to February 1945. Two of the principals in the case, Anton V. Turkul and Ilya Lang, were former White officers who were suspected of having been recruited by the NKVD. Turkul had been a member of the Inner Line of the ROVS with links to General Skoblin. The reputed MAX was one Fritz Kauder, alias Klatt, a Viennese Jew with connections to both Turkul and the Abwehr. The MAX reports dealt with Soviet military matters, strategic and tactical, and were accepted at face value by Gehlen, the Abwehr, and the German General Staff, despite suspicions voiced by others. NKVD Chief Beria is believed to have personally controlled the Moscow end of the operation. Several thousand MAX messages were transmitted to Berlin. The Germans were frequently confronted at critical junctures with more Soviet forces than they had estimated, while the Soviets are reported to have sacrificed considerable numbers of troops to validate the MAX reports. Following the war, U.S. military intelligence discovered the network and determined that Turkul and Lang were Soviet agents and was convinced that Kauder, too, was run by the Soviets.

In his memoirs, Gehlen gives no indication that he was aware that MAX was a notional source directed by the NKVD.[35] One of his tendencies—and of the German High Command—was to rely on MAX because it confirmed German estimates of Soviet strategic intentions, itself an indication of probable Soviet penetration of the Germans.

Was MAX really that good? Probably so, according to Anthony Blunt (as reported by Chapman Pincher) who had served the Soviets while in MI-5 (British Security Service). In this account, Blunt admitted that he passed the deciphered MAX traffic intercepted by the British to his Soviet controller, but was told that Moscow was fully aware of what was going on. From that point, Blunt assumed that the MAX affair was a major Soviet deception operation whose costs in Soviet manpower were sacrificed to promote the deception underscoring its strategic utility.[36]

Operation Scherhorn.[37] One of the more unusual military deception episodes reported on the Eastern Front during World War II was Operation Scherhorn, an elaborate creation of the Soviets centered on a notional group of twenty-five hundred trapped German troops led by Oberstleutnant (Lieutenant Colonel) Heinrich Scherhorn. On 19 August 1944, the German High Command (Oberkommando der Wehrmacht—OKW) received a message from an alleged network in Moscow about Scherhorn and his unit being trapped behind Soviet lines at the Berezina River. From that date until Scherhorn's last message on 4 April 1945, the German SS and OKW expended considerable effort, men, materiel, and aircraft in vain attempts to rescue the trapped unit. In addition to sending numerous radios and radio operators, the Germans reportedly even sent in two SS groups, which never returned. Otto Skorzeny was alerted to create a special air task force to mount a rescue, but that was in March 1945, when the Reich was near collapse. Despite doubts by some German officers, radio messages from Scherhorn and certain of the inserted radio operators kept hopes high that Scherhorn and his men were still operating. Hitler promoted Scherhorn to oberst (colonel), awarded him the Ritterkreuz (Knight's Cross), and promoted all of the officers whose names had been mentioned in messages.

In reality, the group never existed. There had been a fifteen-hundred man German battle group defending the Berezina River during the Belorussian offensive in the summer of 1944, but the group was smashed, and the Soviets took Scherhorn and two hundred survivors as prisoners. Colonel Scherhorn did, indeed, send messages to the OKW, but under Soviet duress. Thus, from 19 August 1944 to 4 April 1945, the Soviets ran a most audacious deception operation against a credulous OKW. Valuable German time, energy, men, and materiel were directed at the chimera, and evidently the Soviets enjoyed the game.

The following case, though it unfolded after the war, was a direct outgrowth of Polish Home Army and Soviet operations (both military and state security) during the last months of World War II. For that reason it is included in this section.

The WiN Operation, 1947–52.[38] In an episode reminiscent of the Trust, both the Soviets and the Polish security service (the UB) succeeded in penetrating a remnant of the World War II Polish Home Army called Wolnosc i Niepodleglosc, (WiN)—Freedom and Independence. After concerted and brutal drives by the Soviets and their UB subordinates in 1946–47, WiN Outside (General Anders and his London group) and U.S. and British intelligence concluded that WiN Inside had been wiped out. Then a controlled UB contact convinced WiN Outside (and the British and Americans) that the Polish underground group was still viable and merited Western support. The support was given, but by that time, WiN Inside was a complete Soviet–UB creature. Its internal purpose was to surface those Polish anti-communists still capable of organizing and running resistance cells and, at the same time, to demonstrate to the Poles that Soviet rule was there to stay. Externally, the Soviets sought to control channels of information to the United States and Britain so as to manipulate and check their anti-Soviet initiatives as well as to pass on spurious intelligence.

It was almost a literal replay of the Trust provocation, even to the extent of using western funds to support the operation. In late December 1952, the Soviets and Poles broke the story with a radio broadcast that stunned the Americans and British, the exiled Polish government in London, and the Polish populace. All of them reacted in a manner similar to that following the Trust exposé. Why Stalin chose that time to wrap it up is unclear and rather odd, because from their shocked reactions, it appears that the principal victims were unsuspecting. It may have had something to do with the impending developments in Moscow leading up to Stalin's death in March 1953. Whatever the motives for the termination, the WiN operation was a signal Soviet success. The scope of compromise was such that no major Western covert action initiatives aimed at tapping Polish unrest were again attempted.

Similar Soviet operations in the Baltic and Ukraine finally put an end to the active guerrilla movements in those regions.[39] Smaller-scale deception and manipulation accompanied the denouement of these groups. U.S. and British covert operations against Albania in the late 1940s and early 1950s were compromised by Kim Philby, a British MI-6 (Secret Intelligence Service) official in Moscow's service.[40]

The Soviet victory on the Eastern Front in cetain key respects was driven by counterintelligence. Beria's and Abakumov's security networks flayed the Germans, but they also worked on their own people. The partisan experience demonstrated how to retain or reintroduce party and state security presence in lost or threatened regions. It also helped the organs to refine their own counterinsurgency skills on recalcitrant populations. The deception and provocation dimension of state security operations before, during, and immediately after the war was a "force multiplier," in contemporary military parlance. Operation Scherhorn may have been a small side game for Moscow Center, but the strategic utility of MAX is hard to contest. As for WiN, the psychological impact of that legend is impossible to calculate but nonetheless devastating. Stalin's divisions grabbed the real estate but his state security won the battle of wits.

7

Transition, 1946–58

B ERIA'S AWARDS and promotion notwithstanding, his accretion of power and prestige gave Stalin pause. Stalin's police boss now faced a period of eclipse from which he did not fully recover until just before the old tyrant's death in March 1953. In December 1945 Beria lost his post of commissar of internal affairs (NKVD) and was replaced by Abakumov's deputy from SMERSH, Sergey Kruglov. Neither Abakumov nor Kruglov were Beria's people. Then in March 1946 both the NKVD and NKGB became ministries, it being deemed politic to dispense with the revolutionary sobriquet of commissariat. Kruglov then became minister of internal affairs (MVD), which post he held until early March 1953. Beria's man Merkulov was dropped from state security in October 1946 and replaced by Abakumov, who held the position of minister of state security (MGB) until August 1951.

In the arcane world of the Soviet counterintelligence state under Stalin, formal organizational lines of control seldom reflected the true balance of authority. By late 1946 Beria had lost direct visible control over the MGB–MVD empire. On the other hand in the same year he received promotion to full Politburo membership (he had been a candidate member) and became deputy chairman of the Council of Ministers. He was also placed in charge of the Soviet nuclear program. This meant overseeing not only the actual research, development, and production of nuclear weapons, but the collection of intelligence on Western nuclear research and capabilities. The latter included the so-called atomic espionage rings in the United States, the United Kingdom, and Canada, as well as the roundup of German scientists, plans, and facilities involved in Hitler's nuclear weapons programs. With such a charge, Beria necessarily was in a position to coordinate and focus the work of both intelligence services, the MGB and the GRU. His positions as Politburo member and deputy chairman of the Council of Ministers provided him official institutional leverage. Practically speaking, since late 1938 he had had the opportunity to place his men throughout both the MGB and MVD, providing him a responsive infrastructure. Security for the whole operation was provided by Abakumov's MGB. Thus, though he officially no longer held the state security portfolio he still enjoyed a degree of entrée, though not as direct as it once was.[1]

Stalin's maneuverings with the two security services and the changes in Beria's fortunes were elements of a broader ominous inward turn in Soviet politics. A more hostile international posture against Moscow's wartime allies was complemented by renewed internal repression throughout the USSR and its new empire in Eastern Europe. Popular hopes for an easing of police pressure in reward for the sufferings and hard-won victory in the war were dashed. A 1930s-style paranoia was revived in a series of campaigns touting vigilance against a new crop of "spies" and other assorted "enemies of the people." The situation was one in which Stalin allowed his minions to work one against the other in increasingly vicious maneuverings to curry his favor and position themselves for the succession when the old man died. This suited Stalin's style in keeping his underlings occupied while precluding the coalescence of any internal forces against him. Such a calculus was behind Stalin's efforts to check Beria's hold over the state security empire.

The opening round of this rush to a renewal of the 1930s atmosphere was Stalin's move to bring a new courtier into his inner circle. Andrey Zhdanov, Leningrad party chief, was brought back to Moscow in 1945 as a Central Committee secretary and potential rival to Beria, Malenkov, and others who had benefited politically from the 1930s purges. Zhdanov launched an ideological vigilance crusade against the arts and writers in general; it soon took on serious anti-Semitic overtones. The crusade became known as the "Zhdanovshchina," evoking the horrors of the "Yezhovshchina" a decade earlier. Abakumov's MGB became the principal enforcer of this new witch hunt.

Associated with the Zhdanov ascendancy was a younger man, Aleksey Kuznetsov, who was emplaced in Moscow as a Central Committee secretary charged with oversight of the MGB and MVD. A point man for Zhdanov, Kuznetsov naturally became the object of intrigue and revenge from Zhdanov's major competitors, Beria and Malenkov; MGB Chief Abakumov likewise viewed Kuznetsov as an incipient threat. But Zhdanov by now was the leader of the pack as Stalin's heir apparent and neither Beria and Malenkov, nor Abakumov, were strong enough to go after Zhdanov's underlings in a blatant frontal attack.

Then suddenly on 31 August 1948 Zhdanov died. The circumstances of his death are still murky; charges were made, and later contradicted, about poisoning by his doctors. Suspicions still linger primarily because of what followed: the so-called Leningrad Affair. Malenkov, the new heir apparent, and Beria launched a purge against Zhdanov's followers and associates from the Leningrad party organization. According to Peter Deriabin, a former MGB bodyguards officer, Malenkov had Abakumov fabricate a case against Zhdanov's supporters, who were then quickly wiped out by the hundreds.[2] The Leningrad Affair removed not only Zhdanov's Central Committee police overseer, Kuznetsov, but Georgiy Popov of the Moscow party organization, who was then replaced by Khrushchev. Another prominent victim was N. A. Voznesenskiy, a Politburo member whose economic views diverged from Stalin's. The whole bloody business was a struggle among Stalin's lieutenants but countenanced by the dictator himself. Malenkov, Beria, and Khrushchev benefited the most. Abakumov, too, gained from the operation but it appears that his actions had nothing to do with Beria. Contrary to some impressions, Abakumov was not one of Beria's supporters, but in this case their interests no doubt converged. Abakumov was to pay a price for going after the Leningraders. In August 1951, following the receipt of a denunciatory letter from Mikhail Ryumin to Stalin in which Abakumov was charged with covering up the facts of Zhdanov's death, Abakumov was arrested. Deriabin attributes this move to Beria.[3]

From August to December 1951 the MGB had an acting chief, General Sergey Ogoltsov, one of Abakumov's surviving deputies. In December 1951 a party apparatchik from the Central Committee, Semyon Ignatyev, took command and ran the MGB until Stalin's death. Though he has often been viewed as one of Beria's men, he was not; Ignatyev was fired when Beria took control of the service in March 1953. Unlike most MGB officials associated with Beria who were executed or imprisoned, Ignatyev died of natural causes in 1983. Still, it was while Ignatyev was MGB minister that Beria made his rebound following the several years of apparent disfavor and intrigues against him by Zhdanov, Poskrebyshev, and Stalin himself.

Concurrent with the maneuverings for leadership of state security and the factional intrigues at the Politburo level, an unusual bureaucratic event occurred among the foreign intelligence–espionage entities of the MGB and military intelligence, the GRU. In October 1947 Stalin decided to fuse all organizations dealing with foreign intelligence and clandestine operations and bring them under one central organization. The new institution, christened the Committee of Information (Komitet Informatsii, or KI) was placed under the Council of Ministers and headed by a succession of senior Foreign Ministry officials from Molotov through Malik, Vyshinskiy, and Zorin. An MGB participant in the KI experiment attributed the idea to Molotov[4]—one more indicator of the struggle among Stalin's minions. The reorganization took the INU (the Foreign Directorate) of the MGB, and the foreign intelligence departments of the GRU and moved them into a central building in what had been the Comintern headquarters in Moscow to perform the following duties:[5]

all military and political espionage work abroad

all counterintelligence work against Soviet embassies, missions, trade delegations, and citizens abroad

operations against Russian émigrés and émigré organizations, defectors, and others considered "traitors"; these actions included penetrations, provocations, and agent recruitments

control of the Soviet intelligence and security advisory network in non-Soviet communist countries.

Apparently, the KI did not receive control over the direct-action–wet affairs activities of Generals Sudoplatov and Eitingon. These remained with Abakumov and his MGB.

Essentially, the KI experiment was a failure. The MGB and MVD had retained all internal security functions; the MGB kept its direct-action account overseas. The counterintelligence state could not function for long with internal and external counterintelligence split in such a fashion. Its very nature mandated a unitary system in its operational expression, even if it were unified at the top under Stalin and Poskrebyshev's secretariat.

The GRU was the first to bail out in mid-1948. Interestingly, Marshal Nikolay Bulganin, a former Chekist himself,[6] convinced Stalin that the KI's military section should revert to the General Staff, which it did. Later that year the counterintelligence, émigré, and satellite advisory elements returned to the MGB, specifically to its First Chief Directorate. Foreign political and economic intelligence collection were all that remained with the KI. These, too, returned to the MGB in 1951 and the KI was then dissolved. Since then, state security has never yielded its foreign accounts and the unity of internal and external counterintelligence was never again tampered with.

The KI interlude was part of the internecine struggles accompanying the last years of Stalin's rule. Molotov's grab at the MGB–Military Intelligence empire undoubtedly had something to do with attempts to get Beria. Stalin's acquiescence in the affair spoke once more to his strategy of letting the wolves have at each other. Yet he and his grey eminence, Poskrebyshev, themselves played provocatory roles in these struggles. The renewed anti-Semitism inherent in the Zhdanovshchina was resurrected in the Crimean Affair and the Doctors' Plot, both of which bore ill omens for Beria. The Mingrelian Affair also carried a distinct anti-Beria odor that seemed to waft from the Stalin–Poskrebyshev axis. Beria was in trouble.

Beria's Georgian home province of Mingrelia sired a number of his close party and police associates in Georgia. In a Stalin-ordered purge, a number of these men, beginning in late 1951 and lasting into 1952, were dismissed from party and government posts—hence the Mingrelian Affair. In the classic Stalinist strategy of indirection some of these people were replaced by Beria's enemies.

The so-called Crimean Affair was the next ominous portent. It actually began in 1948 with the MGB's murder of Solomon Mikhoels on Stalin's orders (the technique was an automobile accident, a favorite service choice).[7] Mikhoels had been a member of the Jewish

Anti-Fascist Committee during the war. Following Mikhoel's murder the committee was suppressed and mass arrests of Jewish cultural and other well-known figures followed—for instance, Molotov's wife, Polina, and Solomon Lozovsky, who had been Litvinov's deputy. On 12 August 1952 Lozovsky and other distinguished Jewish writers were secretly executed, having been charged with conspiring to detach Crimea from the USSR as a new Jewish homeland. Moscow-inspired anti-Semitic fervor spread West to the satellites, especially Czechoslovakia. In November 1952 eleven of fourteen Czech leaders in a Stalin-ordered show trial were Jews, among them Rudolf Slanský and Bedřich Geminder, both believed to have had connections to Soviet state security and specifically Beria. Eleven of the fourteen were executed.

In light of its anti-Semitic focus, the Doctors' Plot of early 1953 was a continuation of the Crimean Affair. But it apparently was also to be the penultimate act before a new and more dramatic purge, one that would have finally hit Beria, Malenkov, and the other senior party acolytes around Stalin. Beria, though, would have headed the list. Even though he technically did not command the MGB–MVD police phalanx, he was the longest-lived state security chief in the thirty-plus year history of the party–state. He knew virtually as much as Stalin did about all the sordid details. And he undoubtedly knew all there was to know about Stalin as well.

On 13 January 1953 a press campaign announced the Doctors' Plot, an alleged terrorist operation that was spiked at the last minute. Several leading Kremlin physicians were arrested, and confessed to the actual and planned medical murders of prominent political and military leaders.[8] Most of the nine doctors arrested bore Jewish surnames; they were charged with espionage for Britain, the United States, and an international bourgeois Jewish nationalist organization. The plot long predated the current alleged crimes, for the doctors were accused of the medical murders of General A. S. Shcherbakov in 1945 (chief of the Main Political Administration of the Army and Navy and an ideologist of anti-Semitism) and Andrey Zhdanov in 1948. This backdating of murder was significant, for both the party and state news organs blamed state security for lack of vigilance in not discovering such long-running conspiracies.[9] This was a direct thrust at Beria, Merkulov and, by time implication,

Abakumov—even though he already had been arrested in 1951 but certainly not for this "crime." It was clear that neither Kruglov (the MVD chief) nor the team of Ignatyev and Ryumin in the MGB were the targets. On reflection, it appears that Ignatyev was but a cipher in this operation; the actual executor of Stalin's and Poskrebyshev's orders was Ryumin. Indeed, Ryumin was arrested by Beria after Stalin's death, but was tried and executed in July 1954, six months after Beria's announced trial and execution.[10] Ignatyev, as seen earlier, survived the cleansing of state security, dying of natural causes in 1983. Neither the Beria connection nor the Doctors' Plot stuck to him. Conquest suspects that Ignatyev and several others enjoyed Khrushchev's protection.[11] This naturally raises suspicions of Khrushchev's role in the affair.

Anti-Semitism was a bona fide feature of the Doctors' Plot but it was not the only motivation. Stalin was preparing another purge and this affair evoked the techniques and rationale of the Kirov murder and subsequent mass arrests and executions. The succession of chiefs of state security between 1946 and Stalin's death struck ominous parallels with the 1930s madness. The fact that Beria's name did not show up on the list of the doctors' intended victims was a confirming indicator that he was being vetted for victim status of another type. Himself an expert practitioner of such Aesopian political chicanery, the message was not lost on him.

In the absence of probative data—which could come only from party–KGB archives or a participating witness—few analysts have been willing to conclude that Stalin's prospective victims chose to preempt him. But this was probably the case. The likely intended targets—Beria, Merkulov, Malenkov, and possibly Molotov, Voroshilov, Bulganin, among others—all were beneficiaries of the 1930s bloodletting and themselves participants to greater or lesser degrees. They knew what to expect and had no claims to higher moral or legal recourse in view of their own compromised histories. They had reasons to concentrate their thinking.

In early October 1952 the first party congress in over thirteen years was held in Moscow. The Nineteenth Party Congress raised the alarm on vigilance, changed the name of the Politburo to Presidium, and then increased that body from eleven to twenty-five full members, diluting the power of the likes of Beria, Malenkov,

Khrushchev, Molotov, and others. Poskrebyshev had disappeared sometime before the Congress but was brought back to stage and run the affair. This time he played a very visible role, sounding the tocsin in a speech linking the lack of vigilance to economic crimes, which were then linked to espionage.[12] Significantly, three Beria men were hurt at the congress. Merkulov was reduced from full to candidate membership in the Central Committee. Gvishiani and Dekanozov were not reelected.

But Beria, probably in league with others, was not idle either. Deriabin insists that Beria worked on purging the Okhrana, as the Bodyguards Directorate of the MGB was called, from early 1952. He steadily reduced their size and poisoned Stalin's thinking on a number of critical Okhrana officers, such as General Nikolay Vlasik, getting them dismissed.[13] On 17 February 1953, MGB General P. Ye. Kosynkin, deputy Kremlin commandant and a loyal Stalinist bodyguard, died a "sudden death."[14] Then, sometime after the Nineteenth Party Congress, Poskrebyshev again disappeared. Stalin's protection apparently was in the hands of Beria. On 22 February the heretofore hysterical vigilance campaign and the screaming about the Doctors' Plot were suddenly terminated. No explanation was given at that time, nor did Khrushchev or his successors ever address this series of suspicious events.

The Soviet press reported on 4 March 1953 that Stalin was stricken ill during the night of 1–2 March.[15] On 6 March it was reported that he died the evening of the fifth.[16] No explanations were offered for the lag between events and official announcements. Deriabin insists that Stalin suffered a stroke in his Kremlin office and was removed by MGB Okhrana men to his dacha at Kuntsevo. (Khrushchev stated that Stalin was at his dacha when he was stricken, but Khrushchev gives no actual dates.) Only then were doctors called.[17] But it was too late.

Stalin's death set in motion a series of events for which the party and police were poorly prepared and that portended serious implications for the survival of the whole system. There was no constitutional mechanism for the succession and no real precedent to follow in the absence of such a mechanism. Lenin's death established no legal precedent, but it did begin the tradition of factional maneuvering.

At the time of Lenin's death state security was more or less an instrument of the party's oppression of the nation. Twenty-nine years later state security had become the action arm of one man, the scourge of nation *and* party.

Without the secret police there might not have been a succession; the whole system would likely have collapsed. With the secret police chances were that the most adept maneuverer among Stalin's courtiers would have seized the moment to use the service against his fellows the way Stalin had done to the whole party during his long rule. Beria made that bid but in the event he was not all that artful, and *that* was surprising. Khrushchev outmaneuvered him.

Two days after Stalin's death Moscow announced that a special plenary session of the Central Committee, together with the Council of Ministers and the Presidium of the Supreme Soviet, had decided to merge the MVD and MGB into one MVD under Lavrentiy Beria. Malenkov was announced as the chairman of the Council of Ministers and Beria as one of four vice chairmen. The Presidium was reduced from twenty-five to ten full members and four candidates. Malenkov and Beria were among the ten, with Malenkov also first secretary.[18]

This was extremely fast bureaucratic movement, especially in view of the fact that on 1 March 1953 Stalin was in apparently good health and in full control of party and police. It argues that things had been set in motion with a degree of confidence and dispatch not in the ordinary mien of that system. Kruglov of the MVD and Ignatyev of the MGB were dropped with equally speedy dispatch, but neither man was arrested or shot, a clear departure from the norm for fallen leaders of the organs. Indeed, Kruglov was retained as Beria's deputy. That was a mistake for Beria.

On the night of the announcement of Stalin's death, state security troops appeared in Moscow, taking complete control of the city. These forces represented Beria's greatest physical asset in his bid for power. Under his newly minted and massive MVD he owned the Border Troops, the Internal Security Troops, the Kremlin Guards and their dedicated units, the Gulag and Convoy Troops, and the OOs that penetrated the Soviet military. Not counting the regular uniformed police (militia) also under his control, Beria could muster approximately a million well-trained and equipped state security military forces that were completely independent of the Ministry of Defense. The specific forces Beria moved into the city were elite state security units—the First Red Banner Dzerzhinskiy Motorized Infantry Division and the Second Motorized Infantry Division.[19]

Beria made the monumental error of returning those troops to their barracks before completing whatever plans he had in mind. This move may have been connected with Kruglov's presence as deputy and Serov's position in the service as well. Neither man at that point could be considered among Beria's people and, in view of their positions after Beria's demise, were surely wired to Beria's Presidium opponents. In Serov's case it was Khrushchev, the latter having sung Serov's praises as an "honest man" whom Khrushchev knew well. Khrushchev claims hardly to have known Kruglov.[20]

Khrushchev's memoirs have Marshal Georgiy Zhukov (who had commanded the final assault on Berlin), General Moskalenko, and nine other marshals and generals in on the conspiracy; he gives no date for the actual Presidium meeting, but it is clear that it was in June.[21] The military were brought into the conspiracy as a counterweight to Beria's MVD forces and different authorities agree that military forces were in place at the time of the coup against Beria, and had occupied Moscow, surrounding MVD establishments.[22] One of these military units is believed to have been an elite, showcase armored division called the Kantemirovskaya Division, stationed near Moscow. Its use against the MVD is the first known instance of the party pitting military forces against state security troops. Usually, it is the other way around. There were rumors of firefights between the military and MVD units but no other information of clashes surfaced.

The Medvedev brothers are distrustful of the Khrushchev memoirs on Beria's fall.[23] Deriabin has Kruglov's men doing the actual arrest as well as the roundup of Beria's lieutenants Merkulov, Kobulov, Dekanozov, and others.[24] Everyone seems to agree that the military kept Beria in custody because of uncertainty over MVD loyalties. It may be presumed that the military were not unhappy with their assigned role in the affair.

There also are differences over the actual date of Beria's arrest. The Medvedevs give 28 June 1953, whereas Deriabin states that the conspirators moved on 26 June, after having learned from Kruglov's wiretapping that Beria had his own coup planned for 27 June.[25] The

Procurator General's Office has the USSR Supreme Soviet Presidium examining a Council of Ministers' report of Beria as a foreign agent and approving his removal and detention for trial on 26 June.[26] However, this smacks of a post facto legalism. Conspirators could not risk security and jeopardize an operation to observe proper judicial protocol.

Beria was immediately replaced by his former deputy Sergey Kruglov, with Ivan Serov as Kruglov's deputy. They were rewarded for their roles in the conspiracy. A *Pravda* announcement in early July claimed that Beria attempted to elevate the MVD above the party and government.[27] The procurator general's charges expanded the indictment to using the MVD to seize power and eliminate the Soviet system so as to restore capitalism on behalf of foreign capital.[28]

On 24 December 1953 it was announced that from 18 to 23 December, the USSR Supreme Court (presided over by Marshal Konev!) had tried Beria and six confederates—V. N. Merkulov, V. G. Dekanozov, B. Kobulov, S. A. Goglidze, P. Ya. Meshik, and L. Vlodzimirsky—on several charges beginning with betrayal of the motherland, and that they were convicted and executed on 23 December 1953.[29] Did the victors really wait that long to get rid of such worrisome figures, especially given the uncertainty caused by Stalin's death and Beria's stillborn coup? They probably shot Beria and at least some of the others as soon as possible; the Medvedevs reported eyewitness accounts of the arrests and executions on the spot of the most prominent and dangerous of Beria's assistants.[30]

Purges, trials, and executions of Beria's men and others from state security continued for several years. Ryumin, of Doctors' Plot fame, was tried and executed in early July 1954. Abakumov was accused of being an accomplice of Beria (debatable) and charged with a variety of offenses including "falsification" of the "Leningrad Case" and, along with three other former MGB officials, was executed in early December 1954.[31] No reason was offered for the year's gap between the Abakumov and Beria trials. In November 1955 still more Beria confederates, led by A. N. Rapava and N. M. Rukhadze, were tried and executed in Tbilisi, Georgia, followed five months later by the trial and execution of M. D. Bagirov and three others in Baku, Azerbaidzhan.

Objectively speaking, Beria should have been able to pull a coup and secure power for himself within weeks, if not days, of Stalin's death. He had amassed enormous punitive power by subordinating the troop elements of the old MGB and MVD to his new MVD. But of equal importance were other directorates that allowed him potential or real control over the totality of Soviet political, economic, and military affairs.[32]

Secret Political Directorate (SPU). This was the heart of the secret police; it controlled party, state–Soviet, informational–educational, religious, scientific, collective farms, and other organizations.

Counterintelligence Directorate (KRU). The KRU ran counterintelligence operations against foreign intelligence services operating on Soviet or bloc territory.

Economic Directorate (EKU). The EKU monitored the economy and all personnel associated therewith; was in charge of economic mobilization; and ran operations against economies and trade of foreign countries.

Foreign Directorate (INU). Conducted espionage, subversion, political action, active measures/wet affairs against foreign countries, groups, émigré organizations, and the like.

Armed Forces Counterintelligence–Directorate of Special Departments (UOO). This was the successor to SMERSH; it carried out counterespionage–counterintelligence in the military; developed informant networks to penetrate and expose dissident or subversive elements; and monitored training and the general political–morale situation.

Road and Transportation Directorate (DTU). The DTU was responsible for security direction and monitoring of all rail, air, and maritime (sea and river) transport.

Guards–Ninth Directorate (Okhrana). This directorate guarded and protected leading party, state, and military officials; provided security for all of the most important party and state installations centrally and locally; and was a critical organ for surveilling and controlling party, state, and military officials.

Other Special Departments. These included technical operations; communications–cryptography; counterpartisan section, and others.

Main Administration of Militia (GUM). Involved civil police plus operations unique to the USSR, such as the Main Passport Administration (which controlled internal movement and residency).

Main Administration of Fire Protection (GUPO). Responsible for fire-fighting and inspection of all premises.

Main Archive Administration (GAU). Controlled the work and archives of various agencies, public organizations, museums, and libraries.

Main Administration of Places of Detention (GUMZ). Oversaw municipal jails, transfer jails, and "inner prisons" (temporary jails where suspects are held during investigation); prepared prisoners to be turned over to the Gulag.

Main Administration of Corrective Labor Camps (Gulag). This is the concentration camp empire that held the overwhelming majority of prisoners; served punitive, and, importantly, economic functions.

There were numerous other directorates, administrations, services, and departments that served both punitive and economic functions. Those identified above highlight the broad scope, functions and, hence, power that Beria actually, not theoretically, exercised. He clearly did not exploit this power in either a timely or adroit manner. Conversely, it was in the interest of his political opponents to dilute such a concentration of power, but only insofar as such dilution would not threaten party control and prerogatives. They also had a concern with economics; a goodly portion of the MVD's economic empire would revert to the appropriate state organizations.

And so, a reining-in occurred, a leashing of sorts. True, the visceral feel of Khrushchev for the mood of the country and the hard facts of explosive ferment in Eastern Europe told him that the USSR could not sustain much more. So amnesties and other administrative or legal measures opened the forced labor camps, thereby reducing the number of prisoners. A well-orchestrated publicity campaign touting "socialist legality," that is, allegedly conforming to Soviet legal statutes, played on the injection of state control into the processes whereby the MVD and its predecessors had hitherto flaunted their special status, answerable only to the person of Stalin or his secretariat. The state procurator was now to oversee the courts, the prisons, and related state security activities. But much of this apparent liberalization masked substance. And politically, the leashing of the police had far more to do with the party's welfare than with that of the citizenry. De-Stalinization carried certain attributes of early "legends" given the pedigree of its sponsor, the realities it masked, and the party's privileged position that it successfully preserved.

The massive MVD continued only for another year when on 13 March 1954 the new Committee for State Security (Komitet Gosudarstvennoy Bezopasnosti, or KGB) was announced.[33] State security, foreign operations, the OOs, and certain troop elements reverted to the KGB, leaving the MVD with purely interior functions. The service no longer enjoyed ministerial status, which enhanced the party's ability to prevent it from being used arbitrarily against the party as it had been under Stalin.

Kruglov remained minister of the MVD and his former deputy, Serov, became the new chairman of the KGB. The purging of Beria's people apparently was accomplished by the time of Khrushchev's secret speech at the Twentieth Party Congress in February 1956. The major police trials were over and it only remained for Khrushchev to dump Kruglov as MVD minister before the congress and replace him with a party apparatchik, Nikolay Dudorov. According to Roy Medvedev, Kruglov later committed suicide in anticipation that the police purges would reach him.[34] It seems then that Serov, as Khrushchev told us, was the latter's man and received his patronage and protection. Kruglov's protectors (Malenkov?) had to have been among the losing faction in the post-Stalin power struggle.

As we have seen, Serov did not come in with clean hands. Khrushchev's laments at the Twentieth Party Congress about the abuses of Stalin and the crimes of Beria could easily have been directed at Serov—or Khrushchev himself for that matter. The handwringing had more to do with appearances and the need to outflank his party rivals. De-Stalinization was a last-minute gambit in the spirit of Khrushchevean audacity, but he was very careful to attribute abuses to *individuals* and not the system or to the police as an institution. In the congress he stressed the unique relationships between the party and the police and pointed out that party and state control *had* been reestablished.[35] This was the beginning of a theme that played up the KGB as the most faithful servant of the party, its "shield and sword." The theme was to be buttressed by linking the KGB to its founder in order to stress the notion of servant of the party. The cult of Dzerzhinskiy had therefore to be created so as to legitimize the service through this sanctified creator.

Khrushchev sought to foster the image of a KGB leavened by fresh, loyal cadres from the party. This was true to an extent but it was not innovative at the time, nor have things changed much since then. The party had always infused state security with new cadres, especially at critical junctures in the regime's life. Khrushchev pretended that the "restoration of Leninist norms" was somehow unique. In reality he was trying to explain away both Stalin and the symbiosis between party and police that had originally been established by Lenin and Dzerzhinskiy. This fused relationship had actually made it much easier for Stalin to savage the party and utilize the police as a personnel instrument. His person and personal secretariat supplanted the party. The symbiosis quite naturally became one of Stalin–police vice party–police. Invoking "Leninist norms" merely reinserted the "party" into that label at the excision of "Stalin." If he were so concerned with violations of "socialist legality," Khrushchev would not have put a mass killer (Serov) in charge.

Historically, party cadres had been injected at all levels of the state security structure. Recall the Civil War and the massive expansion of the Cheka. The Kronstadt rebellion saw the drafting of party activists to stiffen both the military *and* the Cheka. This event was a particularly brutal "bonding" experience, one of mutual implication in moral compromise. During collectivization and the man-made famine, thousands of party activists were recruited into the OGPU or attached to the requisition and punitive squads. At the level of command, Yezhov was dispatched to the NKVD from the Central Committee secretariat to become Yagoda's successor. This type of command-level assignment from senior party post to state security leadership was to become something of a norm: Ignatyev (MGB minister 1951–53); Shelepin (KGB chief 1958–61); Semichastnyy (KGB chief 1961–67); Andropov (KGB chief 1967–82); Chebrikov (KGB chief 1982–present). Following Yagoda's dismissal (1936) and then Yezhov's sacking, thousands of party staffers were injected in the

NKVD to fill the vacancies caused by Yezhov's and Beria's purges. This happened again with the fall of Abakumov in 1951. Therefore, the fall of Beria and his minions would have precipitated broad personnel movement even had Stalin lived or had Khrushchev not chosen to de-Stalinize and promote a campaign of "socialist legality." And, in the final analysis, with the exception of the senior Beria people and others who may have been axed for other reasons, the turnover of personnel apparently was not that great. Khrushchev, at the Twentieth Party Congress, sought to reassure his Chekists that the party trusted them and placed a high priority on raising "revolutionary vigilance" and strengthening the "organs of state security."[36] A year later in a speech on the Fortieth Anniversary of the KGB, Serov allowed as how the old hands in state security enjoyed the complete backing of the Central Committee and the party.[37]

So yes, there were legal reforms, new laws, rehabilitations of Stalin's victims (selectively), reduction in the size of the prison and camp populations, and a controlled liberalization in the cultural and literary spheres. Actually, the codes were strengthened to permit tighter enforcement under the law and the real authority of the KGB was not all that delimited. In cases of political ferment the party and the KGB retained the same administrative, extralegal prerogatives dating back to the Cheka. And when, with the sacking of Serov and the appointment of Shelepin in 1958, Khrushchev and Shelepin embarked on a rehabilitation of the KGB (or more precisely its image— actual rehabilitation had been under way since the last of the major police trials in 1956), the "organs" became the object of official adulation that persists into the 1980s.

If there was a meaningful reining-in of the instruments of repression, it was at the MVD level. The party could ill afford a policy of KGB-bashing if the party meant to survive the widespread disillusionment and the bitterness manifested in the camp uprisings and the explosions in Eastern Europe. But it could safely allow the less-sensitive security elements such as the Militsiya (uniformed police of the MVD) to become the lightning rod for the rest of the system. Beginning in 1957, when it lost control over the Border Troops, the MVD was subject to several humiliating measures such as being fragmented into Republic MVDs (1960) with no national ministry; redesignation as Republic MOOPs (Ministries for the Maintenance of Public Order) in 1962 with no national ministry; and finally a national MOOP in 1966. It was not until 1968 that the old title

MVD was restored. The MVD is that instrument of state authority against which most Soviet citizens run into in the course of their daily lives, namely, the militia, internal passport officers, and camp guards. If there was to be a denegration of or challenge to an institution, let it be a state one—the MVD—and not the party's action arm. Khrushchev's safety valve devolved down to the MVD. He set a precedent. Both Andropov's and Gorbachev's anticorruption campaigns have made a public point of fingering corruption in the MVD, knowing that this evokes responsive sympathy from the masses and deflects resentment away from the party–KGB phalanx.

Deceptive conditioning, manipulative inspiration, reflexive control—techniques common to the counterintelligence state—were practiced by Stalin and continued by his successors. Khrushchev's de-Stalinization, though a calculated risk, preserved the privileged positions of party and police while appearing to humanize the system and restraining the praetorians.

In one arena of state security operations Khrushchev chose not to temper his actions or to dissemble for public consumption: direct action (or wet affairs) beyond Moscow's frontiers. Assassinations and other Soviet-sponsored terrorism actually accelerated during the period of Khrushchev's ascendancy. Although General Sudoplatov (of partisan fame) and General Eitingon (the contracting authority for Trotsky's murder) were imprisoned after Stalin died, it was not because Moscow disowned their methods. Both men were pawns in a larger factional struggle. The increased momentum of Soviet terrorist actions seemed, in part, to be related to ferment within the USSR and its satellites in the wake of Stalin's death and to the accelerated role of defections from state security itself. Additionally, Khrushchev was planning a more active and dynamic foreign policy than had occurred during Stalin's last years (notwithstanding Korea and the Berlin blockade). This included selected direct action operations against foreign governments. Thus, though Khrushchev gave the appearance of restraining the service domestically, internationally he revived the Yezhovian practice of employing mobile killer squads to handle troublesome émigrés, defectors, or other persons or groups considered dangerous to the USSR. There was no break in that tradition inherited from Stalin.

As under Stalin, the KGB used combinations of indigenous agents (local nationals recruited by the KGB), Soviet illegal staff officers located in the target area, or it dispatched KGB staffers. The groups were known in the tradecraft jargon as combat groups or *boyevye gruppy*.[38] Sometimes murders or kidnappings involved singleton operations, but even these required a covert support structure to provide logistics, intelligence, and command and control.

There have been very few defectors from the KGB's wet affairs organization but a number of these came out during the Khrushchev era and after, providing a view into the actual operations and the attitude of the Soviet leadership on such activity. Nikolay Khokhlov, a KGB captain, had been dispatched in 1954 to West Germany to supervise two German indigenous agents in the attempted assassination of NTS leader Georgiy Okolovich.[39] (The NTS [Narodno-Trudovoy Soyuz Rossiyskikh Solidaristov], or Popular Labor Alliance of Russian Solidarists, was and still is an anti-Soviet opposition organization based in West Germany.) After he defected, Khokhlov himself nearly died in a retaliatory attack by another KGB group. Another officer from the KGB wet affairs department, Bogdan Stashinskiy, defected in 1961 and divulged that he indeed had murdered two Ukrainian émigré leaders in West Germany by using vapor guns to project prussic acid. Lev Rebet was murdered in 1957 and Stepan Bandera in 1959. Both Khokhlov and Stashinskiy testified that the Khrushchev-led collective leadership actually reviewed in advance and approved such operations. Stashinskiy personally received the order of the Red Banner from Aleksandr Shelepin, chairman of the KGB and later Politburo member, for the Bandera assassination.[40] They were supported in their testimony by Peter Deriabin, who defected in 1954 after having served in KGB counterintelligence and in Stalin's bodyguard unit.[41]

There were dozens of other operations or suspected ones by such combat groups during the Khrushchev years. A more recent source, but contemporary to that period, had been a member of one of those combat groups in Iran in the late 1940s. He recalled that in 1956 the KGB received special orders from Moscow to prepare teams for special operations in foreign countries to destroy or commit terrorist acts against government officials, facilities, and the like. Control was to be exercised by the KGB chairman and deputy chairman.[42]

Institutionally, the organizational lines for these KGB combat groups traced back to Yezhov's Administration for Special Tasks (see appendix B). During World War II they were situated in General Sudoplatov's Fourth Directorate under the NKGB, operating behind German lines. After the war the new MGB took responsibility for the operation, labeling the new unit Spets Byuro No. 1 (Special Bureau No. 1), still under General Sudoplatov. (Although General Eitingon was supposed to have been with Sudoplatov at the time, a Colonel Lev Studnikov, not Eitingon, has been identified as the deputy.)[43] A *kamera* or chamber was identified as the Byuro's laboratory for developing exotic poisons and weaponry. When Sudoplatov was arrested following Beria's failed coup, the Byuro briefly became the Ninth Section of the First Chief Directorate of the MVD. In 1954, when the KGB was formed, the unit was reorganized as the Department Thirteen of the First Chief Directorate and it remained as such until the late 1960s, when it was rechristened Department "V". Following the defection of a KGB officer, Oleg Lyalin, in Britain in 1971, where he organized sleeper sabotage networks, Department "V" apparently went for a bolthole and it was thought by many observers that the KGB actually went out of that type of enterprise. But in 1982, with the defection of a KGB major in Iran, it was learned that wet affairs was reorganized and reconstituted as Department Eight of the First Chief Directorate's Illegals Directorate.[44]

Khrushchev and KGB Chiefs Serov and Shelepin carried the service intact from its exclusive subordination to Stalin into the opening of a new era as servant of the party. It now remained for Khrushchev to chart the course for the KGB into this era. In doing so, he established the operational framework that carried the KGB into the 1980s. At the same time, he failed to secure his own future. General Serov had served him well. Shelepin would not.

8

The Return to Dzerzhinskiy

I N EARLY December 1958, General Ivan A. Serov was relieved as chairman of the KGB and moved to the General Staff as chief of the Main Intelligence Directorate, the GRU. He was replaced later that month by Aleksandr N. Shelepin who, like Yezhov in 1936 and Ignatyev in 1951, had come in from the Central Committee's Party Organs Department. Prior to that Shelepin had spent years as secretary and first secretary of the Komsomol Central Committee.

Serov's tenure as KGB chairman had been marred by a number of highly sensational and damaging defections. Although several of these occurred before Serov took charge, he had been Kruglov's deputy in the MVD at the time. So, theoretically, he could have borne some of the responsibility. The subsequent adverse publicity that defector testimony, articles, and books generated did not help either the KGB's or Serov's image. It is worth noting the more significant of these defections, which are listed in appendix C. Of course, Serov could not but assist. His notoriety was enhanced in Budapest during the 1956 Hungarian uprising. After then-Ambassador Yuriy Andropov lured a Hungarian delegation headed by Defense Minister Pal Maleter to negotiations, Serov and a KGB group stormed into the meeting with weapons drawn. Maleter and the head of the new Hungarian government, Imre Nagy, were later executed—in Romania. For some reason only Serov was remembered for this sordid affair. Andropov was later touted in the West as a liberal.

Despite this Serov had actually served Khrushchev well and we can only speculate if the hemorrhage of KGB operatives in the 1950s and early 1960s factored into Serov's dismissal. Colonel Oleg Penkovskiy, the GRU officer working for the United Kingdom and the

United States (a defector in place, so to speak), insinuated that Serov's help and support were the only things that allowed Khrushchev to handle the military and force his modernization program on the military establishment. The military, according to Penkovskiy's account, were the triggermen for Beria's execution in 1953. The operation occurred in the basement of Moscow Military District Headquarters and was witnessed by a number of general officers. The military feared an attempt by the MVD to rescue their boss, so they deployed their own armor and troops, brought them to a state of combat readiness, and completely surrounded their headquarters. Following the execution of the police boss, they burned his corpse in the cellar of the building. Penkovskiy stated that military hatred for Serov was of the same intensity as for Beria, and they bitterly resented his presence at the helm of the GRU.[1]

Serov undoubtedly also gave Khrushchev valuable KGB support in his struggle with the so called Anti-Party Group. While Zhukov and the military helped out by flying in Khrushchev's supporters for the critical Central Committee plenum in June 1957, Serov was providing the needed intelligence on Khrushchev's opponents. He was also in charge of security at the Kremlin and probably alerted Khrushchev supporters to the secret Presidium meetings where Khrushchev had been dismissed by a vote of eight to four. The Medvedevs claim that a task force of Marshal Zhukov, Serov, and Frol Kozlov then arranged for that military airlift of Khrushchev men for the decisive Central Committee plenum.[2] The transfer of the Border Troops, and possibly the Internal Troops, back to the KGB between March and June 1957 was calculated to send a message to Khrushchev's opponents—and maybe to the military as well. In this regard it has been observed that in a June 1957 *Red Star* (*Krasnaya zvezda*, the daily of the Ministry of Defense), General of the Army Serov was listed *ahead* of nine marshals of the Soviet Union, an intended infringement of military protocol.[3]

Nonetheless, Serov was dumped. Penkovskiy attributes this to the ingrate nature of Khrushchev's character. After Khrushchev had implanted his own party cadres from the Central Committee and the Ukraine into the leading KGB slots, he dumped Serov on the military and replaced him with his "toady Shelepin."[4]

Penkovskiy is probably right, as far as he goes. But there was one other dimension that he either was not privy to or did not care to share. That was the Popov case. Lieutenant Colonel Pëtr Popov, a GRU officer, was among the first well-placed agents recruited by the CIA within Soviet military intelligence. More precisely, Popov initiated the contact. He worked in place from 1952 until exposed by the KGB in 1958. The writer who chronicled the Popov case concluded that Serov was moved to the GRU because the scandal was so devastating and required the replacement of the GRU chief on whose watch the penetration occurred.[5] This was Lieutenant General Mikhail A. Shalin, who ran the GRU from 1951 to 1956 and from 1957 to 1958. The case was a serious one and pointed to a clear counterintelligence failure. It must be recalled, though, that military counterintelligence was and is a KGB responsibility. On the other hand, if Serov were truly disgraced he would have been fired, imprisoned, or executed. This was, after all, a bona fide hostile intelligence penetration. Thousands of Soviets earlier had been executed on the basis of phony, trumped-up cases.

Serov was destined to suffer real disgrace just a few years later. In 1962 a second GRU officer, Colonel Oleg Penkovskiy, was arrested as a British–U.S. agent. He too had worked in place following his own approach to the West in 1961. The shock and scandal were too much for Serov to survive. He and a number of KGB and GRU officers were summarily fired and hundreds of Soviet operatives called back to the center. A senior KGB officer, General Pëtr Ivashutin, was dispatched to take over and cleanse the GRU. Ivashutin sits there to this day.

Whatever the specific motivations for the 1958 succession, Khrushchev was planning a new course for the service. He considered Shelepin his man and the two moved the KGB into an era of higher operational sophistication.

According to Anatoliy Golitsyn, a former First Chief Directorate officer, Nikolay R. Mironov (the chief of the Leningrad KGB) and Aleksandr Shelepin had proposed to Khrushchev and Brezhnev the idea of transforming the KGB into a true instrument of party policy, the way it had been intended under Lenin and Dzerzhinskiy.[6] Mironov had convinced Shelepin that the NEP of the 1920s and the OGPU's role in its implementation should serve as the paradigm for the new party–KGB policy that Khrushchev wanted implemented. The Trust, as we have seen, was the kind of state security operation that helped to make the NEP successful and it was a return to such political operations that Mironov and Shelepin had in mind for the reoriented KGB.

At first Shelepin was assigned control of the Party Organs Department of the Central Committee, a key post controlling party assignments. By the end of December 1958, Khrushchev gave him the KGB and Mironov was made head of the powerful Administrative Organs Department of the Central Committee. This was and is the controlling mechanism for the KGB, MVD, courts, procuracy, the military, the GRU, DOSAAF (Volunteer Society for Cooperation with the Army, Aviation, and the Fleet), the Main Political Administration of the Army and Navy, and even civil aviation.[7] Then, with full concurrence from Khrushchev, Shelepin created Department D (disinformation) within the KGB's First Chief Directorate and assigned it to Colonel Ivan I. Agayants, a man of no small reputation for his successful work in the KGB's Paris residency a number of years earlier.

Agayants generally was believed to be the guiding spirit behind a spate of spurious books originating in France, some probably written by Grigoriy Bessedovskiy, a former Soviet diplomat who had defected in Paris in 1929.[8] Bessedovskiy has been suspected of literary enterprises ranging from fabrication for profit to outright disinformation on Moscow's behalf. The books at issue included such titles as *My Career at Soviet Headquarters*, *The Soviet Marshals Address You*, and *My Uncle Joe*—all by invented authors—and the phony Litvinov diaries, *Notes for a Journal*. While making light of one of the most vicious epochs of Soviet history, the themes of the books tended to cast Stalin's Russia in benign hues and at the same time stress its military strengths—echoes harking back to the Trust. This period of Agayants's career is seen by some as the early laboratory for his later efforts as chief of Department D. Disinformation and other forms of active measures were to have critical roles in the redirection of party policy and KGB strategy under the guidance of Agayants's Department D.

At the same time, the International Department of the Central Committee under the veteran Comintern apparatchik Boris N. Ponomarev grew in visibility and importance. Thus, in a few swift moves, a stable institutional network was emplaced that exists to this day with few modifications and, obviously, led by new faces.

To execute the reorientation and return to the positive, creative political focus that Mironov and Shelepin associated with Dzerzhinskiy and his Cheka–OGPU, Shelepin called a major conference of senior KGB officers, the ministers of defense and internal affairs, and senior Central Committee members. Over two thousand participants were reported in attendance.[9] Golitsyn identified the following as among the principal tasks the attendees and their organizations were to understand and accomplish.

The main "enemies" of the Soviet Union were the United States, Britain, France, West Germany, Japan, and all countries of NATO and other Western-supported military alliances.

The security and intelligence services of the whole bloc were to be mobilized to influence international relations in directions required by the new long-range policy, and, in effect, to destabilize the "main enemies" and weaken the alliances among them.

The efforts of the KGB in the Soviet intelligentsia were to be redirected outwardly—against foreigners, with a view to enlisting their help in the achievement of policy objectives.

The newly established disinformation department was to work closely with all other relevant departments in the party and government apparatus throughout the country. To this end, all ministries of the Soviet Union, and all first secretaries of republican and provincial party organizations, were to be acquainted with the new political tasks of the KGB to enable them to give support and help when needed.

Joint political operations were to be undertaken with the security and intelligence services of all communist countries.

The contemporary period of Soviet active measures and strategic deception was thus ushered in. By the time Agayants (head of Department D) died, he was a KGB general. By 1970–71, his creation had been elevated from a department (*otdel*) to a service (*sluzhba*), known today as Service A. In the Soviet operational tradition, such changes connote much more than mere bureaucratic honorifics; undoubtedly the elevations were in keeping with performance and importance of function.

The organizational layout for coordinated deception operations gradually took shape, with the party and the KGB leading a condominium of players throughout the party and state bureaucracies. Ponomarev's International Department seemed to become something of a Politburo "general staff," providing the overarching initiative and policy guidance for the KGB and others to follow. Similar developments occurred in Eastern Europe in view of the coordination requirements called for in Shelepin's conference.

It should be stressed that Golitsyn was not the only source talking about long-term deception planning and operations. But Golitsyn did not formulate his conception of a long-range strategic plan until he was in the West for several years. Still, the themes and specifics from the 1959 conference were reflected in the data and insights brought out later by defectors from other communist countries, especially from Czechoslovakia. General Major Jan Sejna (assistant secretary to the Czech Defense Council, chief of staff to the Czech Ministry of Defense, member of Parliament, and member of the Czech Communist Party Central Committee) is one of the most senior, well-placed officials to defect from the Soviet bloc. His unusual access was the basis for his detailed exposition of the early-1960s Soviet Strategic Plan, which he insists set out Moscow's long-term objectives.[10] According to Sejna, direction for strategic deception was included in the Strategic Plan for the USSR and for each of the Warsaw Pact countries.[11] Specific military deception actions would be part of the military operational plan for each Warsaw Pact country and each action would have to be approved by the commander of the Warsaw Pact Forces, a Soviet officer.[12]

Another Czech, Ladislav Bittman, had been an intelligence officer whose service included that of deputy chief of Department D of the Czech intelligence service from 1964 to 1966. Bittman spoke of the work of his service on long-term deception plans covering a period of five to seven years; the service was required to follow basic guidelines articulated by Moscow. This was to ensure that satellite deception planning was synchronous with Moscow's own long-range plan.[13] In addition to oversight on these matters by local KGB advisors, Bittman observed that General Agayants himself periodically checked in person on Bittman's organization and was the approving authority for Czech deception operations and even phases of operations.[14] According to Bittman, Agayants was a dedicated, stern professional, almost ascetic in his commitment to Soviet objectives.[15] Shelepin and Khrushchev had picked the right man to help return the KGB to the style and spirit of Dzerzhinskiy.

The new age of active measures was ushered in by two state security professionals (Mironov and Agayants), an old party survivor
and intriguer (Khrushchev), a young party intriguer trying to climb
higher (Shelepin), and a veteran Comintern workhorse (Ponomarev)
who would outlast them all, surviving up to the Gorbachev era.
(Ponomarev in turn would be replaced by Anatoliy Dobrynin, former ambassador to the United States.) Ponomarev's success as party
overseer of the active measures offensive initiated by the men discussed above accounted, in part, for his longevity. The stature he
brought to the International Department is gauged by the importance and reputation it acquired as the actual focal point of foreign
policy. The assignment of Dobrynin to the ID rather than to the
Foreign Ministry (run by a former police general, Edward Shevar-
nadze, inexperienced in foreign affairs) shows that Gorbachev has a
keen appreciation for the distinction.

Bittman, Sejna, and Golitsyn correctly evaluated the unique elements of the Khrushchev, Shelepin, and Mironov policies, but it was
the internal counterintelligence dimension that characterized the
true rehabilitation of state security. Khrushchev and Mironov had
reputations for being concerned with "socialist legality." Mironov
specifically used his position as head of the Administrative Organs Department (AOD) to promote Khrushchev's de-Stalinization
schemes and the campaign against arbitrariness by the punitive organs. As head of the AOD he also was in a position to reinforce
Khrushchev's control over the military, which might have factored
into Mironov's death several years later (more on this later in this
chapter).

Whether Mironov was truly concerned with the observation of
socialist norms by the organs is subject to debate. What *is* known
about his and Shelepin's tenures (in their respective posts of security
oversight and leadership) is that they consciously sought to refurbish
and enhance the image of the organs. Penkovskiy characterized Mironov as an all powerful tsar and god over the GRU and KGB, one
before whom even General Serov stood at attention.[16] Under both
men a literary campaign of sorts expanded efforts begun slightly earlier to publicize the service and its heroic efforts to protect party and
state. Mironov himself contributed to this operation with articles and
books that, though stressing socialist legality, also played on the positive contributions that state security made on behalf of party and
state, while criticizing the MVD, the courts, and even the party.[17]

The themes set by Mironov—socialist legality coupled with the heroic efforts of the service—seemed to resonate in the works of the KGB literary renaissance. A veritable cult of Dzerzhinskiy and the heroic Cheka, begun earlier in the 1950s, expanded and never really abated.[18] Old Chekists were rehabilitated and espionage in the service of socialism was finally acknowledged.[19] This even extended to the world of philately, with stamps not only of Dzerzhinskiy but of hitherto denied and unsung heroes such as Richard Sorge.

Attending the rehabilitation of state security was a gradual reaffirmation of its powers. We have seen how the burden of irresponsibility tended to be placed on the MVD. Its redesignation in 1962 as the Ministry for Maintenance of Public Order (MOOP) had the effect of perpetuating its negative image in the eyes of the Soviet public. At the same time Shelepin worked hard to ensure that de-Stalinization did not erode the ethos of KGB authority. Serov may have had the well-earned reputation of a thug, and the party may have believed that in Shelepin they would at least have a "respectable" apparatchik at the helm of the service. But among the Soviet intelligentsia, according to two former Soviet scholars who knew the scene, Shelepin was nicknamed "Iron Shurik," a not-so-subtle play on Shelepin's pretensions to be another Dzerzhinskiy.[20] And given the kind of authority and power Mironov had as head of the Administrative Organs Department, it is doubtful that Shelepin was re-Stalinizing the service on his own. Rehabilitation of state security was the mission of both men and Mironov was the party man in charge.

Shelepin was ambitious and his attitude on "vigilance" and repression of the restive tendencies unleashed by Khrushchev's gamble with de-Stalinization certainly did not hurt his reputation among nervous party bureaucrats and state security cadres. These had all sensed an incipient danger in a loosening of restraints. He was rewarded in November 1961 when he was promoted into the Central Committee secretariat, whence it is believed he still exercised control over the service. This was not too difficult to accomplish. His successor, Vladimir Semichastnyy, had virtually the same boot size. He succeeded Shelepin as first secretary of the Komsomol Central Committee and then followed his boss into the Party Organs Department when Shelepin moved into the KGB. He also had the reputation of a brutish reactionary who believed that an unfettered KGB, the action arm of the party, could best provide the "tranquility" absent since the days of Stalin. Both Semichastnyy and Shelepin became a pair, uncontrolled by a Khrushchev who made an error not unlike Beria before him. In short, Semichastnyy was Shelepin's man.

Internally, the rehabilitation of the KGB received reinforcement with the events in the city of Novocherkassk in the southern USSR near Rostov in June 1962.[21] These events demonstrated, once again, the continuity of KGB control over special troops to handle internal unrest and insurgencies. What started as a workers' protest against the raising of food prices and production quotas turned into a mass protest involving over ten thousand workers.[22] Party offices were sacked and the regular militia of the MVD could not handle the situation. The troops brought in to replace the militia and stop the protest fired on the crowds with automatic weapons, causing an estimated seventy to eighty deaths in the first round of shooting, according to Solzhenitsyn.[23] Solzhenitsyn referred to the troops as if they were from the regular military. They were not. They were KGB, at least those who did most of the firing, and they comprised non-Russian soldiers plus a heavy ratio of officers.[24] Some of those who fired did come from the militia but the local military garrison officers and men were reported to have refused to carry out orders. Arrests, trials, and courts marshal were accompanied by threats of mass deportations if striking workers did not return to work.[25]

This event is instructive on several counts. It showed the fragility of party and internal security control even in the Soviet heartland— Novocherkassk is Russian-Ukrainian, *not* a non-Slavic minority region—when economic and social conditions deteriorate below some undetermined threshold of popular toleration. Related to this is a Soviet strength: that of keeping the news of such happenings from reaching the West. Only the stature of Solzhenitsyn got the tragedy the little notice that it did attract outside the USSR. The unreliability of the regular military (reserves too, because some of these were reported ordered into the city) when it comes to suppressing civil disturbances was also demonstrated. This is balanced off by the very evident willingness of the KGB troops to do what they were ordered by the party.

This last item is extremely important in assessing the longevity and persistence of the counterintelligence state. We too often forget or ignore the fact that the KGB has its own forces, and not just

Border Troops, which do not necessarily appear in the published data the Soviets allow on their armed forces. Additionally, the Internal Security Troops nominally subordinated to the MVD—which *are* admitted to by Soviet authorities—can readily and administratively remand to KGB control at the discretion of the senior leadership, as former officers from state security have been telling the West for decades. But in their way, accidently or not, the Soviets admit to this. Soviet legal textbooks, for instance, tell us that there are KGB "special" troops and that other forces could fall under KGB jurisdiction because of the political needs of the party and because the KGB is a political organization:

> The KGB conducts the practical management of the whole system of organs and of special troops (state security troops, border troops) performing functions for the protection of the state security of the USSR.[26]

Or:

> The KGB conducts the practical management of the whole system of organs and of state security troops.[27]

And

> the organs of the KGB actively participate in the development and coordination of state measures for securing state security. . . . The activity of the organs has a clearly expressed political and policy nature. They are political organs that put into practice the policies of the Central Committee of the Party and the Soviet Government for the defense of the socialist state.[28]

In sum, the KGB has the troops for doing special missions along with the political and "legal" mandate from the party. Institutional boundaries between it, the MVD, the military, and other state organizations are readily overcome in favor of the KGB if the security of the state requires it.

That Khrushchev was having apparent problems with the KGB supporting his policies was not a problem of uncontrolled state security but rather a symptom of his own difficulties with the rest of the party leadership. It was observed earlier that Shelepin, and by extension Semichastnyy, would not prove as reliable or loyal as Serov. In the last year of Khrushchev's tenure several KGB provocations against Westerners in the USSR seemed timed to conflict with Khrushchev's Western initiatives and cause him international embarrassment. These were the arrest of U. S. Professor Frederick Barghoorn in October 1963 on espionage charges, which generated a stiff protest from President Kennedy and resulted in Barghoorn's release; the attack on U. S. and British military attachés in Khabarovsk in September 1964; and the vicious poison gas attack on a West German Embassy security specialist before a planned meeting by Khrushchev with West German leaders. Khrushchev extended sincere apologies to the West Germans, with a clear statement that the operation was not of his sponsorship: "Those who indulge in such actions are trying to undermine the good relations between our two countries."[29]

Comparing these events to the Brezhnev succession, which showed signs of similar provocations (aimed internally, however), it is clear that a palace coup was in the offing and that the KGB leadership had been co-opted by the conspirators. So, too, had the military. Unlike 1957 when Khrushchev had Zhukov and Serov in his corner, in the fall of 1964 both the military and state security were aligned with his new party enemies, prominent among whom were Brezhnev, Shelepin, Mikhail Suslov, and Gromyko.

Khrushchev was at his Black Sea dacha in Sochi when his opponents convened a Presidium meeting on 11 October 1964. According to the Medvedevs, Brezhnev called Khrushchev that day to inform him of the meeting and that he was expected to be there or it would go on without him.[30] Khrushchev at first demurred, but then left immediately. Other accounts differ, having him arrive on 13 October in the afternoon, where he had to face his opponents alone after they successfully prevented him from contacting his Central Committee supporters as he had done in 1957.[31] This could only have been accomplished with the direct collusion of Semichastnyy's KGB. Rumors circulated that both Semichastnyy and Shelepin met Khrushchev at the airport and "escorted" him directly to the Presidium meeting. On 15 October a large portrait of Khrushchev hanging in

Red Square was removed: the next day his "resignation" was announced.[32]

If Shelepin had hoped to gain the position of first secretary through his deliverance of the KGB to the conspirators, he miscalculated. Solzhenitsyn suggests that Shelepin originally had been the choice of the Stalinists who asked what "had been the point of overthrowing Khrushchev if not to revert to Stalinism?"[33] But the drama was still not completely played out. On 20 October 1964, *Red Star* carried the stunning announcement that on 19 October a Soviet military transport carrying KGB General Nikolay R. Mironov (the head of the party's Administrative Organs Department), Marshal Sergey Biryuzov (the chief of the General Staff), and several other senior military officials and air crew crashed on a mountainside in Yugoslavia.[34] There were suspicions that Shelepin, Semichastnyy, and even the new party First Secretary Brezhnev somehow were linked to the accident. Mironov, with his "legality" and de-Stalinization efforts, might have stood in the way of a full rehabilitation of the service and could have crimped Shelepin's style in controlling the KGB via his protégé, Semichastnyy. Marshal Biryuzov, the next senior victim on board the ill-fated flight and also a Khrushchev man, was suspected by some in the senior leadership of harboring attitudes similar to those of Zhukov, that is, he wanted less party interference in purely professional military affairs.[35] Whether or not a KGB-staged "accident" occurred, the only apparent obstacle remaining from Khrushchev's entourage, Mironov, had been removed. Virtually everyone else had moved over to the conspirators. All that remained now was for Suslov and Brezhnev to secure control of state security from Shelepin and Semichastnyy, who already had demonstrated that they could not be trusted.

Although Shelepin moved into the Politburo as a full member in November 1964—an apparent reward for the success of the coup—the next several years were marked by a steady diminution of his party authority and prestige, and hence his access to the KGB. As is standard in factional warfare, the target is seldom confronted frontally. It was easier to go after Semichastnyy who, besides Shelepin, had no influential patrons at that level. Additionally, the festering residue of the Penkovskiy scandal gave Brezhnev and Suslov a hook on which to hang charges of grave counterintelligence failures.

On 18 May 1967, Semichastnyy was fired as KGB chairman after having served about five-and-one-half years. Five months later Shelepin was removed from the secretariat and given the time-consuming but not dangerous post of trade union chief.

Yuriy Andropov's accession on 18 May 1967 began a long period of stabilization and growth for the service. Within a month he was given candidacy membership in the Politburo (it had been renamed at the Twenty-third Party Congress the year before) and, in 1973, along with the Foreign Minister Gromyko and the Defense Minister Marshal A. A. Grechko, became a full voting member of that all-important body. Reigning until May 1982 as KGB chief and retaining his levers of control as a secretary and then general secretary until his death in February 1984, Andropov gave the longest uninterrupted leadership to the organs in Soviet history. Even Beria's tenure could not compare because from 1945 until early 1953 he technically was not in control. Andropov logged fifteen years as chief and then another one-and-one-half years from his party perch.

Though not a Chekist by profession, Andropov had important experience with security matters dating back to his party–NKVD work in the partisan movement in Karelia in 1941 (but apparently without combat behind the German lines), his ambassadorship to Hungary (1954–57), and his Central Committee duties as head of the Department for Liaison with Socialist Countries. Comparatively speaking, then, he was better prepared for the KGB position than any of his non–state security predecessors (Semichastnyy, Shelepin, Ignatyev, and Yezhov). He was not a mere party apparatchik foisted on a resentful professional brotherhood.

It may have been recognition of this experience that reinforced Brezhnev in his decision to stack the leading KGB positions with his appointees, several of whom came to be known as the "Dneprope-trovskaya Banda" or Mafia. They included the following figures.[36]

General Semyon Tsvigun, who was KGB deputy chairman and then first deputy chairman and was Brezhnev's brother-in-law. His service with the general secretary dated to the early 1950s in Moldavia.

General Vitaliy Fedorchuk served as chief of Military Counterintelligence (Third Chief Directorate) and then as KGB chief in the Ukraine. Though he was not known specifically as a Brezhnev protégé, he was close to such Brezhnev KGB men as Tsvigun, Tsinev, and Chebrikov.

General Georgiy Tsinev was deputy KGB chairman by 1970. He graduated from Dnepropetrovsk Metallurgical Institute with Brezhnev and served with him on the First Ukrainian Front during the war, and also had a Military CI background.

General Vadim Matrosov, chief of the Main Directorate of Border Troops. Though technically not a member of the Banda, he was close to others who were.

General Viktor Chebrikov became chief of the KGB Personnel Directorate after being brought in by Brezhnev in 1967. He served in Dnepropetrovsk in the late 1950s and early 1960s. From 1968 to April 1982 he was deputy chairman of the KGB; from April to December 1982, was first deputy chairman; and from December 1982 to the present, has been chairman of the KGB.

On two other institutional levels, Brezhnev retained a "safe" individual and put one of his Banda into another critical post. At the GRU, General Pëtr Ivashutin was kept on as chief, where he had been assigned by Khrushchev after the Penkovskiy counterintelligence scandal. With a Military CI pedigree, Ivashutin had links to Tsinev, Fedorchuk, Tsvigun, and General Aleksandr Yepishev, chief of the Main Political Administration of the Army and Navy and former MGB deputy minister. Ivashutin was viewed as reliable not only by Brezhnev, but apparently by Andropov and Gorbachev. As of this writing, he is still in place. It is worth noting that Soviet Military Intelligence has now been run by former KGB senior officials for the last twenty-eight plus years.

The other individual from Brezhnev's Dnepropetrovsk crowd was General Nikolay Shchelokov, who was brought in to head the Ministry for Maintenance of Public Order (MOOP) in July 1966. Two years later, in an effort to revive the prestige of that ministry and possibly to reestablish it as an institutional counterweight to the KGB, the MOOP was redesignated the Ministry of Internal Affairs (MVD). In view of the growth of the dissident movement in the 1960s, the change was also intended as a message to evoke images of a sterner past. Shchelokov became a close crony of Brezhnev, later being rewarded with the rank of full army general in 1976. He would not last much beyond Brezhnev's death in late 1982. As in the late 1950s and early 1960s, Andropov and then Gorbachev would target the MVD as an engine of corruption in their efforts to have a foil to absorb the blame for the ills of the system that they hoped to jury-rig.

There seems to be no compelling evidence that Brezhnev had any reason to fear that these arrangements were not working or that Andropov was attempting to align the KGB with some anti-Brezhnev faction as the Shelepin–Semichastnyy team had done. It was not until the last year of Brezhnev's long occupancy that evidence surfaced of an Andropov-linked conspiracy. In the interim, Andropov had carried the service through the reorientation and restructuring begun by Khrushchev and Shelepin. On the whole, his efforts must be judged successful. But, what he did *not* do was elevate state security over the party as some writers recently have suggested.[37]

It is instructive to look at the accomplishments insofar as these were beneficial to the long-term survival interests of the party and state security itself. Andropov successfully built on the renovations begun by Shelepin by transforming the KGB into an effective servant of the party in the tradition of the counterintelligence state. This restoration and renaissance removed the tarnish and pathos of de-Stalinization. Internally, this was accomplished with the steady and unrelenting drive against political, intellectual, nationality, and religious dissidence, accompanied by the expansion of the labor camp system, internal exile, and the use of psychiatric wards. Andropov accommodated this by a tightening of the criminal codes. Thus, it was easier for the KGB to intrude into broader reaches of Soviet society to prosecute offenders and to spread itself into areas hitherto reserved for other state agencies.[38] Where the codes got in the way, they were ignored. Mironov's legacy, if it were bona fide, did not survive the plane crash in 1964.

Andropov was not content to just raise the *image* of the service; he wanted to *codify* its elevation. In 1956 the Supreme Soviet had "legally" established the KGB as a state committee under, or attached to, the Council of Ministers. This codified the 1954 decree by the same body. Then in July 1978, the wording on subordination was changed by a new law making the KGB a "state committee of the

USSR."[39] Not only was the KGB elevated back to ministerial status with the prestige that this entailed, but the legal change made its unique relationship to the party even more specific. Party and legal texts had always stressed that the KGB was a *political* organ and therefore in a unique alignment relative to other state institutions. The "KGB *of* the USSR" underscored that distinction. Prime Minister Aleksey Kosygin, then chairman of the Council of Ministers, reportedly contested the name change, even though he exercised no control over the service through his ministerial structure.[40] It could be that he sensed that Andropov would bid for power by employing his KGB base.

Externally, Andropov concentrated on improving the KGB's performance (1) in the areas of scientific and technical intelligence acquisition; (2) by the expansion of General Agayants's active measures work begun under Khrushchev and Shelepin; and (3) by enhancing the direct-action capacity and programs of state security to allow Moscow to better exploit the so-called national liberation struggles and other revolutionary and terrorist movements. In this latter area the party and KGB leadership sensed a convergence of interests with these various tendencies but always at Western expense.

In the first area, Andropov was able to build on an organizational infrastructure already in existence at the time of the Penkovskiy affair. Penkovskiy was a GRU officer assigned to the GKNT, the State Committee for Science and Technology, a collector and central processor for Western technology. The same organization exists today but as part of an expanded condominium embracing the following.[41]

Politburo–Central Committee—Council of Ministers

Ministry of Defense—General Staff—GRU

Military Industrial Commission (VPK)—key defense manufacturing ministries

KGB—East European intelligence services

GKNT

Academy of Sciences

Ministry of Foreign Trade

State Committee for Foreign Economic Relations (GKES)

other defense manufacturing ministries

In this condominium of collectors and users of science and technology data and hardware, an elaborately coordinated process of collection tasking, validation, acquisition, and utilization by the appropriate design bureau and defense industry is overseen by the highest political levels. The principal coordinator for this overall operation is the Military Industrial Commission (VPK, Voyenno-promyshlennaya Kommissiya), which orchestrates the development of Soviet weapons and the national-level program to acquire pertinent Western technology. The KGB serves, with the GRU, as the principal collector of both data and hardware although at least four other national entities and the East European services contribute. Additionally, KGB officers in the other organizations (such as the GKNT) expand the KGB role in the process even further.

Andropov, in his fifteen-year tenure as KGB chief, was a major architect in the design of this elaborate mechanism. Despite its cumbersome appearance, it works remarkably well, especially in view of standard Soviet bureaucratic performance. Does it produce? Two end-use results are offered as examples.[42]

Approximately 70 percent of the documents and hardware acquired in the tenth and eleventh five-year plans (to date), judged by Moscow to be the most significant to their military research projects, probably were embargoed, export controlled, classified, or under some sort of Western government control.

Two ministries (for defense industry and aviation industry) realized their greatest savings in research project costs from 1976 to 1980—almost one half billion rubles (or $800 million at 1980 dollar cost of equivalent research activity). Manpower savings translate roughly into over a hundred thousand man-years of scientific research. Despite a Soviet tendency to inflate savings, these figures appear conservative.

When Agayants organized the KGB's Department D in 1959, state security already had been in the business of provocational manipulation as part of its counterintelligence tradition since the Lockhart

Plot of 1918. However successful the Trust and other operations proved to have been, the organizational focus for such actions appeared to approach the casual, albeit centralized at the highest levels. Agayants and his KGB superiors retained the centralization, but instituted a programmatic mechanism to assure continuity, a relationship of active measures to party policy and strategy, and a long-term vision to allow state security to target the enemy on a long-term basis. One of Agayants's first operations in the context of these guidelines was to fragment NATO, or at the least to drive a wedge between certain of the key NATO members. The French were his principal target. Whether or not Agayants and his Department D should receive all or any credit for the French withdrawal from active military participation in the alliance, Agayants and his creation received recognition for something. Agayants died a KGB general in the late 1960s. By 1971 his creation was no longer a department but a service (*sluzhba*), a higher-level structure denoting larger size, scope, and responsibility.[43] Both promotions occurred during the first years of Andropov's chairmanship of state security.

More was to come. The 1970s and 1980s seemed to explode with KGB initiatives or KGB exploitation of popular movements or grievances, all in the noncommunist world. From forgeries, to the anti-neutron warhead campaign, to penetration agents cum influence agents (Arne Treholt, Pierre-Charles Pathe), to the anti-INF modernization campaigns in Western Europe[44]—Service A and the International Department carried Agayants's creation far beyond the Bessedovskiy fabrications of the 1950s. It seems that in every area to which Andropov pushed the KGB, the ensuing operations were marked by a gigantism of scale.

In 1971, Oleg Lyalin defected from the Soviet Embassy in London where he had been a KGB officer, under legal cover, from Department V, or the wet affairs department.[45] Following his defection the Soviets were forced to call back officers from around the world because of compromise. It was generally felt that the KGB went out of the assassination and sabotage business because of Lyalin's disclosures and because they had developed a distaste for direct-action operations. Wish preempted fact, as it turned out.

A little over a decade later another KGB defector, via Iran, updated the skeptics.[46] Vladimir Kuzichkin was from the Illegals Directorate (Directorate S) of the KGB and brought the information that Department V was alive and kicking (or shooting), had been hidden in Directorate S for security, and was now called Department Eight. Not only that, it had been involved in the training of foreign terrorists at Soviet camps, the commander of one of these having carried out the operation to kill President Hafizullah Amin in Afghanistan in December 1979. The commander, a colonel, died in the operation.

Not only Department Eight of the KGB, but major elements of the GRU have the forces and the ability to mount special operations or direct-action missions and to support insurgencies and terrorist groups with weapons, training, and logistics. The GRU deploys sizable special operations forces (*voyska spetsial'nogo naznacheniya*, or spetsnaz) organized as Spetsnaz Brigades (900–1200 men) stationed in the Soviet military districts, the four Soviet fleets, in groups of forces outside the USSR, and in Afghanistan. The GRU operates these forces, but the KGB has responsibility under Politburo and Central Committee guidance for the operational planning, coordination, and political control of such forces in peacetime.[47] Whereas the GRU focuses on military targets for direct-action operations, the KGB's Department Eight would direct its clandestine assets primarily to civil targets for assassination and wartime sabotage. Additionally, the GRU's spetsnaz capability embraces two major elements for supporting and studying insurgencies and "national liberation" movements, including training facilities within the USSR and Third World countries.

It seems that here, too, Andropov enlarged on a tradition bequeathed him by his predecessors, going back to Yezhov's precedent. When Yezhov created the Administration for Special Tasks, its principal mission was to externally project the purge psychosis then under way in the USSR. The activities of his mobile teams in Europe in the 1930s were an extreme form of external counterintelligence. Under Andropov the direct-action tradition, like technology acquisition, became carefully structured, was expanded considerably, especially in its military (spetsnaz) dimension, and was subjected to a scrutinizing top–down command chain. Nor were the satellites and surrogates left out. Counterpart entities are found in most East European states (always within the intelligence and security organs) and such surrogates as Cuba and Vietnam. The "intimacy" of the connection between those services and the KGB is such that the former must be considered extensions (intimacy depending on the country), of Soviet state security. It is therefore difficult to impute ignorance to Moscow for operations conducted by those services.

I observed earlier that despite the powers that accrued to the KGB under Andropov, I felt that it had not supplanted or overshadowed the party. One hears about the Polish example where the military for all practical purposes is running the country. Couldn't one argue for the same type of development in the USSR, but with the KGB, not the military, in charge? Two things militate against that. First, the party is not moribund (yet) in the Soviet Union, and second, whereas the Polish military still evokes positive, patriotic responses among many Poles, the KGB enjoys nowhere near such prestige in the USSR.

There were clear signs that the KGB was being used by Andropov in the months before Brezhnev's death in a rather open effort to "propel" the succession. There was the *Avrora* affair in early 1982 in which the publication by that name in Leningrad ran a lightly masked satire on aged leaders who would not step down. There was the investigation of Brezhnev's daughter and son for bribery, corruption, illegal speculation, and misuse of state funds. The expanding dimensions of the investigation and scandal precipitated a heated clash between KGB First Deputy Chairman Tsvigun (Brezhnev's brother-in-law) and Mikhail Suslov. On 19 January 1982 Tsvigun died suddenly at KGB headquarters. Rumors floated that he committed suicide because of his impossible position relative to the investigation of "his" family. Tsvigun's obituary was *not* signed by Brezhnev, whereas he did sign those of far lesser figures.[48] Then a week later Suslov "suddenly" died. He had been in good health. An increasingly critical campaign against corruption in the MVD had become even shrill—Brezhnev's son-in-law, Yuriy Churbanov, was first deputy minister there. Something odd was happening, not unlike the harassment of Khrushchev in his last year as first secretary. The succession process had been accelerated by Andropov and he was using his KGB to help it along.

Interestingly, Andropov first placed Vitaliy Fedorchuk, former Ukrainian KGB boss, in the KGB chairman's seat when Andropov moved up to the secretariat in May 1982. But in December 1982, a month after Brezhnev's death and Andropov's actual succession, Fedorchuk moved over to the MVD and was told to clean house. In Fedorchuk's place Andropov elevated Viktor Chebrikov, first deputy KGB chairman and a former Dnepropetrovsk Mafia associate of Brezhnev! Chebrikov was made army general, but not until the following November. Then in December he was brought into the Politburo as a candidate member. Finally in April 1985 he became a full voting member, more than a year after Andropov's death.

Throughout all of this Andropov and his successor once removed, Gorbachev, continued their anticorruption campaigns long after taking charge. The MVD, again, became a highly visible target; Minister of the Interior Nikolay Shchelokov was not only fired, but was dropped from the Central Committee in June 1983. Numerous other firings occurred, with the replacements arriving from—the KGB. It was rumored that Shchelokov later committed suicide.

This chapter began with General Serov's dismissal as KGB chief and concluded with Andropov's arrival at the pinnacle of the party pyramid, only to be brought low by the vagaries of health. In that space of twenty-five years the KGB was revitalized after the "humiliation" of de-Stalinization, and was groomed as the party's cutting edge. As the leading organ in the defense of the counterintelligence state it has been granted unique privileges by the party relative to the rest of Soviet society. It has a vested interest in perpetuating its preferred place in that system.

9

Conclusions: Whither the Counterintelligence State?

On Continuities and Discontinuities

The Bolsheviks and their Cheka learned some interesting but incorrect lessons from the last years of tsarist Russia. By the early twentieth century the worst of tsarist despotism had passed into history. The continued erosion of autocratic power appeared to be the norm. Had not World War I intervened and applied the brakes to this liberalization, it is fascinating to speculate on what might have developed. But it was not to be. The Bolsheviks had learned to emulate tsarism's declining, but worse, side: its political police. At the same time they displayed complete contempt and hatred for the positive face of the system, namely the growing political freedom and economic improvement.

However, Bolshevik abuses and arrogance did not stop there. The tsarist police, for all their arbitrary acts (and incompetence compared to their successor), operated under relatively restrictive constraints, especially when compared with what followed. The courts, after all, were independent of the police and were known for their surprising leniency with political offenders. The Bolsheviks recognized such restrictive "defects" and used them to their advantage, ultimately to overcome the Provisional Government that had expanded such "defects." When they came to power, the Bolsheviks ensured that such "defects" were engineered out of their system. Police power became ascendant, a throwback not to the recently collapsed autocracy of

Nicholas II, but rather to an earlier, darker Muscovite tradition. The Cheka had more in common with Ivan the Terrible's Oprichnina than it had with the Okhrana. Police and state became coterminous.

Political liberalization was not merely halted, it was proscribed. Kadets, anarchists, liberals, Mensheviks, Social Revolutionaries—all were hounded with a hatred and vengeance that smacked of the demonic. The Bolsheviks and their Cheka, the counterintelligence state, reversed the polarity of what had been. Now the police were ascendant and political liberalization obliterated.

Wherever Soviet clone-states emerge, this same pattern repeats itself—whether it is a Cuba or Nicaragua in Latin America, or an Ethiopia or Angola in Africa. The first two products exported to such states invariably are a party or party-type movement to organize and focus political power, and a state security apparatus to secure the monopoly of that power, to organize society in an atomized manner to facilitate control, and to commence the search for "enemies of the people." It is also axiomatic, in practice, that general economic impoverishment soon follows. This, too, is enforced by state security, as in the collectivization and terror-famine of the 1930s in the USSR. The pedigree of the Ethiopian famine traces back to the Ukraine. The counterintelligence state can generate political power and the security to protect it. It cannot generate economic welfare for the common good; but, then, that is not what communist systems are about.

The Durability of the Counterintelligence State

Despite the trendiness of Andropov's and Gorbachev's anticorruption campaigns and the latter's *glasnost'* initiatives, the essential reality of the Soviet system has altered little in its operational demeanor. The state is still above society and the party–state security phalanx sits at the apex of state elites. Analogies are frequently made to the period of "the thaw" under Khrushchev. We forget, however, that under Khrushchev the KGB was still being "disciplined" as part of de-Stalinization and was undergoing reorientation back to the operational style of the Dzerzhinskiy era. The KGB of the Andropov–Gorbachev period has long been rehabilitated and once more is the cutting edge of the party, a circumstance pointedly repeated by the party and KGB alike. This is nowhere better illustrated than by the number of KGB–MVD delegates at Khrushchev's last party congress (the twenty-second, in 1961) and at the most recent congress (the twenty-seventh, in 1986). In 1961 a total of twelve KGB–MVD (ten and two respectively) delegates were in attendance. In 1986 the number was thirty-five (twenty-four and eleven, respectively).

This does not mean that the organs now control the party. It does speak for a higher degree of interpenetration of party and state security cadres. The counterintelligence state is not going to liberalize itself out of existence.

A system annealed and perpetuated in conspiracy will not voluntarily dispense with its raison d'être or with nearly a century of an uninhibited pursuit and exercise of power. The KGB, like the Cheka, considers itself the sword and most trusted servant of the party. Those duties entail striking enemies and preserving the system in its core essentials. Both Chekists and party apparatchiks historically have demonstrated that in the face of the most dangerous challenges they can energize the counterintelligence state into confronting the threat frontally, as at Kronstadt, or through strategem, as with the Trust. Afghanistan and *glasnost'* attest to the survival of that tradition.

Appendixes

Appendix A:

Comparisons of Victims in the Last Ninety Years of Tsarist Rule (1826–1917) with the First Phase of the Cheka–GPU–OGPU (1917–24)

LATE TSARIST PERIOD (1826–1917)

Executions

1826–1906: 894[1]
1866–1917: 14,000 approx.[2]
1866–1900: 48[3]; 94[4]
1906 (six months of the Stolypin military field tribunals):   950[5]
1907: 1,139[6]
1908: 1,340[7]
1908–12: 6,000[8]
"Following the 1905–7 Revolution": 11,000[9]
"Eighty years that preceded the Revolution in Russia":   17/year
  (average)[10]

Deaths from Executions, Pogrom Murders, and Deaths in Prison
1867–1917: 25,000[11]

Convicts at Hard Labor
1913: 32,000 (year largest numbers were reached)[12]

Political Exile without Confinement
1907: 17,000 (year largest numbers were reached)[13]

Maximum Number Imprisoned (Criminals and politicals)
1912: 183,949[14]

EARLY SOVIET PERIOD (1917–24)

Executions by Cheka and Tribunals

1917–23:   200,000[15]
1918 & 1st half of 1919:   8,389[16]
1917–20:   12,733[17]
"Civil War":   50,000[18]
1918–19:   1,700,000[19]
1918–23:   2,500,000 per annum[20]

Deaths Caused by Cheka

1917–22:   250,000–300,000[21]

Deaths from the Suppression of "Rebellions" and from Prison and Camp Treatment

1917–24:   300,000[22]

Executions in the Crimea Following General Wrangel's Defeat and Evacuation

1920–21:   50,000–150,000[23]

Hostages and Prisoners in Camps and Prisons (1917–23)[24]

1918:   42,254 hostages/prisoners in camps and prisons[25]
1919 (to July):   44,639 hostages/prisoners in camps and prisons[26]
1918:   47,348 hostages/prisoners in camps and prisons[27]
1919:   80,662 hostages/prisoners in camps and prisons[28]
1920 (late):   25,336 camp inmates plus 24,400 Civil War prisoners;[29] 48,112 prisoners in RFSFR NKYu prisons;[30] 60,000 NKYu prisoners according to commissar of justice[31]
1921 (Jan.):   51,158[32]
1921 (Sep.):   60,457[33]
1921 (Dec.):   40,913;[34] 73,000 prisoners in NKYu prisons [35]
1922 (Oct.):   60,000[36]
1923 (Oct.):   68,297[37]

Note: The first phase of the Cheka–GPU–OGPU ends with Lenin's death in 1924.

[1]M. N. Gernet, ed., *Protiv smertnoy kazni*, 2nd ed. (1907), pp. 385–423, cited in Solzhenitsyn, *Gulag*.
[2]Conquest, *The Human Cost*.
[3]Ibid., citing a confidential tsarist document.
[4]Ibid., citing the *Small Soviet Encyclopedia*, 1st ed.
[5]*Byloye*, No. 2/14 (February 1907), cited in Solzhenitsyn, *Gulag*, p. 301.
[6]Conquest, *The Human Cost*, citing Soviet sources.
[7]Ibid.
[8]Ibid.
[9]Ibid.
[10]Solzhenitsyn, *Warning to the West*, p. 19.
[11]Conquest, *The Human Cost*.

[12]Walkin, "Some Contrasts," p. 60, citing official tsarist figures; and Gsovski, *Soviet Civil Law*, vol. 1, p. 238.

[13]Walkin, "Some Contrasts."

[14]Conquest, *The Human Cost*.

[15]Ibid., p. 11.

[16]Latsis, *Dva goda bor'by*, pp. 74–76. Latsis was a top Cheka official notorious for his bloody pronouncements on class war.

[17]Latsis, *Chrezvychaynye komissii*, pp. 28–29. Latsis clearly was downplaying his own earlier death figures cited in his 1920 piece above. The 8,389 executed during 1918 and the first half of 1919 were from twenty provinces in central Russia. Central Russia certainly was not the locus of the Civil War; the Cheka execution figures for the more volatile and contested areas necessarily were higher.

[18]Chamberlin, *The Russian Revolution*, vol II, p. 75. Chamberlin does not include in his figure "insurgents who were shot down with arms in their hands or people who were killed by mobs or by uncontrolled bands of soldiers and sailors."

[19]Denikin, *The White Army*, p. 292. This figure is no doubt exaggerated, as Latsis's figures are grossly understated. Denikin states, however, that the actual number is "known but to God."

[20]Egeny [sic] Komnin writing in *Roul*, 3 August 1923, cited in Melgounov [Mel'gunov], *The Red Terror in Russia*, pp. 110–11. Komnin's figures are extrapolations based on Bolshevik execution totals for 1920, whence he derived a daily average for each "torture centre" of the Cheka, Tribunals, Military Tribunals, etc. He calculates an average of five persons per day per center. Given approximately 1,000 centers, that yields 5,000 executions per day or 2,500,000 per annum. This is the highest figure I have come across and it far exceeds the Denikin figure of 1,700,000. For the period of 1918 through 1921 it would mean 10,000,000 executions, a reverse mirror of Latsis's gross understatements.

[21]Leggett, *The Cheka*, p. 467, citing Vladimir Brunovskii, a senior Soviet administrator who reported the opinions of top party officials from that period.

[22]Conquest, *The Human Cost*, p. 11. This figure is in addition to the 200,000 executed in 1917–23.

[23]Melgounov, *The Red Terror in Russia*, pp. 75–76; also Mel'gunov *Krasnyy terror v Rossii (1917–1927): Ofitsial'noye proiskhozhdeniye terrora*, manuscript from "Melgunov Collection on the Red Terror," Box 4, Folder 4, Hoover Archives, pp. 17–19. It is unclear in Conquest that Mel'gunov's 1920–21 Crimean executions are included under Conquest's 1917–24 category of deaths from suppressions, etc. (300,000).

[24]As seen from the source citations, these figures are Soviet ones (Cheka, NKYu and NKVD). They are contradictory and understated. Not accommodated by them are the prisoners held in numerous facilities run by the Militia, Cheka, armed forces, and other punitive organs. Also not included in the figures are the penal battalions of the Red Army.

[25]Latsis, *Dva goda bor'by*, p. 76. As noted with the executions, these and the 1919 (to July) figures are only for twenty provinces in Central Russia.

[26]Ibid.

[27]Latsis, "The Truth about the Red Terror," *Izvestiya*, 6 February 1920, cited in Leggett, *The Cheka*, p. 181.

[28]Ibid. As with his earlier execution figures, the two sets of statistics are plainly inconsistent and reflect an effort to soften the negative image of the Cheka. Latsis's second set of figures for 1918 and 1919 do include executions, but only 6,185 and 3,456, respectively. His figures also include total releases of 54,250 for both years.

[29]Central State Archives of the October Revolution, cited in Solzhenitsyn, *Gulag*, vol 2, p. 21.

[30]*Statisticheskii Ezhegodnik RSFSR, 1918–1920*, vol. 8, Vypusk 2, p. 98; cited in Leggett, *The Cheka*, p. 182.

[31]*Sbornik materialov tsentral'nogo karatel'nogo otdela*, No. 1, (Moscow: 1920), pp. 113–30; cited in Gerson, *The Secret Police*, p. 172.

[32]*Vlast' sovetov*, 1922, no. 1–2, p. 41, cited in Leggett, *The Cheka*, p. 178.

[33]Ibid.

[34]Ibid.

[35]*Sotsialistickeskiy vestnik*, no. 13–14 (20 July 1922), p. 8; cited in Gerson, *The Secret Police*, p. 176.

[36]*Vlast' sovetov*, 1922, no. 10, p. 66, cited in Gerson, *The Secret Police*, p. 149.

[37]Central State Archives, cited in Solzhenitzyn, *Gulag*, vol. 2, p. 21.

Appendix B:
Organization for Direct Action (Wet Affairs) in Soviet State Security

Pre-1936	Foreign Department (INO), with tasking and oversight from Stalin and/or his personal secretariat
1936–41	Administration for Special Tasks, NKVD
1941–46	Fourth Directorate (Partisans), NKGB
1946–53	Spets Byuro No. 1, NKGB–MGB
1953–54	Ninth Section, First Chief Directorate, MVD
1954–late 1960s	Department 13, First Chief Directorate, KGB
Late 1960s–early 1970s	Department V, First Chief Directorate, KGB
Early 1970s–present	Department 8, Directorate S (Illegals), First Chief Directorate, KGB

Appendix C:
Selected Significant Defections during General Serov's Tenure as KGB Chief

Defector	Date	Service Component
Grigoriy S. Burlutskiy	June 1953	Border Troops
Yuriy Rastvorov	January 1954	First Chief Directorate
Peter Deriabin	February 1954	First Chief Directorate
Nikolay Khokhlov	February 1954	Wet Affairs
Vladimir & Evdokia Petrov	April 1954	First Chief Directorate
Reino Hayhanen	April 1954	Illegals
Karlo Toumi	February 1958	Illegals
Aleksandr Kaznacheyev	June 1959	KGB Co-optee in Foreign Ministry
Bogdan Stashinskiy	August 1961	Wet Affairs
Mikhail Goleniewski	January 1961	KGB Co-optee in Polish Intelligence (UB)
Anatoliy Golitsyn	December 1961	First Chief Directorate

Note: Includes cases that occurred both before and after Serov's tenure as KGB chief, either while he was Kruglov's deputy or immediately after his dispatch to the GRU. These are included because Serov was or may have been involved with them at their start.

Appendix D:
State Security Leadership

1917–26	Feliks Dzerzhinskiy
1926–34	Vyacheslav Menzhinskiy
1934–36	Genrikh Yagoda
1936–38	Nikolay Yezhov
1938–41 (Feb.)	Lavrentiy Beria (NKVD)
1941 (Feb.)–1941 (July)	Vsevolod Merkulov (NKGB)
1941 (July)–1943 (Apr.)	Lavrentiy Beria (NKVD)
1943 (Apr.)–1946 (Mar.)	Vsevolod Merkulov (NKGB)
1943 (Mar.)–1946 (Oct.)	Viktor Abakumov (SMERSH)
1946 (Mar.)–1946 (Oct.)	Vsevolod Merkulov (MGB)
1946 (Oct.)–1951 (Aug.)	Viktor Abakumov (MGB)
1951 (Aug.)–1951 (Dec.)	Sergey Ogoltsov (Acting; MGB)
1951 (Dec.)–1953 (Mar.)	Semyon Ignatyev (MGB)
1953 (Mar.)–1953 (June)	Lavrentiy Beria (MVD)
1953–54	Sergey Kruglov (MVD)
1954–58	Ivan Serov (KGB)
1958–61	Aleksandr Shelepin
1961–67	Vladimir Semichastnyy
1967–82	Yuriy Andropov
1982 (May)–1982 (Dec.)	Vitaliy Fedorchuk
1982–present	Viktor Chebrikov

Appendix E:
Development of Soviet Intelligence and Security Services

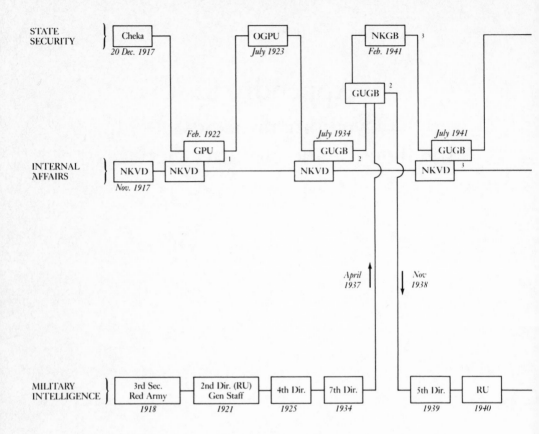

STATE SECURITY }

| Cheka | OGPU | NKGB |
| 20 Dec. 1917 | July 1923 | Feb. 1941 |

GUGB

INTERNAL AFFAIRS }

| NKVD | NKVD | GPU | GUGB | NKVD | GUGB | NKVD |
| Nov. 1917 | | Feb. 1922 | July 1934 | | July 1941 | |

April 1937   Nov 1938

MILITARY INTELLIGENCE }

| 3rd Sec. Red Army | 2nd Dir. (RU) Gen Staff | 4th Dir. | 7th Dir. | 5th Dir. | RU |
| 1918 | 1921 | 1925 | 1934 | 1939 | 1940 |

Copyright © 1985 by John J. Dziak and Raymond G. Rocca.

Note: Over the years the Soviet intelligence and security services experienced a series of fusions, separations, and resubordinations, usually associated with internal party developments and maneuverings. The changes portrayed in this timeline are spelled out at the appropriate chronological points in the body of this book's text. The following notes are offered as brief summaries of these organizational and acronym changes.

[1]In 1922 the Cheka was renamed the State Political Directorate (GPU) and subordinated to the People's Commissariat of Internal Affairs (NKVD). Both organs were headed by Feliks Dzerzhinskiy. This fusion lasted only until 1923, when the United State Political Directorate (OGPU) was separated from the NKVD and headed by Dzerzhinskiy until his death in 1926.

[2]Nine years later, in 1934, state security once more was placed under the NKVD, this time with the title, Chief Directorate for State Security (GUGB), until 1941. During that period, from 1937 to 1938, Soviet military intelligence was controlled by the NKVD–GUGB chief, Nikolay Yezhov. This was at the time when the military, military intelligence, and state security itself were particularly hard hit in the Stalin–Yezhov purges.

[3]In February 1941, a separate People's Commissariat for State Security (NKGB) was created from the GUGB and headed by one of Beria's cronies, V. N. Merkulov. It is believed that this change occurred to more "efficiently" digest the captive populations of the Baltic

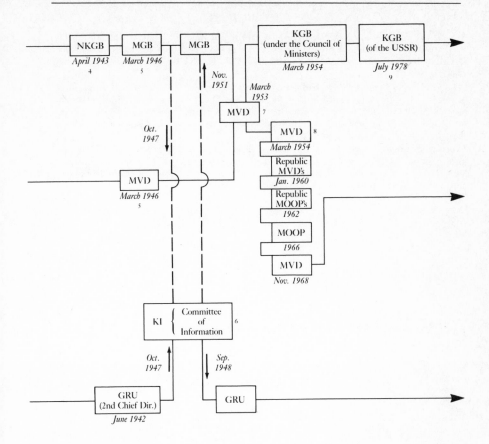

countries, eastern Poland, and the territories of Bukovina and Bessarabia taken from Romania. The German invasion of June 1941 caused Stalin to quickly change back to an NKVD subordinated GUGB, ostensibly for cleaner command lines because of a real danger of collapse of the whole Soviet political system. Beria was NKVD commissar.

[4] Sensing an ultimate victory over the Germans and with the need to reabsorb previously occupied lands and people, state security was once again recreated as a separate commissariat, the NKGB, again under Merkulov. Beria continued as NKVD commissar.

[5] As part of a retitling of all commissariats, the NKGB and NKVD became the Ministry of State Security (MGB) and the Ministry of Internal Affairs (MVD), respectively. V. S. Abakumov headed the MGB until 1951, when he was replaced first by S. I. Ogoltsov and then S. D. Ignatyev. S. N. Kruglov headed the MVD until 1953.

[6] From 1947 until 1951 MGB foreign intelligence functions passed to a new Committee of Information (KI) under the USSR Council of Ministers. GRU foreign intelligence functions likewise were absorbed by the KI, but only from 1947 to 1948. Chairmen of the KI were V. N. Molotov, Ya. Malik, A. Vyshinskiy, and V. Zorin. The idea for the KI apparently came from Molotov and was one of several indicators of a struggle among Stalin's minions. Precedent for the KI may have come from the 1937–38, when Yezhov, as NKVD chief, also directed military intelligence. The experiment was viewed as a failure.

[7] In March 1953, immediately following Stalin's death, Beria caused the MGB and MVD

to be fused into a massive MVD. Beria was arrested in June 1953, but it was not until a year later that the MVD was broken up into a new delimited Committee for State Security (KGB) under the Council of Ministers, and an MVD. The KGB and MVD have not been rejoined since.

[8]The MVD, from 1954 to 1968, had gone through a series of title changes and diminution of stature, including a period from 1960 to 1966 when there was no all-union MVD or all-union MOOP (Ministry for the Maintenance of Public Order), its successor. In 1968 it was retitled MVD. In the period of the Andropov–Gorbachev reforms and *glasnost'*, the MVD came under attacks for corruption.

[9]The latest nomenclature change for state security came in July 1978 when it became known as the KGB of the USSR, succeeding the KGB under the Council of Ministers. This has been interpreted as one element of the steady rehabilitation of the KGB's image and stature and one of the legacies of Andropov's tenure.

Notes

NOTE: Full citations for works mentioned in these notes (with the exception of newspapers) may be found in the selected bibliography.

INTRODUCTION

1. The Soviets prefer that everyone forget that bit of history. When I referred to the 1939 pact and its consequences at an October 1986 symposium on Soviet military history at the U.S. Air Force Academy, I was charged by the Soviets with spreading "disinformation about the prewar policy of the USSR" and repeating the "hackneyed lie that the Soviet–German Treaty of 1939 opened the path to the second world war." *Voyenno-istoricheskiy zhurnal*, no. 3 (March 1987), p. 96.

1. THE FORMATION OF THE STATE SECURITY TRADITION

1. The pervasiveness of the Soviet police state renders it different from the police systems in more traditional, authoritarian societies. The police in the latter systems tend to overtly enforce the political will of a ruling group or clique, frequently allowing important margins of social, cultural, and even ideological elbow room in society. The Soviet system uses the police, among other party–state institutions, to overtly *and* covertly enforce unitary social, cultural, and ideological norms determined and articulated by a single center, the party.

2. On the issue of "Oriental" or "Asiatic" despotism and the USSR as an evocative variation of these, see Wittfogel, *Oriental Despotism*.

3. When the Bolsheviks took power, Russia was still using the Julian calendar. By that time, the "Old Style" calendar, introduced in 46 B.C., was thirteen days behind the "New Style," or Gregorian, calendar that had been generally used in the West since the late sixteenth century. On 1 February 1918 (OS), the Bolsheviks adopted

the Gregorian calendar, and that day became 14 February 1918 (NS). Thus the fact that the anniversary of the "October Revolution" is now celebrated in November.

4. Zinoviev, *History of the Bolshevik Party*, p. 158.

5. Possony, *Lenin*, p. 388.

6. *Vestnik vremenogo pravitel'stva*, 16 June 1917, p. 3. For the full commission report see *Padeniye tsarskogo rezhima*.

7. Smith, *The Young Stalin*, p. 282.

8. Lenin, *Selected Works*, vol. 3, pp. 238, 260–61.

9. Ibid., vol. 8, p. 318. The date here is New Style, as are all dates in this book, unless otherwise noted.

10. *Poslednye novosti*, 1 January 1934, p. 3.

11. Tennant, *The Department of Police*, pp. 26–29.

12. See, for instance, Antonov-Ovseyenko, *The Time of Stalin*, p. 148. See also *Voprosy istorii KPSS*, no. 11, 1965, where Beria's links to the intelligence service of the Moslem Democratic Party (Mussavat) are alleged. This charge was first raised in 1953 when Beria was tried and executed for a variety of treasonous activities. Beria was also charged with serving British intelligence through the Mussavat service and through the Georgian Menshevik government.

13. Medvedev, *Let History Judge*, pp. 312ff.

14. Ibid., p. 312.

15. Mel'gunov and Tsyavlovskiy, *Bol'sheviki*, p. ix.

16. Medvedev, *Let History Judge*, p. 315. For another well-informed dissident's view that gives credence to the same sources dispar-

aged by Medvedev, see Antonov-Ovseyenko, *The Time of Stalin*, pp. 240–41.

17. Orlov, "The Sensational Secret;" Senate Committee on the Judiciary, *The Legacy of Alexander Orlov.*

18. Levine, *Stalin's Great Secret*. A facsimile of the Okhrana letter—also known as the Eremin Letter—was reproduced in the book as well as in the 23 April 1956 *Life* issue (pp. 47–51) that carried Orlov's piece.

19. Litvinov, *Notes for a Journal*. Bessedovskiy, a Soviet diplomat when he defected in Paris in 1929, was the author or suspected author of a number of literary fabrications and was suspected, with cause, of being under Soviet control. On this point see Brook-Shepherd, *The Storm Petrels*, pp. 70–90.

20. Smith, *The Young Stalin*, pp. 308–9.

21. Katkov, *Russia 1917*, pp. 119–32.

22. Bradley, "The Russian Secret Service", p. 243.

23. Bonch-Bruyevich, *Vsya vlast' sovetam*, pp. 55–65.

24. Katkov, *Russia 1917*, pp. 128–29. Keskula, an Estonian Bolshevik and adventurer, was part of the German–Lenin connection that included, among others, Alexander Helphand (Parvus) and Jacob Hanecki (Ganetsky). See Futrell, *Northern Underground*, pp. 119–96; and Carmichael, "German Money and Bolshevik Honor."

25. Golovine, *The Russian Campaign of 1914*, p. 40.

26. *Dekrety*, vol. 1, p. 522.

27. Possony, *Lenin*, p. 167.

28. For the actual protocol, see Belov et al., eds., *Iz istorii*, p. 78.

29. "From Our Moscow Correspondent."

30. Lenin, "Speech Delivered . . .

December 6, 1920."

31. Tishkov, *Perviy chekist*, p. 100. Agabekov, a former member of the INO in 1921, claims that it was then still called the Fourteenth Special Section, which would suggest that there was an institutional predecessor to the INO within the Cheka; Agabekov, *G.P.U. (Zapiski chekista)*, pp. 43–44.

32. Kolakowski, "Marxist Roots of Stalinism," pp. 283–98.

33. Ibid., p. 287. Emphasis added.

34. Ibid., p. 289.

35. Leggett, *The Cheka*, p. 359.

2. THE CLASSICAL PERIOD OF LENIN AND DZERZHINSKIY

1. Tsvigun et al., *V. I. Lenin i VChK*.

2. Ibid., p. 9.

3. For instance, in his dogmatic and dismissive approach to Alexander Orlov's claims on the Stalin–Okhrana file, Medvedev seems unaware that Orlov did not agree with the authenticity of the Eremin letter and so told the editors of *Life* magazine and Isaac Don Levine (Medvedev, *Let History Judge*, pp. 316–18). Medvedev is no less condescending in his handling of the testimony of those Old Bolsheviks and other victims of Stalin who in various ways gave hints or testimony on Stalin's days as a police provocateur (ibid., pp. 315–24). For example, an Old Bolshevik, "G. B——v," wrote to Medvedev, chiding him that [i]t goes against your grain . . . to admit that for thirty years the party was headed by an agent of the tsarist Okhrana. But your counter arguments are not convincing. Stalin knew that if he were exposed and removed from office, he would be shot, as Malinovsky was. But precisely in 1935 certain documents that compromised Stalin came into the hands of some prominent people in the Party . . . and NKVD. . . . However, Stalin forestalled the plans of those who would have exposed him, and they themselves were shot." Medvedev wrote in reply: "G. B——v cites no evidence in support of . . . his allegations. He has none. Therefore there is no reason to reply to them here." (Medvedev, "New Pages," p. 200). Yet Medvedev adduces precisely the same type of evidence in support of his arguments. In fact, G. B——v's statements appear to be concordant with Orlov's information.

4. Medvedev, *The October Revolution*.

5. Pipes, *Russia under the Old Regime*, p. 317.

6. Schapiro, *The Russian Revolution of 1917*, p. 185.

7. Johnson, *Modern Times*, p. 53.

8. The full minute and resolution may be found in Tsvigun et al., *V. I. Lenin i VChK*, pp. 36–37. An earlier, shorter version may be found in Belov et al., eds. *Iz istorii*, p. 78. Belov carries the resolution as a protocol.

9. The actual text of the resolution was not published for external consumption until 1922 in *Izvestiya* (10 February), although it had circulated within the Cheka earlier. Leggett observes that there was only one attempt by the Soviets to label it a decree in 1927, but this was countered by a *Pravda* article the very same day (18 December) by the very same

author (the historian, Pokrovskiy). Leggett, *The Cheka*, pp. 18, 371, 372.

10. Tsvigun et al. *V. I. Lenin i VChK.* In the resolution, a question mark follows the names *Sergo* and *Vasilevskiy.*

11. Lenin, *Collected Works*, vol. 26, p. 109.

12. Ibid.

13. *Dekrety*, vol. 1, p. 124.

14. Matthews, ed., *Soviet Government*, p. 233.

15. Ibid., pp. 233–36.

16. Lenin, *Collected Works*, vol. 26, pp. 501–4.

17. Steinberg, *In the Workshop of Revolution*, p. 145.

18. Lenin, *Collected Works*, vol. 27, pp. 30–35. Emphasis in original.

19. Steinberg, *In the Workshop of Revolution*, p. 146.

20. Golinkov, *Krakh vrazheskogo podpol'ya, pp. 67–68.*

21. "From Our Moscow Correspondent." Dzerzhinskiy may have been speaking of the regular Revolutionary Tribunal. The central Revolutionary Military Tribunal was not formed until October 1918. He seemed to be saying that he was not bound by legalities that were the stuff of the tribunals.

22. Ibid.

23. Ibid.

24. Ibid.

25. Quoted in Belov et al., eds., *Iz istorii*, pp. 182–83.

26. Latsis, *Chrezvychaynye komissii*, pp. 28–29; Robert Conquest, "The Human Cost of Soviet Communism," Senate Committee on the Judiciary (Washington, D.C.: GPO, 1971), p. 11.

27. Both Boris Nikolaevsky and George Leggett have called attention to the suppression of a Chekist literary endeavor, *Krasnaya kniga VChK* (a projected four-volume collection), and the probable destruction of the Cheka archive on orders from Lenin some time in late 1921 or early 1922. See Nikolaevsky, "Iz istorii," and Leggett, "Lenin's Reported Destruction of the Cheka Archives." A rare typescript copy of volume 1 of *Krasnaya kniga VChK* (526 pp.) may be found in the Nikolaevsky collection at the Hoover Archives (files 143-1, 143-2, 143-3). The same collection also holds a rare typescript copy of S. S. Dukel'skiy, *Cheka-GPU*, pt. 1, (Kharkov: Gosudarstvennoy Izdatel'stvo Ukrainy, 1923), 167 pp. Dukel'skiy's volume is one of the few surviving regional imitations of the *Krasnaya kniga* effort, all of which suffered the same fate.

28. Melgounov [Mel'gunov], *The Red Terror in Russia*, p. 111, citing a Professor Sarolea writing in the Edinburgh *Scotsman*.

29. *Vlast' sovetov*, no. 1–2 (1922), p. 42, cited in Leggett, *The Cheka*, p. 178.

30. Pipes, *Russia under the Old Regime*, p. 301.

31. Tennant, *The Department of Police*, p. 5.

32. Ibid., p. 17.

33. *Bol'shaya sovetskaya entsiklopediya*, 3rd ed., vol. 9, p. 120.

34. For greater detail on the Okhrana and its Foreign Agency see Smith, "*The Okhrana*"; Zuckerman, "The Russian Political Police"; and Martynov, *Moya sluzhba.*

35. Zubov, *F. E. Dzerzhinskiy*, p. 183. Another Soviet author gives a

slightly higher figure: "In the initial stages the Cheka was assigned 30 of the most tested and true Red Guards. A little later they were joined by a group of soldiers from the Sveaborg regiment. This small armed detachment was the embryo of the Cheka forces." See Sofinov, *Ocherki*, p. 22.

36. Leggett, *The Cheka*, p. 100. Leggett feels that 37,000 is far too conservative, or about 17,000 below authorized level. Also left out are a central reserve for the Corps of Cheka Troops.

37. Latsis, *Chrezvychaynye komissii*, p. 12 for the 31,000 figure; for the troop figures, M.I.D. report, from Riga, Latvia, no. 02021, 23 September 1921 (20037-10084/5), National Archives, RG 165.

38. "Za chto my boremsia," *Izvestiia vremennogo revoliutsionogo komiteta* (8 March 1921), in *Pravda o Kronshtadte* (Prague: 1921), pp. 82–84, cited in Avrich, *Kronstadt 1921*, p. 241.

39. Ibid., p. 242.

40. "Sotsializm v Kavychkakh," *Izvestiia vremennogo*, in ibid., p. 245.

41. Lenin, *Collected Works*, vol. 45, p. 694.

42. Leggett, *The Cheka*, pp. 353–55.

43. Trotsky, *Stalin*, pp. 305, 417.

44. Wolin and Slusser, eds., *The Soviet Secret Police*, p. 13.

3. THE COUNTERINTELLIGENCE–
ACTIVE MEASURES TRADITION

Portions of this chapter first appeared in Dziak, "Soviet Deception." For incisive coverage on deception as a feature of the Slavic, Russian, and Soviet traditions see Baczkowski, *Toward an*

Understanding of Russia, and Hingley, *The Russian Mind*.

1. According to a former Polish intelligence official, Stetskevich–Kiyakovskiy and Dobrzynskiy–Sosnowskiy came to play major roles in the Trust legend. See Wraga, "Trest"; Voytsekhovskiy, "Trest: Vospominaniya V. T. Drimmer."

2. A recent Soviet work lionized both the Cheka and Artuzov (since rehabilitated) and his role in the Trust. See Gladkov and Zaytsev, *I ya emu ne mogu ne verit'* . . .

3. Rezanov, *Le Travail Secret*, pp. 80–82.

4. "The Embassies and Foreign Affairs," p. 8.

5. Ibid., p. 9.

6. Ibid., p. 8.

7. *Geroi oktyabrya*, pp. 486–87.

8. *Segodnya* (Riga), 27 October 1927.

9. *Segodnya* (Riga), 4 November 1927.

10. N. Chebyshev, "Trest," *Vozrozhdeniye* (5 September 1935).

11. Leggett, *The Cheka*, p. 296. One of these sources, Eduard Opperput (also known as Selyaninov and Staunitz, among other names), was a principal in the Trust and has been the object of intense controversy ever since.

12. Chebyshev, "Trest."

13. Grant, *Dezinformatsiya*.

14. The fiction of Comintern independence of Moscow is no longer seriously debated, but it is still worth noting that Feliks Dzerzhinskiy represented the Polish Communist Party at the Fourth Comintern Congress in 1922, *after having represented the Russian Communist Party at the first three Comintern congresses.*

15. Peters, "Vospominaniya."
16. Kravchenko, "Pervye shagi VChK"; and Kravchenko, "Pod imenem Shmidkhena."
17. Ibid.
18. Lockhart, *British Agent*, pp. 319–22.
19. Ibid., p. 321. Another author, writing in 1971, feels that Lockhart was indeed innocent of the Lockhart Plot, but had been a witting conspirator earlier with Boris Savinkov in other disruptive actions. Debo, "Lockhart Plot or Dzerzhinskiy Plot?"
20. Pimenov, *Kak ya iskal shpiona Reili*. Pimenov, a dissident writer, was supposed to have received a camp sentence for this and other manuscripts.
21. Lockhart, *Reilly*, pp. 13–14.
22. *Novyi zhurnal* (New York) no. 65 (1961), pp. 146–47, cited in Lazich and Drachkovitch, *Lenin and the Comintern*, vol. 1, p. 549.
23. The Okhrana tradition here is raised with caution. Dzerzhinskiy's state security and its successors took counterintelligence type provocations far beyond even the most audacious Okhrana initiatives without losing detailed centralized control. It is inconceivable that the chief of service, the prime minister, and the tsar were ever simultaneously aware of any given Okhrana provocation. In the Soviet context provocations frequently originated and most definitely were overseen by comparable levels of state leadership, from Lenin through Gorbachev.
24. Churchill, *Great Contemporaries*, pp. 103–4.
25. The Soviets have published several versions of their efforts to get Savinkov. The most comprehensive (though unreliable), covering events in both Sindikat I and II, is Ardamatskiy, *Vozmezdiye*. In 1966 the Soviets had serialized a novel about Savinkov by the same Ardamatskiy in *Krasnaya zvezda* (3, 10, 17, and 24 September 1966). In 1922 Opperput, under the name Selyaninov-Opperput, himself apparently published a booklet of what happened to Savinkov's union, titled *Narodnyy soyuz zashchity rodiny i svotody* (Berlin, 1922, no publisher listed). The most recent Soviet account is Gladkov and Zaytesev, *I ya emu ne mogu ne verit'*, pp. 107–43. Each of these accounts, including Opperput's to an extent, contrives to portray Savinkov as unreliable and volatile and to demonstrate the futility of anti-Soviet actions.
26. *Segodnya* (Riga), no. 235, 18 October 1927.
27. Tobenkin, "Boris Savinkov."
28. *Pravda*, 30 August 1924.
29. From the stenographic record of the "Trial of Boris Savinkov," published in *Pravda*, 30 August 1924, trans. and signed by E. Aronsberg, New York City. From the Hoover Archives (TS Russia S 268).
30. Heller, "Krasin–Savinkov." The article includes a reproduction of the Savinkov–Piłsudski letter in Russian.
31. This account of the Trust draws principally from the following sources: Bailey, *The Conspirators*, pp. 1–86; Voytsekhovskiy, *Trest*; Struve, Shulgin, and Voytsekhovskiy, "New about the Trust"; Voytsekhovskiy, "Conversation with Opperput"; Wraga, "The Trust: The History of a Soviet Provoca-

tion"; Burtsev, "Police Provocation in Russia"; and Shulgin, "How I Was Hoodwinked by the Bolsheviks."

32. Lenin, *Selected Works*, vol. 3, pp. 744–46. From Lenin's 27 March 1922 report to the Eleventh RKP (b) Party Congress.

33. Williams, "Changing Landmarks in Russian Berlin."

34. See Wraga, "The Trust." Polish intelligence had a respectable record against the USSR during the interwar period. For instance, from 1920 to 1932 a Polish officer by the name of Poleshchuk had penetrated the Soviet government under the name of "Konar" (a Red Army soldier shot in the Russo-Polish War), rising to a high position in the Commissariat of Agriculture. Interestingly, he reportedly developed a close friendship with Yezhov, who later (1936) rose to the NKVD leadership. It may have been the Konar penetration that confirmed for Piłsudski that the Trust was spurious. See Orlov, *The Secret History*; Fisher, *Men and Politics*; and Rowen, *Terror in Our Time*.

35. See Wraga, "Trest—Vnutrennaya Liniya"; Bailey, *The Conspirators*; and Wraga, "Cloak and Dagger Politics."

4. THE SECOND REVOLUTION: ARMAGEDDON AT HOME

1. *Izvestiya*, 22 March 1925.
2. Leggett, *The Cheka*, p. 364.
3. For a Soviet history of the Special Departments in all their variants (SMERSH, the Third Directorate, and others), see Ostryakov, *Voyennye chekisty*.
4. For a first-hand account by a later member of one of these state security formations see Deriabin, *Watchdogs of Terror*. Soviet accounts of these forces and their origins may be found in Yakovlev et al., *Vnutrenniye voyska*; and Belikov et al., *Imeni Dzerzhinskogo*.
5. For some trenchant accounts of this phenomenon, see Hollander, *Political Pilgrims*, chaps. 3 and 4; Carynnyk, "The Famine," pp. 32–40; and Conquest, *The Harvest of Sorrow*, pp. 308–21.
6. Deutscher, *Stalin*, p. 325.
7. Belikov, *Imeni Dzerzhinskogo*, pp. 46–62.
8. Akhmedov, *In and Out of Stalin's GRU*, pp. 80–81.
9. Interviews with Ismail Akhmedov, 7 and 21 June 1985; and ibid., p. 81.
10. Lyons, *Assignment in Utopia*, pp. 489–90.
11. Ibid., p. 490.
12. Conquest, *The Harvest of Sorrow*, pp. 237, 327–28.
13. Ibid., p. 301.
14. Ibid., p. 303.
15. Orlov, *The Secret History*, p. 28.
16. Ibid.
17. Nicolaevskiy, *Power and the Soviet Elite*.
18. Stalin, "Speech to the Seventeenth Party Congress," p. 629.
19. The most complete study of this organization under Stalin is Rosenfeldt's *Knowledge and Power*. See Schapiro, "The General Department," pp. 53–65; and Bazhanov, *Avec Staline*.
20. Orlov, *The Secret History*, pp. 6–8.
21. Ibid., ch. 1.
22. Krivitsky, *In Stalin's Secret Service*, p. 183.
23. Ibid., pp. 183–84.
24. Ibid., ch. 1.
25. For instance, of the top six

NKVD officials directly under Yagoda—Ya. Agranov, V. Balitsky, T. Deribas, G. Prokofiev, S. Redens, and L. Zakovskiy—only Prokofiev was not an Old Bolshevik. For the revolutionary pedigrees of these men, see Conquest, *Inside Stalin's Secret Police*, chap. 1.

26. Krivitsky's accounts of Soviet actions in Spain played heavily on his claimed personal role in certain clandestine enterprises there (arms procurement). This was largely hype and is generally attributed to his ghostwriter and publishers. See the 1984 preface by William Hood to Krivitsky, *In Stalin's Secret Service*.

27. These include not only Conquest's *The Harvest of Sorrow* and *Inside Stalin's Secret Police*, but Solzhenitsyn's *The Gulag* and the works of such important on-scene observers as Antonov-Ovseyenko, *The Time of Stalin*; and Gnedin, *Iz istorii otnosheniy*. The massive and penetrating history of the USSR, Heller and Nekrich's *Utopia in Power*, by two former Soviet historians, also utilizes Orlov's and Krivitsky's accounts and confirms them from other sources.

28. *The Soviet Secret Police*, edited by Wolin and Slusser, remains one of the core writings on the subject, though the chronicle carries only through the immediate post-Stalin era. Conquest's *The Great Terror*, *Inside Stalin's Secret Police*, and *The Harvest of Sorrow* are considered the definitive Western analyses for the 1930s.

29. Petrov and Petrov, *Empire of Fear*, p. 69.

30. Conquest, *The Great Terror*, pp. 497–98; and Ponomarev, *The Plot*.

31. Orlov, *The Secret History*, p. 141;

and Fischer, *Men and Politics*, pp. 227–28. Fischer claims that Stalin probably held Yagoda responsible for the penetration. Orlov insists the entrée was through Yezhov.

32. From "Khrushchev's Secret Speech," carried as app. 4 in *Khrushchev Remembers*, p. 575.

33. *Pravda*, 27 September 1936.

34. *Pravda*, 4 April 1937.

35. Antonov-Ovseyenko, *The Time of Stalin*, p. 124.

36. Petrov and Petrov, *Empire of Fear*, pp. 73–74.

37. Ibid., p. 74.

38. Ibid., pp. 74–75. The Petrovs do not identify Lyushkov by other than Lt. B——. However, they do admit that B—— later was in charge of NKVD frontier troops in the Far East whence he defected to Japan. The commander was General Lyushkov. He provided the Japanese with valuable intelligence on the political and military situation in the USSR. Lyushkov was reported to have been executed at the end of World War II by the Japanese. Other rumors had him disappearing in Manchuria in 1945 when the Soviets invaded.

39. Ivanov-Razumnik, *Memoirs*, p. 149.

40. Krivitsky, *In Stalin's Secret Service*, p. 232. Krivitsky cites 35,000. See also Erickson, *The Soviet High Command*, pp. 505–6. Erickson gives a range of 15,000–30,000 out of an officer corps of 75,000–80,000. He opts for 20,000–25,000 military victims for the period of late summer 1937 to late autumn 1938.

41. Rapoport and Alexeev, *High Treason*, pp. 277–78.

42. Petrov, *Partiinoye stroitel'stvo*, pp. 298–317.

43. Krivitsky, *In Stalin's Secret Service*, chaps. 1 and 2; Antonov-Ovseyenko, *The Time of Stalin*, pp. 186–87.

44. Orlov, "The Sensational Secret."

45. Krivitsky, *In Stalin's Secret Service*, p. 230.

46. Orlov, "The Sensational Secret," p. 38.

47. 6 June 1954, Memo of SAC, New York to Director FBI re SAC interviews with Alexander Orlov on 1/11/54, 2/16/54, and 5/18/54.

48. Orlov, "The Sensational Secret," p. 38.

5. THE SECOND REVOLUTION: THE EXTERNAL DIMENSION

1. *Sotsialisticheskiy vestnik*, No. 8–9, (August–September 1959), p. 171 (pp. 167–72 for whole article).

2. *Byulleten' oppozitsii*, no. 11 (May 1930), pp. 10–11.

3. Serge, *Memoirs*, pp. 356–57.

4. Orlov, *The Secret History*, pp. 192–93. Orlov gives the impresion that Blyumkin was a bona fide Trotskyite. But Blyumkin had a rather strange career in state security, beginning as a Left Socialist Revolutionary when he assassinated Count Mirbach, the German ambassador, in 1918. There are strong suspicions that this itself was a Cheka provocation because Blyumkin was allowed to continue in state security long after the other Left SR Chekists had been purged. As for Liza Gorskaya, the OGPU woman who entrapped Blyumkin, she later became Mrs. Vasili Zubilin (alias Zarubin, among others). He was an important state security operative who conducted atomic espionage

efforts in the United States in the early 1940s. See Dallin, *Soviet Espionage*, pp. 405–6.

5. Stalin, *Works*, vol. 10, August–December 1927, p. 193.

6. Schapiro, *The Communist Party of the Soviet Union*, p. 306.

7. Orlov, *The Secret History*, p. 311.

8. Ibid., pp. 311–12.

9. Sayers and Kahn, *The Great Conspiracy*, p. 227. This particular work is a pro-Soviet slant on, among others, Sidney Reilly, Savinkov, the Trust, and Trotsky and the Opposition—dubbed "Russia's Fifth Column" by the authors. The book, basically a period piece of Stalinist historiography, devotes a lot of space to alleged anti-Soviet intrigues of Trotsky and his followers. The book was promoted by the CPUSA; Soviet sponsorship of the book was identified in congressional testimony in 1952 by Igor Bogolepov, a former Soviet foreign affairs official who says he saw the original manuscript at the Foreign Ministry in Moscow before it was sent to the United States. See Senate Committee on the Judiciary, pp. 4513–14.

10. They were also known as Sobol, Schmidt, Well, Sobolev, Senin, and Sobolevich. Sons of a wealthy Jewish–Lithuanian merchant, they were most likely already OGPU agents before showing up in the Trotskyite movement in the later 1920s. They publicly broke with Trotsky in 1932–33, declaring for Stalin.

11. For accounts of these splitting activities see Vereeken, *The GPU*, pp. 16–31. This is a Trotskyist work that suffers from an inability to draw the appropriate conclu-

sions from the evidence it adduces: that the Soblen brothers were OGPU operatives from the very beginning, sent to spy on, manipulate, and disrupt the Trotsky movement. See also Deutscher, *The Prophet Outcast.*

12. A fair amount is known of the Zborowskiy penetration of the Trotskyite movement. I have drawn principally on the following: Senate Committee on the Judiciary, *Scope of Soviet Activity,* pp. 77–101, 103–36; Senate Committee on the Judiciary, *The Legacy of Alexander Orlov,* pp. 9–10, 16, 20–23, 27–31, 35–36, 38–41, 73; Vereeken, The GPU, chap. 1; Dallin, "Mark Zborowski, Soviet Agent."

13. Vereeken, *The GPU,* p. 378.

14. Senate Committee on the Judiciary, *The Legacy of Alexander Orlov,* pp. 20–22. More recently, another source has disclosed that, unrelated to the Dallin–Orlov event, Bernaut *did* warn Zborowskiy, this time of FBI interest in his actions after she was questioned by the FBI about him. See Lamphere Shachtman, *The FBI–KGB War,* pp. 87–88.

15. *The Legacy of Alexander Orlov,* pp. 18–20. David Dallin, in a two-part article two years after he and Lilia met with Orlov, wrote a scathing piece on Etienne–Zborowskiy, accusing him of complicity in NKVD murders, among other serious crimes. Other than admitting knowing Zborowskiy, he provides no details on either his or Lilia's relationship with the man. Neither does he refer to his and Lilia's meeting with Orlov; however, he refers to Orlov's warning to Trotsky but gives Orlov the pseudonym of "Nick Pavlov." See Dallin, "Mark Zborowski, Soviet Agent."

16. Deutscher, *The Prophet Outcast,* p. 349.

17. Ibid.

18. Senate Committee on the Judiciary, *Scope of Soviet Activity,* pp. 95–96.

19. Ibid., pp. 94–95.

20. Dallin, "Mark Zborowski, Soviet Agent," p. 9.

21. Ibid., p. 95.

22. Dallin, "Mark Zborowski, Soviet Agent," p. 16.

23. The charge and the trial are written up in Kravchenko's second book, *I Chose Justice,* 1950. *I Chose Freedom* was published in 1946.

24. See Heller and Nekrich, *Utopia in Power,* chaps. 6 and 7, for one of the most incisive treatments of this phase of Soviet foreign policy.

25. Krivitsky, *In Stalin's Secret Service,* p. 2.

26. Gnedin, *Iz istorii otnosheniy,* pp. 22–27.

27. This diplomat, one Gelfand, passed this on to a British diplomat following the former's defection. British Foreign Office, file 24845, p. 47, document 371. Quoted in Heller and Nekrich, *Utopia in Power,* p. 322.

28. Krivitsky, *In Stalin's Secret Service,* p. 10; Gnedin, *Iz istorii otnosheniy,* p. 37.

29. Heller and Nekrich, *Utopia in Power,* p. 327.

30. Krivitsky, *In Stalin's Secret Service,* pp. 12–15.

31. Artuzov and a number of his old Cheka colleagues killed during the purges have been rehabilitated. They are lionized in the Gladkov

and Zaytsev's *I ya emu ne mogu ne verit'.* . . .

32. A set of the 1934–36 documents is held at the Hoover Institution, Stanford, California, under the title "Postanovleniia Politbiuro VKP(b)." This collection of alleged Politburo resolutions covers the period from 27 January 1934 to 14 March 1936. Originals are in handwritten Russian with verbatim German translations. English translations are from the Russian and German copies. The Russian and German copies were acquired together.

33. Bertram Wolfe and Alexander Orlov were vociferous believers that the documents were forgeries. Detailed correspondence between Wolfe and a researcher by the name of Milton Loventhal—a believer in the documents—may be found in the "Postanovleniia Politbiuro VKP(b)" archive at the Hoover Institution.

34. 13 September 1945 Memorandum (Secret), from Captain O. J. Lissitzyn to Dr. G. T. Robinson, subject *Materials from Germany,* RG226, entry 1, box 5, "USSR Division–1945" Folder, National Archives.

35. Bessedovskiy's book, *Na putyakh" K" termidoru,,* went through English, French, and German editions and versions. All troublesome, they deal with his official experiences and the circumstances of his defection. A pungent examination of Bessedovskiy may be found in Brook-Shepherd, *The Storm Petrels,* chap. 5.

36. See the lengthy exchange of correspondence between Wolfe and Milton Loventhal, a supporter of the authenticity of the Politburo documents, Bertram D. Wolfe Collection, box 103, file 103-6, "Literary forgeries and Mystifications—Correspondence—Loventhal."

37. Brook-Shepherd, *The Storm Petrels,* p. 89.

38. For example, see the 2 July 1924 Riga dispatch No. 2244 (National Archives, N.A. 861.00/10403).

39. N.A. 861.00/10208; N.A. 861.00B/201; N.A. 861.00B/316; N.A. 861.00/10404; N.A. 861.00/10434; N.A. 861.00/10382.

40. Brook-Shepherd, *The Storm Petrels,* p. 59.

41. Ibid., pp. 59–61.

42. See Reyman, "Agent v politbyuro."

43. Reyman, "Agent v politbyuro," 8 (1985), p. 68.

44. Hoover Archives, "Postanovleniia Politbiuro VKP(b)." Apparently only two documents from 1931 and 1933 showed up in the German materials held in the U. S. National Archives, which led researchers to concentrate on those covering the 1934–36 period. Unaware of the Gaidouk documents and the large number surfaced by Reyman for 1931–33, analysts such as Milton Loventhal and Bertram Wolfe argued over the authenticity of only one piece of a broader mosaic.

45. N.A. 861.00B/316 (14 April 1925).

46. Reyman, "Agent v politbyuro," 8 (1985), pp. 72–73.

47. Ibid., p. 74.

48. Ibid., p. 75.

49. Reyman, "Agent v politbyuro," 9 (1985), p. 37.

50. "Postanovleniia Politbiuro VKP

(b), " 24 October 1934, 7 November 1934, 10 November 1934.

51. Ibid., 5 November 1934; 24 May 1934. This latter resolution was to be kept "absolutely secret from all comrades" because of its exceptional nature, that is, for tactical reasons "the Soviet government must, for a while, stop being communist in its acts and measures. . . ."

52. Ibid., 24 October 1934.

53. Loventhal and McDowell, *Soviet Intelligence Material*, p. 18; and Loventhal, "The Politburo's Resolutions," no date, 7 pp., box 4, "Postanovleniia Politbiuro VKP(b)."

54. Loventhal and McDowell, *Soviet Intelligence Material*, p. 19.

55. Ibid.

56. Ibid., p. 21, citing Alfred Rosenberg, *Das politische Tagebuch Alfred Rosenbergs* (Göttingen: Musterschmidt Verlag, 1956), p. 29.

57. Natalie Grant, *Disinformation*, unpublished manuscript, 1980, pp. 25–34.

58. Ibid., p. 31.

59. Loventhal and McDowell, *Soviet Intelligence Material*, pp. 15, 19; letter of Witold S. Sworakowski to Henri E. Ruffin, Washington, D.C., 20 June 1956, in "Postanovleniia Politbiuro VKP(b)," box 3.

60. Letter of Bertram Wolfe to Milton Loventhal, 14 September 1960, Hoover Archives, Bertram D. Wolfe Collection, box 103.

61. Letter of Bertram Wolfe to Milton Loventhal, 17 October 1960, Hoover Archives, Bertram D. Wolfe Collection, box 103.

62. Ibid.

63. Agursky, "Soviet Disinformation and Forgeries."

64. Ibid., p. 22.

65. *Der Stern*, no. 47 (19 November 1967), p. 142.

66. Hilger and Meyer, *The Incompatible Allies*, p. 256.

67. Wraga, *Disinformation*, pp. 35–36.

68. Senate Committee on the Judiciary, *The Legacy of Alexander Orlov*, pp. 147–48.

69. Krivitsky, *In Stalin's Secret Service*, p. 239. Skoblin was linked to the Nazi SD through the Guchkov Circle, a group of Russian émigrés around Aleksandr Guckhov, former Duma member and plotter against Nicholas II. Though linked to the SD, the circle was also penetrated by the NKVD.

70. Rapoport and Alexeev, *High Treason*, pp. 258–62; Conquest, *The Great Terror*, pp. 300–302.

71. Bailey, *The Conspirators*, pt. 2. Conquest, in his *The Great Terror*, feels that this "definite 'proof' of treason seems now to have produced a final decision on the conduct of the blow against the generals," p. 302.

72. Krivitsky, *In Stalin's Secret Service*, chap. 7; Rapoport and Alexeev, *High Treason*, pp. 325–26.

73. Brook-Shepherd, *The Storm Petrels*, pp. 63–69.

74. Wraga, "Trest"; *Segodnya* (Riga), 2 November 1927.

75. *Krasnaya zvezda*, 22 September 1965. Emphasis added. The author of this item, Colonel General of Air Reserves N. Shimanov, chastizes another Soviet writer for giving Puzitskiy only two lines out of a 263-page book. The other writer was Lev Nikulin, whose book *Mertvaya zyb'* dealt with the Trust and ROVS.

76. Valtin, *Out of the Night*.

77. Gitlow, *The Whole of Our Lives*, pp. 343–44.
78. Heller and Nekrich, *Utopia in Power*, p. 352.
79. There is considerable confusion over the activities of the two Eitingon brothers. Mark was linked to Nadezhda Plevitskaya and her husband General Skoblin. However, a Soviet dissident work has Naum as the one who probably recruited Plevitskaya in 1919 and directed the kidnappings of Generals Kutyepov and Miller. See Rapoport and Alexeev, *High Treason*, app. 5. Other sources that finger Mark as the one linked to Plevitskaya are *Vozrozhdeniya* (9 December 1938), and "The Case of General Miller," unsigned Russian manuscript (December 1937).
80. James Yuenges, "Brutality, Terror Emerge in Soviet Spy Apparatus," *Chicago Tribune* (21 November 1971).
81. Ibid.
82. Details on this penetration and sketches of Skoblin and Plevitskaya may be found in B. Pryanishnikov, *Nezrimaya pautina* (Silver Spring, Md.: published by author, 1979); see also Fedor Raskolnikov's "Open Letter to Stalin," in *Sotsialisticheskiy vestnik* (19 October 1939). Raskolnikov had been Soviet ambassador to Bulgaria when he defected during the purges. He too died under mysterious circumstances in Nice; also, Wraga, "Trest—Vnutrennaya Liniya."
83. *Vozrozhdeniya* (9 December 1938); Bailey, *The Conspirators*, chap. 12.
84. Bailey, *The Conspirators*, p. 257.
85. Rapport and Alexeev, *High Treason*, app. 5.
86. "The Case of General Miller," unsigned manuscript, 14 December 1937.
87. Krivitsky, *In Stalin's Secret Service*, pp. 213, 239.
88. Nekrich, "Stalin and the Pact with Hitler."
89. Ibid.

6. WAR AND EXPANSION

1. Conversations with Peter Deriabin, former MGB officer, May 1984.
2. G. M. Maksimov, ed., *Vsesoyuznaya perepis' SSSR 1970: Statistika* (Moscow, 1976), cited in Dyadkin, *Unnatural Deaths*, p. 16.
3. "Glavnoye Upravlenie Kontrrazvedki," *Sovetskaya voyennaya entsiklopediya*, vol. 2 (Moscow: Voyenizdat, 1976), p. 564.
4. A very credible history of SMERSH may be found in Stephan, "Death to Spies." Stephan lists all the political security reasons for the creation of the organization.
5. Ostryakov, *Voyenniy chekisty*, pp. 178–79.
6. Conversations with Deriabin, May 1984; see also Deriabin's *Watchdogs of Terror*, chap. 6.
7. Bor-Komorowski, *The Secret Army*, pp 46–47.
8. Karski, *Story of a Secret State*, chaps. 2 and 3.
9. Buber, *Under Two Dictators*, p. XII.
10. The most definitive study of the Katyn massacre is Zawodny's *Death in the Forest*. Among the senior NKVD officials suspected of major roles in the Katyn massacre under Beria were Merkulov,

Kruglov, Zarubin, Serov, and Raikhman. Of these the latter two are especially suspect because of their roles in the deportations of millions from the annexed territories during the Hitler–Stalin Pact and the deportations of suspect peoples during the war. Serov survived Beria and went on to command both the KGB (1954–58) and the GRU (1958–63). Raikhman was promoted to general in 1945 but was arrested in 1954 in the purge of Beria's lieutenants. Deriabin feels that Raikhman was the NKVD commander in charge of the actual operation (discussions with Deriabin, May 1984).

11. Kahn, *The Codebreakers*, p. 1083, fn. 650.

12. McSherry, *Stalin, Hitler, and Europe*, vol. 2, p. 229.

13. The relevant telegrams are found in the National Archives (N.A. 105-104/113116, 113131, 113283). Others of the Ponschab telegrams pertinent to this issue include 113116-7, 113138, 113257, 113283, 113293, 113323, 113331, 113383, 113409, 113417, 113424, 113431, 113432, 113434, 113435, 113437, 113438, 113441, 113445, 113451, 113463, 113465, 113469, 113471.

14. Conquest, (*Inside Stalin's Secret Police*, p. 156), observes that General Mikhail M. Gvishiani, one of the most notorious of Beria's henchmen, not only survived but apparently escaped prison as well. Penkovskiy claims that Gvishiani was a distant relative of Stalin (*The Penkovskiy Papers*, p. 170). Gvishiani's son, Dzermen, was Penkovskiy's superior in the GKNT, the State Committee for Science and Technology, a major S&T intelligence collection coordinating body. Young Gvishiani was married to Kosygin's daughter. Conquest feels that the elder Gvishiani may have protected Kosygin during the notorious Leningrad case in the late 1940s and that Kosygin may then have protected Gvishiani when Khrushchev was killing Beria's thugs in the 1950s. Dzermen Gvishiani later became chief of the GKNT.

15. Anders, *Memoires*, p. 86.

16. This is why the contemporary Defense Council appears so important to analysts of Soviet strategic leadership. Today's Defense Council is based, by Soviet account, on its World War II analogue, the GKO. Then and now, the KGB chairman is a member.

17. V. F. Nekrasov, "Vklad vnutrennikh voysk," p. 29.

18. War Department, *Handbook*, pp. iv–4.

19. E. A. Andreevich, "Structure and Function of the Soviet Secret Police," in Wolin and Slusser, eds., *The Soviet Secret Police*, p. 135.

20. War Department, *Handbook*, pp. iv–5.

21. Interview with Ilya Dzirkvelov, June 1986. Dzirkvelov said this organization was a special assault unit called the Pervaya Osobaya Diviziya or "First Special Division."

22. Wolin and Slusser, eds., *The Soviet Secret Police*, pp. 20, 248.

23. Erickson, *The Road to Stalingrad*, pp. 378–79.

24. Senate Committee on the Judiciary, *The Legacy of Alexander Orlov*, pp. 25, 70, 75.

25. Aleksandrovskaya, *My internatsion-alisty*, pp. 46–58.

26. Interview with Ismail Akhmedov, former GRU officer, June 1985.

27. Penkovskiy, *The Penkovskiy Papers*, pp. 69–70.

28. Suvorov, *Soviet Military Intelligence*, pp. 136–40.

29. An excellent analysis of these aspects of partisan war is found in Gaerlitz, *Der zweite Weltkrieg*, pp. 57–171.

30. This section is drawn from the following works: Aleksandrov, et al., eds., *Partiya vo glave*; Belikov, et al., *Imeni Dzerzhinskogo*; Emelyanov, *Sovietskiye podvodnye lodki*; Endzheyak and Kuznetsov, *Osobaya partizansko-diversionnaya*; Manayenkov, et al., eds., *Partizanskie formirovaniya Belorussii*; Fyodorov, *The Underground R. C. Carries On*; Abwehr (Ostfront), *Organisation und Aufgaben*; deWitt, *The Role of Partisans*; Yudin, *Pervaya partizanskaya*.

31. Discussion with Ilya Dzirkvelov, June 1986.

32. The cases summarized here first appeared as part of a chapter of mine that appeared in Dailey and Parker, eds., *Soviet Strategic Deception*, chap. 1.

33. Reference number SAIC/R/2, 24 June 1945; RG238. Records of the National Archives Collection of World War II War Crimes, entry 160, SAID/R/2, folder 87 (box 18).

34. See Kahn, *Hitler's Spies*, pp. 312–17, 335, 368–69; Gehlen, *The Service*, pp. 57–58. The most incisive summary of the MAX case is found in Thomas, "The Legend of Agent 'MAX'." Also see CSDIC Special Interrogation Report No. 1716, 9 August 1945, "Notes on

Gruppe I Luft"; CSDIC Special Interrogation Report No. 1727, 16 September 1945, "Notes on Abwehr I, Appendix I"; CIA, no date, "The German Intelligence Service and the War," declassified report, National Archives, per FOIA; U.S. Army Intelligence and Security Command, Richard Kauder, interrogation file, No. XE O111758, National Archives, per FOIA; and U.S. Political Advisor for Germany, "Russian Emigre Organizations," 10 May 1949, NA RG 59 861.20262/5-1049.

35. Gehlen, *The Service*, pp. 57–58.

36. Pincher, *Their Trade Is Treachery*, pp. 104–7.

37. Front Reconnaissance Unit 103, Report No. 90/45, 12 February 1945, to General Staff of the Army/Foreign Armies East [translation of FHO Report German Records Group, National Archives, Washington, D.C.]. See also Sevin, "Operation Scherhorn."

38. Rositzke, *The CIA's Secret Operations*, pp. 169–72; and Powers, *The Man Who Kept the Secrets*, pp. 41–43.

39. Tawcas, *Guerrilla Warfare*.

40. Bethell, *Betrayed*; and Philby, *My Silent War*. Philby discusses the Anglo-American Albanian venture, but says nothing of his treacherous role in compromising it.

7. TRANSITION, 1946–58

1. Some authorities feel that despite Beria's postwar decline he still exercised significant influence over the security organs. See Hing-

ley, *The Russian Secret Police*, p. 203; Conquest, *The Soviet Police System*, p. 21; Levytsky, *The Uses of Terror*, p. 178; Commonwealth of Australia, *Report*, p. 433.

2. Deriabin, *Watchdogs of Terror*, p. 313.

3. Ibid.

4. Petrov and Petrov, *Empire of Fear*, p. 210.

5. Ibid., p. 431.

6. *Sovetskaya voyennaya entsiklopediya*, vol. 1, p. 620.

7. Allilueva, *Tol'ko Odingod*, p. 134; Deriabin, *Watchdogs of Terror*, p. 371.

8. *Pravda*, 13 January 1953.

9. Ibid., and *Izvestiya*, 13 January 1953.

10. *Pravda*, 23 July 1954.

11. Conquest, *Power and Policy*, p. 190.

12. *Pravda*, 13 October 1952.

13. Deriabin, *Watchdogs of Terror*, chap. 7.

14. *Izvestiya*, 17 February 1953.

15. *Pravda*, 4 March 1953.

16. *Izvestiya*, 6 March 1953.

17. Deriabin, *Watchdogs of Terror*, pp. 326–27; Khrushchev, *Khrushchev Remembers*, pp. 316–320.

18. *Pravda*, 7 March 1953.

19. Deriabin, *Watchdogs of Terror*, p. 328. Soviet sources are silent on the role of the MGB troops in Stalin's succession and prefer to concentrate on their prewar and World War II exploits. See, for instance, Belikov, et al., eds., *Imeni Dzerzhinskogo*; and "Vnutrenniye voyska," *Sovetskaya voyennaya entsiklopediya*, vol. 2 pp. 164–65.

20. Khrushchev, *Khrushchev Remembers*, p. 338.

21. Ibid., p. 336.

22. Deriabin, *Watchdogs of Terror*, pp.

332–33; and Medvedev and Medvedev, *Khrushchev*, p. 10.

23. Medvedev and Medvedev, ibid., p. 7.

24. Deriabin, *Watchdogs of Terror*, p. 333.

25. Medvedev and Medvedev, *Khrushchev*, p. 10; Deriabin, ibid., p. 332.

26. *Pravda*, 17 December 1953.

27. *Pravda*, 10 July 1953.

28. *Pravda*, 17 December 1953.

29. *Pravda*, 24 December 1953. They were executed by firing squads.

30. Medvedev and Medvedev, *Khrushchev*, p. 10.

31. *Pravda*, 24 December 1954. This case was tried in Leningrad.

32. The organizational structure outlined here relies on Artemiev and Viktorov, *Organizatsiya*; Intelligence Division, *Survey*; and Wolin and Slusser, eds., *The Soviet Secret Police*.

33. *Pravda*, 28 April 1954.

34. Medvedev, *Khrushchev*, pp. 113–14.

35. *Pravda*, 15 February 1956.

36. *XXs"ezd KPSS*, p. 95.

37. *Pravda*, 15 February 1956.

38. From a declassified CIA report to the general counsel of the President's Commission on the Assassination of President Kennedy, in "From Azeff to Agca."

39. See Khokhlov, *In the Name of Conscience*, 365 pp. The Russian edition of this work is considerably larger and more detailed. See *Pravo na sovest'*, 612 pp.

40. Khokhlov, *Pravo na sovest'*; Barron, *KGB*, pp. 311–15.

41. Senate Committee on the Judiciary, *Murder International, Inc.*

42. Discussions with Ilya Dzirkvelov, June 1986. Dzirkvelov, a former KGB officer involved in such

operations, reported that within the KGB they did not use the term "wet affairs," which had a purely criminal connotation, but rather *voyennaya podgotovka* or "military drill."

43. Barron, *KGB*, p. 310.
44. "Coups and Killings in Kabul"; Barron, *KGB Today*, pp. 15–16, 445.

8. THE RETURN TO DZERZHINSKIY

Portions of this chapter dealing with Shelepin, Mironov, Agayants, and the reorientation of the KGB first appeared in my "Soviet Deception."

1. Penkovskiy, *The Penkovskiy Papers*, chaps. 2, 5, 6, and 7.
2. Medvedev and Medvedev, *Khrushchev*, p. 77.
3. *Krasnaya zvezda*, June 1957.
4. Penkovskiy, *The Penkovskiy Papers*, p. 272.
5. Hood, *Mole*, chap. 25.
6. Golitsyn, *New Lies for Old*, chap. 6. Golitsyn is central to one controversy that is still raging, that is, the bona fides of KGB defector Yuriy Nosenko, and is criticized for his persistent view of the Sino-Soviet split as a grand deception. Nonetheless, his grasp of internal party–KGB interaction and his own participation in KGB actions in Finland make him a valuable source of primary information. For a broader critique of Golitsyn's work see my review essay "Soviet 'Active Measures.' "
7. See Manokhin, ed., *Sovetskoye administrativnoye pravo*, chap. 36–39.
8. Grant, *Dezinformatsiya*, chap. 9; Brook-Shepherd, *The Storm Petrels*, chap. 5; Agursky, "Soviet Disinformation and Forgeries." Dzirkvelov contends that Agayants also had the charge, at that time, to organize direct action (for example, sabotage) in Western Europe and that Agayants wanted to make his operation stronger and more effective than Sudoplatov's. Discussions with Dzirkvelov, June 1986.
9. Golitsyn, *New Lies for Old*, pp. 48–49. The conference was reported in *Pravda*, 18 May 1959, but without the details Golitsyn provided. Several months later it was written up in an émigré journal: Minyailo, "The Conference of the State Security Organs."
10. Sejna, *We Will Bury You*.
11. Discussions with General Sejna, 1978–80.
12. Ibid.
13. Bittman, *The Deception Game*, p. 86.
14. Ibid., pp. 112–13, 153–55.
15. Discussions with Ladislav Bittman, June 1984.
16. Penkovskiy, *The Penkovskiy Papers*, p. 275.
17. See *Voprosy istorii KPSS*; *Partinaya zhizn*'; and Mironov's *Ukrepleniye*.
18. For instance: *Feliks Edmundovich Dzerzhinskiy 1877–1926*; Belov et al., eds., *Iz istorii*; Sofinov, *Ocherki*; Zubov, *F. E. Dzerzhinskiy*; Fomin, *Zapiski starogo chekista*; and Viktorov, *Podpol'shchik voin, chekist*.
19. For more of these works lionizing the service see Rocca and Dziak, *Bibliography on Soviet Intelligence and Security Services*; and Library of Congress, *Soviet Intelligence and Security Services*.
20. Heller and Nekrich, *Utopia in Power*, p. 605; and Solzhenitsyn, *The Oak and the Calf*, pp. 98–100, 554.

21. Solzhenitsyn, *The Gulag*, 3, pp. 507–14. Solzhenitsyn is one of very few writers in the West to call attention to the riots and repressions in Novocherkassk. But his account was originally written in the USSR and then published in the West—but not until 1978. The only other Western account that appeared fairly close to the event was that by Boiter, "When the Kettle Boils Over."

22. Alexeeva and Chalidze, *Mass Rioting in the USSR*, p. 129 b.

23. Solzhenitsyn, *Gulag*, p. 510.

24. Alexeeva and Chalidze, *Mass Rioting in the USSR*, pp. 74–78.

25. Ibid.

26. Kozlov et al., *Sovetskoye administrativnoye pravo* (1968), p. 524.

27. Kozlov et al., *Sovetskoye administrativnoye pravo* (1973), p. 532.

28. Bakhov et al., *Upravleniye*, pp. 77–78.

29. Cited in Tatu, *Power in the Kremlin*, p. 390.

30. Medvedev and Medvedev, *Khrushchev*, p. 172.

31. Tatu, *Power in the Kremlin*, p. 412. The Medvedevs give legal sanction to the coup claiming that "the organizers took elaborate care to keep all measures within the limits of constitutional and Party procedure and to avoid any possible cause for unrest in the country at large." (*Khrushchev*, p. 173). It is unusual to find the Soviet constitution invoked to legitimize a palace coup by a party faction. The very fact that the conspirators felt constrained to wait until Khrushchev was away from Moscow and then prevent him from turning to the Central Committee for support suggests something less than

constitutional was afoot. In the final analysis, the Soviet constitution is not the fundamental law of the land.

32. *Pravda*, 16 October 1964.

33. Solzhenitsyn, *The Oak and the Calf*, p. 98.

34. *Krasnaya zvezda*, 20 October 1964.

35. Discussions with General Sejna, Winter 1980.

36. For more details on these men see the following: Deriabin with Bagley, "Fedorchuk, the KGB, and the Soviet Succession"; *Sovetskaya voyennaya entsiklopediya*, vols. 1–8; Beichman and Bernstam, *Andropov*; Zemtsov, *Andropov*; Knight, "Andropov."

37. Corson and Crowley, *The New KGB*; and Solovyov and Klepikova, *Behind the High Kremlin Walls*.

38. See Alexeeva, *Soviet Dissent*; Podrabinek, *Punitive Medicine*; Kaminskaya, *Final Judgment*; Grigorenko, *Memoirs*; and Bukovsky, *To Build a Castle*.

39. *Pravda*, 8 July 1978. The new law applied to a number of other state committees as well but the significance for the KGB was greater because of its sensitive missions.

40. Deriabin with Bagley, "Fedorchuk, the KGB, and the Soviet Succession," p. 627.

41. See Department of Defense, *Soviet Acquisition of Militarily Significant Western Technology*.

42. Ibid., p. 6.

43. See Barron, *KGB*.

44. See Shultz and Godson, *Dezinformatsia*. Arne Treholt, a high official in Norway's Foreign Ministry, was sentenced to twenty years' imprisonment for his service to the KGB. Pierre-Charles Pathe

was tried and convicted of espionage in France in 1979. Both men, but especially Pathe, were also viewed by many observers as agents of influence.

45. On the Lyalin affair see Barron, *KGB*, pp. 320–21. This portion of the chapter draws on Dziak, "Military Doctrine and Structure," pp.

77–92; and Dziak, "The Soviet Approach to Special Operations," 95–133.

46. "Coups and Killings in Kabul" for a complete account of Kuzichkin's interview.

47. Department of Defense, *Soviet Military Power 1987*, p. 89.

48. *Pravda*, 21 January 1982.

Selected Bibliography

Abwehr (Ostfront). *Organisation und Aufgaben des sowjetischen Geheimdienstes im Operationsgebiet der Ostfront*. 1944. (Abwehr manual from German archives, declassified 15 August 1946)

Agebekov, G. *G.P.U. (Zapiski chekista)*. Berlin: Izdatel'stvo "Strela," 1930.

Agursky, Mikhail. "Soviet Disinformation and Forgeries: An Historical Background." Paper presented at Soviet Active Measures, a conference sponsored by the USIA, 10–11 March 1987, American Cultural Center, Jerusalem, Israel.

Akhmedov, Ismail. *In and Out of Stalin's GRU: A Tatar's Escape from Red Army Intelligence*. Frederick, Md.: University Publications of America, 1984.

Aleksandrovskaya, S. M. *My internatsionalisty*. Moscow: Politizdat, 1975.

Aleksandrov, P. A., et al., eds. *Partiya vo glave narodnoy bor'by v tylu vraga, 1941–1944*. Moscow: Izdatel'stvo "Mysl'," 1976.

Alexeeva, Ludmilla, and Valery Chalidze. *Mass Rioting in the USSR*. Report 19, prepared for the Office of Net Assessment, Department of Defense. Silver Spring, Md.: The Foundation for Soviet Studies, January 1985.

Alexeeva, Ludmilla. *Soviet Dissent: Contemporary Movements for National, Religious, and Human Rights*. Middletown, Conn.: Wesleyan University Press, 1985.

Allilueva, Svetlana. *Tol'ko odin god*. Translated by Paul Chavchavadze. London: 1969.

Anders, Władysław. *Memoires, 1939–46*. Translated from the Polish by Jan Rzewuska. Paris: 1948.

Anin, David. "Lenin and Malinovsky." *Survey* 21, no. 4 (97) (Autumn 1975), pp. 145–156.

Antonov-Ovseyenko, Anton. *The Time of Stalin: Portrait of a Tyranny*. Translated by George Saunders. New York: Harper & Row, 1981.

Ardamatskiy, V. I. *Vozmezdiye*. Moscow: Molodaya Gvardiya, 1968.

Artemiev, V. P., and G. M. Viktorov. *Organizatsiya i deyatel'nost' KGB i MVD*. Oberammergau, West Germany: Detachment "R," U.S. Army, 1962.

Avrich, Paul. *Kronstadt 1921*. New York: W. W. Norton, 1974.

Baczkowski, Wlodzimierz. *Toward an Understanding of Russia: A Study in Policy and Strategy*. Jerusalem: Lipshutz Press, 1947.

Bailey, Geoffrey. *The Conspirators*. New York: Harper & Bros., 1960.

Bakhov, A. S., et al. *Upravleniye v oblasti administrativno-politicheskoy deyatel'nosti.* Moscow: Izdatel'stvo "Yuridicheskaya Literatura," 1979.

Barron, John. *KGB: The Secret Work of Soviet Secret Agents.* New York: Reader's Digest Press, 1974.

————. *KGB Today: The Hidden Hand.* New York: Reader's Digest Press, 1983.

Bazhanov, Boris G. *Avec Staline dans le Kremlin.* Paris: Les Editions de France, 1930.

Beichman, Arnold, and Mikhail S. Bernstam. *Andropov: A New Challenge to the West.* New York: Stein and Day, 1983.

Belikov, I. G., et al. *Imeni Dzerzhinskogo.* Moscow: Voyenizdat, 1976.

Belov, G. A., et al., eds. *Iz istorii vserossiyskoy chrezvychaynoy komissii 1917–1921 gg. Sbornik dokumentov.* Moscow: Gospolitizdat, 1958.

Bessedovskiy, Grigoriy Z. *Na putyakh" k" termidoru.* Paris: Mishen', 1930.

Bethell, Nicholas. *Betrayed.* New York: Times Books, 1985.

Bittman, Ladislav. *The Deception Game.* New York: Ballantine Books, 1981.

Boiter, Albert. "When the Kettle Boils Over." *Problems of Communism* (January–February 1964).

Bol'shaya sovetskaya entsiklopediya. 3rd ed. Moscow: Sovetskaya Entsiklopediya Izd., 1970–78.

Bonch-Bruyevich, M. D. *Vsya vlast' sovetam.* Moscow: Voyenizdat, 1957.

Bor-Komorowski, T. *The Secret Army.* London: Victor Gollanz Ltd., 1950.

Bradley, J. F. N. "The Russian Secret Service in the First World War." *Soviet Studies* 20, no. 2 (October 1968), pp. 242–48.

Brook-Shepherd, Gordon. *The Storm Petrels.* New York: Ballantine Books, 1982.

Buber, Margarete. *Under Two Dictators.* New York: Dodd, Mead & Co., 1949.

Bukovsky, Vladimir. *To Build a Castle.* Translated by Michael Scammell. New York: Viking Press, 1978.

Burtsev, Vladimir. "Police Provocation in Russia." *The Slavonic Review* 6 (December 1927), pp. 311–20.

Carmichael, Joel. "German Money and Bolshevik Honor." *Encounter* 42, no. 3 (March 1974), pp. 81–90.

Carynnyk, Marco. "The Famine the 'Times' Couldn't Find," *Commentary* (November 1983), pp. 32–40.

"The Case of General Miller," Author and publisher unknown, 14 December, 1937.

Chamberlin, William Henry. *The Russian Revolution.* 2 vols. New York: Grosset & Dunlap, 1935/1965.

Chebyshev, N. "Trest." *Vozrozhdeniye* (5 September 1935).

Churchill, Winston S. *Great Contemporaries.* New York: Putnam, 1937.

Committee on Public Information, The (George Creel, chairman). *The German–Bolshevik Conspiracy.* War Information Series, no. 20 (October 1918). Washington, D.C.: U.S. Government.

Commonwealth of Australia. *Report of the Royal Commission on Espionage,* 22 August 1955. Sydney: Government Printer for New South Wales, 1955.

Conquest, Robert. *The Great Terror.* Rev. ed. New York: Macmillan, 1973.

————. *The Harvest of Sorrow: Soviet Collectivization and the Terror-Famine.* New York: Oxford University Press, 1986.

————. "The Human Cost of Soviet Communism," prepared for Senate Committee on the Judiciary, Subcommittee to Investigate the Administration of the Internal Security Act and Other Internal Security Laws. Washington, D.C.: GPO, 1971.

————. *Inside Stalin's Secret Police: NKVD Politics, 1936–1939*. Stanford: Hoover Institution Press, 1986.

————. *Power and Policy in the USSR*. New York: Harper and Row, 1967.

————. *The Soviet Police System*. New York: Praeger, 1968.

Corson, William R., and Robert T. Crowley. *The New KGB: Engine of Soviet Power*. New York: William Morrow & Co., Inc., 1985.

"Coups and Killings in Kabul." *Time* (22 November 1982), pp. 33–34.

Dailey, Brian D., and Patrick J. Parker, eds. *Soviet Strategic Deception*. Lexington, Mass.: Lexington Books, 1987.

Dallin, David J. "Mark Zborowski, Soviet Agent." *The New Leader* (19 March 1956), pp. 8–10; (26 March 1956), pp. 15–16.

————. *Soviet Espionage*. New Haven, Conn.: Yale University Press, 1955.

Dallin, David J., and Boris I. Nicolaevsky. *Forced Labor in Soviet Russia*. New Haven, Conn.: Yale University Press, 1947.

Debo, Richard K. "Lockhart Plot or Dzerzhinskiy Plot?" *Journal of Modern History* 43, no. 3 (September 1971), pp. 413–39.

Dekrety sovetskoy vlasti. Vol. 1. Moscow: Voyenizdat, 1957.

Denikin, Anton I. *The White Army*. London: Jonathan Cape, 1930.

Department of Defense. *Soviet Acquisition of Militarily Significant Western Technology: An Update*. Washington, D.C.: Department of Defense, 1985.

————. *Soviet Military Power 1987*. Washington, D.C.: GPO, 1987.

Deriabin, Peter. *Watchdogs of Terror*. 2nd ed. Frederick, Md.: University Publications of America, 1984.

Deriabin, Peter, with T. H. Bagley, "Fedorchuk, the KGB, and the Soviet Succession." *Orbis* (Fall 1982), pp. 611–35.

Deutscher, Isaac. *The Prophet Outcast: Trotsky, 1929–1940*. New York: Oxford University Press, 1963.

————. *Stalin: A Political Biography*. New York: Vintage Books, 1962.

deWitt, Kurt. *The Role of Partisans in Soviet Intelligence*. Maxwell Air Force Base, Ala.: Human Resources Research Institute, War Documentation Project, 1954.

Dukel'skiy, S. S. *Cheka-GPU*. Pt. 1. Kharkov: Gosudarstvennoy Izdatel'stvo Ukrainy, 1923, 167 pp. In the Hoover Archives.

Dyadkin, Iosif G. *Unnatural Deaths in the USSR, 1928–1954*. New Brunswick, N. J.: Transaction Books, 1983.

Dziak, John. "Military Doctrine and Structure." In *Hydra of Carnage*. Edited by Uri Ra'anan et al. Lexington, Mass.: Lexington Books, 1986.

————. "Soviet 'Active Measures'." *Problems of Communism* 33 (November-December 1984), pp. 66-69.

————. "The Soviet Approach to Special Operations." In *Special Operations in U.S. Strategy*. Edited by Frank R. Barnett et al. Washington, D.C.: National Defense University Press and the National Strategy Information Center, 1984.

————. "Soviet Deception: The Organizational and Operational Tradition." In *Soviet Strategic Deception*. Edited by Brian D. Dailey and Patrick J. Parker. Lexington, Mass.: Lexington Books and Hoover Institution Press. 1987.

————. "Soviet Intelligence and Security Services in the 1980s: The Paramilitary Dimension." In *Intelligence Requirements for the 1980s: Counterintelligence*. Edited by Roy Godson. Washington, D.C.: National Strategy Information Center, 1980.

"The Embassies and Foreign Affairs." *The Whitehall Gazette and St. James Review* (May 1926), pp. 6–9.

Emelyanov, A. *Sovietskiye podvodnye lodki v Velikoi Otechestvennoi Voine*. Moscow: Voyenizdat, 1981.

Endzheyak, V., and A. Kuznetsov. *Osobaya partizansko-diversionnaya*. Kiev: Politizdat Ukrainiy, 1977.

Erickson, John. *The Road to Stalingrad*. New York: Harper & Row, 1975.

————. *The Soviet High Command*. London: St. Martin's Press, 1962.

Feliks Edmundovich Dzerzhinskiy 1877–1926. Moscow: Marx-Engels-Lenin Institute, 1951.

Fischer, Louis. *Men and Politics: An Autobiography*. New York: Duell, Sloan & Pearce, 1941.

Fomin, F. T. *Zapiski starogo chekista*. Moscow: Politizdat, 1962; 2nd ed., 1964.

"From Azeff to Agca." *Survey* 27 (118/119) (Autumn–Winter 1983), pp. 1–89.

"From Our Moscow Correspondent." *Novaya zhizn'*, 9 June 1918, p. 4 (signed by B. Rossov). From the Bertram Wolfe Collection, Hoover Archives, box 110, file 110-2.

Futrell, Michael. *Northern Underground: Episodes of Russian Revolutionary Transport and Communications through Scandinavia and Finland 1863–1917*. London: Faber & Faber, 1963.

Fyodorov, A. *The Underground R. C. Carries On*. 2 vols. Moscow: Foreign Language Publishing House, 1949–50.

Goerlitz, Walter. *Der zweite Weltkrieg, 1939–1945*. Stuttgart: Steingrubon-Verlag, 1952.

Gehlen, Reinhard. *The Service*. New York: World Publishing, 1972.

Geroi oktyabrya: Biografii aktivnykh uchastnikov podkotovki i provedeniya oktyabrskogo voorozhennogo vosstaniya v Petrograde. Vol. 1. Leningrad: Leninizdat, 1967.

Gerson, Leonard D. *The Secret Police in Lenin's Russia*. Philadelphia: Temple University Press, 1976.

Gitlow, Benjamin. *The Whole of Our Lives*. New York: Charles Scribner's Sons, 1948.

Gladkov, Teodor, and Nikolay Zaytsev. *I ya emu ne mogu ne verit'*. . . . Moscow: Politizdat, 1983, 1986.

Gnedin, Evgeniy. *Iz istorii otnosheniy mezhdu SSSR i fashistkoy Germaniey*. New York: Izdatel'stvo "Khronika," 1977.

————. *Katastrofa i vtoroye rozhdeniye*. Amsterdam: Fond Imeni Gertsena, 1977.

Golinkov, D. L. *Krakh vrazheskogo podpol'ya: Iz istorii bor'by s kontrrevolyutsiyey v sovetskoy Rossii v 1917–1924 gg*. Moscow: Izdatel'stvo Politicheskoy Literatury, 1971.

Golitsyn, Anatoliy. *New Lies for Old: The Communist Strategy of Deception and Disinformation*. New York: Dodd, Mead & Co., 1984.

Golovine, Nicholas N. *The Russian Campaign of 1914*. Ft. Leavenworth, Kans.: The Command and General Staff School Press, 1933.

Gouzenko, Igor. *The Iron Curtain*. New York: E. P. Dutton, 1948.

Grant, Natalie. *Dezinformatsiya*. Unpublished manuscript. Lovettsville, Va., 1974. Used with permission.

———. *Disinformation*. Unpublished manuscript. Lovettsville, Va., 1980. Used with permission.

Grigorenko, Petro, G. *Memoirs*. Translated by Thomas P. Whitney. New York: W. W. Norton, 1982.

Gsovski, Vladimir. *Soviet Civil Law*. Vol. 1. Ann Arbor: University of Michigan Law School, 1948.

Heller, Michel. "Krasin–Savinkov: Une Rencontre Secrete." *Cahiers du Monde Russe et Sovietique* 26 (i) (January–March 1985), pp. 63–67.

Heller, Mikhail, and Aleksandr M. Nekrich. *Utopia in Power: The History of the Soviet Union from 1917 to the Present*. New York: Summit Books, 1986.

Hilger, Gustav, and Alfred G. Meyer. *The Incompatible Allies*. New York: Macmillan, 1953.

Hingley, Ronald. *The Russian Mind*. New York: Charles Scribner's Sons, 1977.

———. *The Russian Secret Police: Muscovite, Imperial Russian, and Soviet Political Security Operations, 1565–1970*. New York: Simon & Schuster, 1971.

Hollander, Paul. *Political Pilgrims*. New York: Harper Colophon, 1983.

Hood, William. *Mole*. New York: W. W. Norton, 1982.

Intelligence Division, General Staff, U.S. Army. *Survey of Soviet Intelligence and Counterintelligence*. Washington, D.C. 9 January 1948. Declassified NND770011.

Ivanov-Razumnik, R. V. *The Memoirs of Ivanov-Razumnik*. Translated and annotated from *Tyur'my i ssylki*, by P. S. Squire. London: Oxford University Press, 1965.

Johnson, Paul. *Modern Times: The World from the Twenties to the Eighties*. New York: Harper & Row, 1983.

Kahn, David. *The Codebreakers*. New York: Macmillan, 1967.

———. *Hitler's Spies*. New York: Macmillan, 1978.

Kaminskaya, Dina. *Final Judgment: My Life as a Defense Attorney*. Translated by Michael Glenny. New York: Simon & Schuster, 1982.

Karski, Jan. *Story of a Secret State*. Boston: Houghton Mifflin, 1944.

Katkov, George. "German Foreign Office Documents on Financial Support to the Bolsheviks in 1917." *International Affairs* 32, no. 2 (April 1956), pp. 181–89.

———. *Russia 1917: The February Revolution*. New York: Harper & Row, 1967.

Khokhlov, Nikolai Y. *In the Name of Conscience*. Translated by Emily Kingsbury. New York: David McKay Co., 1957.

———. *Pravo na sovest'*. Frankfurt am Main: Possev Verlag, 1957.

Khrushchev, Nikita S. *Khrushchev Remembers*. Introduction and commentary by Edward Crankshaw; translated and edited by Strobe Talbott. Boston: Little, Brown, 1970.

Knight, Amy. "Andropov: Myths and Realities." *Survey* 28, no. 1 (Spring 1984), pp. 22–44.

Kolakowski, Leszek. "Marxist Roots of Stalinism." In *Stalinism: Essays in Historical Interpretation*. Edited by Robert C. Tucker. New York: W. W. Norton, 1977.

Kozlov, Yu. M., et al. *Sovetskoye administrativnoye pravo*. Moscow: Izdatel'stvo "Yuridicheskaya Literatura," 1968.

———. *Sovetskoye administrativnoye pravo*. Moscow: Izdatel'stvo "Yuridicheskaya Literatura," 1973.

Kravchenko, Victor. *I Chose Freedom*. New York: Scribner's, 1946.

———. *I Chose Justice*. New York: Scribner's, 1950.

Kravchenko, Vladimir F. "Pervye shagi VChK." *Sovetskoye gosudarstvo i pravo*, no. 3 (March 1967), pp. 67–102.

———. "Pod imenem Shmidkhena." *Nedelya* (6–12 March 1966), p. 7.

Krivitsky, Walter. *In Stalin's Secret Service*. Reprint. Frederick, Md.: University Publications of America, 1985.

Lamphere, Robert J., and Tom Shachtman. *The FBI–KGB War: A Special Agent's Story*. New York: Random House, 1986.

Latsis, M. Ya. *Chrezvychaynye komissii po bor'be s kontrrevolyutsiey*. Moscow: Gosizdat, 1921.

———. *Dva goda bor'by na vnutrennom fronte*. Moscow: Gosizdat, 1920.

Lazich, Branko, and Milorad M. Drachkovitch. *Lenin and the Comintern*. Vol. 1. Stanford: Hoover Institution Press, 1972.

Leggett, George. *The Cheka: Lenin's Political Police*. Oxford: Oxford University Press, 1981.

———. "Lenin's Reported Destruction of the Cheka Archives." *Survey* 24, no. 2 (107) (Spring 1979), pp. 193–99.

Lenin, V. I. *Collected Works*, vols. 26, 27, 31, 45. Moscow: Progress Publishers, 1964, 1966.

———. *Selected Works*, vol. 3. Moscow: Foreign Languages Publishing House, 1961, pp. 744–46.

———. *Selected Works*, vols. 3, 8. New York: International Publishers, 1943.

———. "Speech Delivered at a Meeting of Activists of the Moscow Organization of the R.C.P.(B.), December 6, 1920." *Collected Works*, vol. 31. Moscow: Progress Publishers, 1966, p. 444.

Levine, Isaac Don. *Stalin's Great Secret*. New York: Coward-McCann, 1956.

Levytsky, Boris. *The Uses of Terror*. New York: Coward-McCann, 1972.

Library of Congress, Congressional Research Service. *Soviet Intelligence and Security Services*. Vol. 1, 1964–70; vol. 2, 1971 and 1972. Washington, D.C.: GPO, 1972, 1975.

Litvinov, Maxim. *Notes for a Journal*. Introduction by E. H. Carr; prefatory note by General Walter Bedell Smith. New York: William Morrow & Co., 1955.

Lockhart, R. H. Bruce. *British Agent*. New York: G. P. Putnam's Sons, 1933.

———. *Reilly: The First Man*. New York: Penguin Books, 1987.

Loventhal, Milton. "The Politburo's Resolutions on Soviet Foreign Policy: 1934–35." No date, 7 pp., box 4, "Postanovleniia Politbiuro VKP(b)" archive at the Hoover Institution.

Loventhal, Milton, and Jennifer McDowell. *Soviet Intelligence Material from the German Archives*. Unpublished manuscript, no date.

Lyons, Eugene. *Assignment in Utopia*. New York: Harcourt, Brace & Co., 1937.

McSherry, James E. *Stalin, Hitler, and Europe*. Vol. 2. New York: World Publishing Co., 1970.

Manayenkov, A. L., et al., eds. *Partizanskiye formirovaniya Belorussii v gody Velikoy Otechestvonnoy Voiny, 1941–1944*. Minsk: Izdatel'stvo "Belarus," 1983.

Manokhin, V. M., ed. *Sovetskoye administrativnoye pravo*. Moscow: Izdatel'stvo "Yuridicheskaya Literatura," 1977.

Marchenko, Anatoliy. *My Testimony*. Translated by Michael Scammell. London: Pall Mall Press, 1969.

Martynov, A. P. *Moya sluzhba vo otdelnom korpuse zhandarmov: Vospominaniya*. Edited by Richard Wraga. Stanford: Hoover Institution Press, 1972.

Matthews, Mervyn, ed. *Soviet Government: A Selection of Official Documents on Internal Policies*. New York: Taplinger Publishing Co., Inc., 1974.

Medvedev, Roy. *Khrushchev*. Anchor Press, 1983.

———. *Let History Judge: The Origins and Consequences of Stalinism*. Translated by Colleen Taylor. New York: Alfred A. Knopf, 1972.

———. "New Pages from the Political Biography of Stalin." In *Stalinism: Essays in Historical Interpretation*. Edited by Robert C. Tucker. New York: W. W. Norton, 1977.

———. *The October Revolution*. Translated by George Saunders. New York: Columbia University Press, 1979.

Medvedev, Roy A., and Zhores A. Medvedev. *Khrushchev: The Years in Power*. New York: Columbia University Press, 1976.

Melgounov, S. P. [Mel'gunov]. *The Red Terror in Russia*. London: J. M. Dent & Sons Ltd., 1926.

Mel'gunov, S. P., and M. A. Tsyavlovskiy, eds. *Bol'sheviki: Dokumenty po istorii bol'shevizma s 1903 po 1916 god byushego Moskovskogo Okhrannogo Otdeleniya*. Moscow: Zadruga, 1918.

Minyailo, V. "The Conference of the State Security Organs." *Bulletin: Institute for the Study of the USSR* (September 1959), pp. 21–23.

Mironov, Nikolay R. *Ukrepleniye zakonnosti i pravoporyadka v obshchenoradnom gosudarstve: Programmnaya zadacha partii*. Moscow: Izdatel'stvo "Yuridicheskaya Literatura," 1964.

Nekrasov, V. F. "Vklad vnutrennikh voysk v delo pobedy sovetskogo naroda v Velikoy Otechestvonnoy voyne." *Voyenno-istoricheskiy zhurnal*, no. 9 (September 1985), pp. 29–35.

Nekrich, Aleksandr. "Stalin and the Pact with Hitler." *Russia*, no. 4 (1981), p. 48.

Nikolaevsky [Nicolaevsky], Boris. "Iz istorii mashiny sovetskogo terrora." *Sotsialisticheskiy vestnik* (New York), no. 8–9 (1959), pp. 167–72.

———. *Power and the Soviet Elite: Letter of an Old Bolshevik and Other Essays*. New York: Praeger, 1965.

Nikulin, Lev Ven'yaminovich. *Mertvaya zyb'*. Moscow: Voyenizdat, 1965.

Orlov, Alexander. *Handbook of Intelligence and Guerrilla Warfare*. Ann Arbor, Mich.: University of Michigan Press, 1963.

————. *The Secret History of Stalin's Crimes.* New York: Random House, 1953.

————. "The Sensational Secret behind Damnation of Stalin." *Life* (23 April 1956), pp. 34–38, 43–45.

Ostryakov, Sergey Z. *Voyennye chekisty.* Moscow: Voyenizdat, 1979.

Padeniye tsarskogo rezhima. Stenograficheskiye otchëty. 7 vols. Moscow: Gosizdat, 1924–27.

Penkovskiy, Oleg. *The Penkovskiy Papers.* Translated by Peter Deriabin. Introduction and commentary by Frank Gibney. New York: Doubleday & Co., Inc., 1965.

Peters, Ya. "Vospominaniya o rabote v VChK v pervyi god revolyutsii." *Proletarskaya revolyutsiya,* no. 10 (33) (October 1924), pp. 5–32.

Petrov, Vladimir, and Evdokia Petrov. *Empire of Fear.* New York: Praeger, 1956.

Petrov, Yuriy P. *Partiinoye stroitel'stvo v Sovetskoy Armii i Flote.* Moscow: Voyenizdat, 1964.

Philby, Kim. *My Silent War.* New York: Ballantine Books, 1983.

Pimenov, Revolt I. *Kak ya iskal shpiona Reili* [samizdat manuscript]. Leningrad, 1968. Published by Radio Liberty in Samizdat Archive AS 1089. Munich, 1972. 22 pp.

Pincher, Chapman. *Their Trade is Treachery.* London: Sidgwick & Jackson, 1981.

————. *Too Secret Too Long.* New York: St. Martin's Press, 1984.

Pipes, Richard. *Russia under the Old Regime.* New York: Charles Scribner's Sons, 1974.

Podrabinek, Alexander. *Punitive Medicine.* Ann Arbor, Mich.: Karoma Publishers, 1979.

Ponomarev, B., comp. *The Plot against the Soviet Union and World Peace: Facts and Documents. Compiled from the Verbatim Report of the Court Proceedings in the Case of the Anti-Soviet "Bloc of Rights and Trotskyites."* New York: Workers Library Publishers; printed in the USSR, n.d.

Poretsky, Elizabeth. *Our Own People: A Memoir of Ignace Reiss and His Friends.* Ann Arbor, Mich.: University of Michigan Press, 1970.

Possony, Stefan. *Lenin: The Compulsive Revolutionary.* Chicago: Henry Regnery Co., 1964.

Powers, Thomas. *The Man Who Kept the Secrets.* New York: Alfred A. Knopf, 1979.

Pryanishnikov, B. *Nezrimaya pautina.* Silver Spring, Md: Published by author, 1979.

Rapoport, Vitaly, and Yuri Alexeev. *High Treason: Essays on the History of the Red Army 1918–1938.* Edited by Vladimir G. Treml, and translated and coedited by Bruce Adams. Durham, N. C.: Duke University Press, 1985.

Reiman, Michael [Mikhail Reyman]. *The Birth of Stalinism: The USSR on the Eve of the "Second Revolution."* Translated by George Saunders. Bloomington: University of Indiana Press, 1987.

Reyman, Mikhail. "Agent v politbyuro: K istorii sovetskoy politiki v 1932–1933 gg." *Strana i mir* 8 (1985), pp. 68–78; 9 (1985), pp. 28–38.

Rezanov, Colonel A. *Le Travail secret des Agents Bolchevistes.* Paris: Editions Bossard, 1926.

Rocca, Raymond G., and John J. Dziak, with the staff of the Consortium for the Study of Intelligence. *Bibliography on Soviet Intelligence and Security Services.* Boulder, Colo.: Westview Press, 1985.

Romanov, A. I. [pseud.] *Nights Are Longest There: A Memoir of the Soviet Security Services*. Boston: Little, Brown, 1972.

Rosenfeldt, Niels Erik. *Knowledge and Power: The Role of Stalin's Secret Chancellery in the Soviet System of Government*. Copenhagen: Rosenkilde & Bogger, 1978.

Rositzke, Harry. *The CIA's Secret Operations*. New York: Reader's Digest Press, 1977.

Rowen, Richard Wilmer. *Terror in Our Time*. New York: Longmans, Green & Co., 1941.

Sayers, Michael, and Albert E. Kahn. *The Great Conspiracy: The Secret War against Soviet Russia*. Boston: Little, Brown, 1946.

Schapiro, Leonard. *The Communist Party of the Soviet Union*. New York: Random House, 1960.

————. "The General Department of the Central Committee of the CPSU." *Survey* 21 (Summer 1975), pp. 53–65.

————. *The Russian Revolution of 1917: The Origins of Modern Communism*. New York: Basic Books, Inc., 1984.

Schurer, H. "Karl Moor: German Agent and Friend of Lenin." *Journal of Contemporary History* 5, no. 2 (1970), pp. 131–52.

Senate Committee on the Judiciary, Subcommittee to Investigate the Administration of the Internal Security Act and Other Internal Security Laws. *Institute of Pacific Relations, Part 13. Testimony of Igor Bogolepov*. 82nd Cong., 2nd sess. Washington, D.C.: GPO, 1952.

————. *The Legacy of Alexander Orlov*. 93rd Cong., 1st sess. Washington, D.C.: GPO, 1973.

————. *Murder International, Inc.: Murder and Kidnapping as an Instrument of Soviet Police. Testimony of Peter S. Deriabin*. 89th Cong., 1st sess. Washington, D.C.: GPO, 1965.

————. *Scope of Soviet Activity in the United States, Part 4. Testimony of Mark Zborowsky*. 84th Cong., 2nd sess. Washington, D.C.: GPO, 1956.

Senja, Jan. *We Will Bury You*. London: Sidgwick & Jackson, 1982.

Serge, Victor. *Memoirs of a Revolutionary, 1901–1941*. Edited and translated by Peter Sedgwich. London: Oxford University Press, 1963.

Sevin, Dieter. "Operation Scherhorn." *Military Review* 46 (March 1966), pp. 35–43.

Shifrin, Avraham. *The First Guidebook to Prisons and Concentration Camps in the Soviet Union*. New York: Bantam Books, 1982.

Shulgin, Basil. "How I Was Hoodwinked by the Bolsheviks." *The Slavonic Review* (March 1928), pp. 505–19.

Shultz, Richard H., and Roy Godson. *Dezinformatsia*. New York: Pergammon-Brassey's, 1984.

Smith, Edward Ellis. *"The Okhrana": The Russian Department of Police*. Hoover Institution Bibliographic Series 33. Stanford: Hoover Institution Press, 1967.

————. *The Young Stalin*. New York: Farrar, Straus & Giroux, 1967.

Sofinov, P. G. *Ocherki istorii vserossiyskoy chrezvychaynoy komissii 1917–1921 gg.* Moscow: Gospolitizdat, 1960.

Solovyov, Vladimir, and Elena Klepikova. *Behind the High Kremlin Walls*. Translated by Guy Daniels in collaboration with the authors. New York: Berkley Books, 1987.

————. *Yuri Andropov: A Secret Passage into the Kremlin*. Translated by Guy Daniels in collaboration with the authors. New York: Macmillan, 1983.

Solzhenitsyn, Aleksandr. *The Gulag Archipelago, 1918–56*. Translated by Thomas P. Whitney and Harry Willetts. New York: Harper & Row, 1974–76.

————. *The Oak and the Calf: A Memoir*. New York: Harper & Row, 1980.

————. *Warning to the West*. New York: Farrar, Straus & Giroux, 1976.

Sotsialisticheskiy vestnik, no. 8–9 (August–September 1959), p. 171 (pp. 167–72 for whole article).

Sovetskaya voyennaya entsiklopediya. Moscow: Voyenizdat, 1976; 1976–86.

Stalin, J. V. "Speech to the Seventeenth Party Congress." In *Problems of Leninism*. Moscow: Foreign Languages Publishing House, 1953.

————. *Works*. Vol. 10, August–December 1927. Moscow: Foreign Languages Publishing House, 1954.

Steinberg, I. N. *In the Workshop of Revolution*. London: Victor Gollancz Ltd., 1955.

Stephen, Robert W. "Death to Spies: The Story of SMERSH." Master's thesis, American University, Washington, D.C., 1984.

Stone, Helena M. "Another Look at the Sisson Forgeries and Their Background." *Soviet Studies* 37, no. 1 (January 1985), pp. 90–102.

Struve, G., V. Shulgin, and S. Voytsekhovskiy. "New about the Trust." *Novyy zhurnal*, no. 125 (1975), pp. 194–214.

Suvorov, Viktor. *Soviet Military Intelligence*. London: Hamish Hamilton, 1984.

Tatu, Michel. *Power in the Kremlin*. Translated by Helen Katel. New York: Viking Press, 1968.

Tawcas, K. V. *Guerrilla Warfare on the Amber Coast*. New York: Voyager Press, 1962.

Tennant, Ellis [Edward Ellis Smith], comp. and ed. *The Department of Police, 1911–1913. From the Recollections of Nikolai Vladimirovich Veselago*. Manuscript. Stanford: Hoover Institution Archives, 1962.

Thomas, David L. "The Legend of Agent 'MAX'." *Foreign Intelligence Literary Scene* 5, no. 1 (January 1986), pp. 1-2, 5.

Tishkov, A. V. *Perviy chekist*. Moscow: Voyenizdat, 1968.

Tobenkin, Elias. "Boris Savinkov: The Conversion of the Soviets' Most Spectacular Foe." *Current History Magazine* (December 1924), p. 392.

Trotsky, Leon. *Stalin: An Appraisal of the Man and His Influence*. New York: Harpers, 1946.

Tsvigun, S. K., et al. *V. I. Lenin i VChK: Sbornik dokumentov (1917–1922 gg)*. Moscow: Politizdat, 1975.

XX s"ezd KPSS: Stenograficheskiy otchët. Vol. 1. Moscow: Gosizdat, 1956.

Valtin, Jan. *Out of the Night*. New York: Alliance Book Corporation, 1941.

Vereeken, Georges. *The GPU in the Trotskyist Movement*. London: New Park Publications, 1976.

Viktorov, I. V. *Podpol'shchik, voin, chekist*. Moscow: Molodaya Gvardiya, 1961; 2nd ed. 1967.

Voprosy istorii KPSS, no. 2 (February 1964), pp. 17–29.

Voslensky, Michael. *Nomenklatura: The Soviet Ruling Class: An Insider's Report.* Translated by Eric Mosbacher. Garden City, N. Y.: Doubleday & Cᵒ , 1984.

Voytsekhovskiy, S. L. "Conversation with Opperput." *Vozrozhdeniy.,* no. 16 (July–August 1951), pp. 129–37.

———. *Trest: Vospominaniya i dokumenty.* London, Ontario, Canada: Zarya Publishers, 1974.

———. "Trest: Vospominaniya V. T. Drimmer." *Pereklichka* (New York); January–February 1967, pp. 11–15; March–April 1967, pn. 6–10; May–June 1967, pp. 9–16.

Walkin, Jacob. "Some Contrasts between the Tsarist and Communist Political Systems." *New Review of East European History* 15, no. 3–4; 16, no. 1 (March 1976), pp. 55–66.

War Department. *Handbook on the USSR Armed Forces.* TM 30-430, sect. iv. Washington, D.C.: GPO, 1945.

Williams, Robert C. "Changing Landmarks in Russian Berlin: 1922–1924." *Slavic Review* 27 (December 1968), pp. 581–93.

Wittfogel, Karl A. *Oriental Despotism: A Comparative Study of Total Power.* New Haven, Conn.: Yale University Press, 1957.

Wolin, Simon, and Robert M. Slusser, eds. *The Soviet Secret Police.* New York: Praeger, 1957.

Wraga, Richard. "Cloak and Dagger Politics." *Problems of Communism* 10, no. 2 (March–April 1961), pp. 56–59.

———. "Trest." *Vozrozhdeniye,* no. 7 (January–February 1950), pp. 123-33.

———. "Trest—Vnutrennaya liniya." *Vozrozhdeniye,* no. 11 (September–October 1950), pp. 138–43.

Wright, Peter. *Spy Catcher.* New York: Viking Penguin Inc., 1987.

Yakovlev, I. K., et al. *Vnutrenniye voyska sovetskoy respubliki (1917–1922 gg.).* Moscow: Izdatel'stvo "Yuridicheskaya Literatura," 1972.

Yudin, N. F. *Pervaya partizanskaya.* Moscow: Izdatel'stvo "Moskovskiy Rabochiy," 1983.

Zawodny, J. K. *Death in the Forest: The Story of the Katyn Forest Massacre.* South Bend, Ind.: University of Notre Dame Press, 1962.

Zemtsov, Ilya. *Andropov: Policy Dilemmas and the Struggle for Power.* Jerusalem: IRICS Publishers, 1983.

Zinoviev, Grigorii. *History of the Bolshevik Party: A Popular Outline.* Translated by R. Chappell. London: New Park Publications Ltd., 1973.

Zubov, Nikolay I. *F. E. Dzerzhinksiy: Biografiya.* 3rd ed. Moscow: Politizdat, 1971 (1st ed., 1963/ 2nd ed., 1965).

Zuckerman, Frederic S. "The Russian Political Police at Home and Abroad, 1880–1917." Ph.D. diss., New York University, 1973.

Index

About the Author

J OHN J. DZIAK has served in the Defense Intelligence Agency (DIA) for over twenty-two years, specializing in Soviet political-military affairs. He received his Ph.D. in Russian history from Georgetown University and is a graduate of the National War College. He is the author of the book *Soviet Perceptions of Military Doctrine and Military Power* (1981 and 1984) and co-editor of the *Bibliography on Soviet Intelligence and Security Services* (1985), and he has contributed to several books and written numerous articles on Soviet intelligence and political-military affairs. Dr. Dziak is an Adjunct Professor of History and International Affairs, Institute for Sino-Soviet Studies, of The George Washington University. He also is an Adjunct Professor of Government at Georgetown University, where he teaches a graduate course on the Soviet intelligence and security services.